EQUITY AND TRUSTS

EQUITY AND TRUSTS

Fifth Edition

Paul Todd, MA, BCL

Cardiff Law School, University of Wales

Series Editor: C.J. Carr, MA, BCL

BLACKSTONE
PRESS LIMITED

This edition published in Great Britain 1996 by Blackstone Press Limited, 9–15 Aldine Street, London W12 8AW. Telephone: 0181–740 1173.

© Paul Todd, 1986

First edition, 1986
Second edition, 1989
Third edition, 1991
Fourth edition, 1994
Fifth edition, 1996

ISBN: 1 85431 500 5

British Cataloguing in Publication Data
A CIP catalogue record for this book is available from the British Library

Typeset by Montage Studios Ltd, Tonbridge, Kent
Printed by Bell & Bain Limited, Glasgow

CONTENTS

PREFACE

This is not intended to be another introductory trusts textbook. If you want a conventional textbook on the subject there are plenty to choose from, in varying degrees of clarity and detail (and price). In common with other books in the series its purpose rather is to help students who have already embarked on a study of the law of trusts (or equity and trusts) to succeed as well as possible in assessment in the subject, at degree or equivalent level.

Unlike normal textbooks, therefore, this book concentrates primarily on the assessment process itself, which in most trust courses is still likely to be primarily examination based, and though the substance of the subject is by no means relegated to second place, you will not find here an overview of equity and trusts in the didactic style that textbooks usually adopt.

It does not follow that this book is aimed at the weak student. Far from it. Under-performance in exams is just as likely to pull a student down from an upper to a lower second as it is to pull a weaker student down from a pass to a fail.

Nobody would suggest that you can succeed at exams without a sound grasp of the subject. But every university teacher is familiar with students who apparently under-perform in exams. Such students work hard and attend classes diligently, only to produce an examination performance which fails to do justice to their effort or ability.

The reason for poor achievement is usually rooted in failure to appreciate the purpose of exams, without which appreciation it is impossible to acquire the skills necessary for a creditable performance. This book seeks to remedy that, and the first chapter is directed to an examination of the assessment process itself. Only once you have understood the system can you hope to beat it, and chapter 2 is about working during the course to achieve that aim. The rest of the book deals with the substance of the subject, the emphasis again being directed towards success in the assessment.

How then in detail does this book differ from a conventional textbook? There are three main ways. First, it is assumed that you are already a student of trusts (or equity and trusts), and so there is no need for material which is purely introductory, or setting the scene. Secondly, not all subjects are covered, but rather the material is selective. Thirdly, each substantive chapter is directed primarily towards the type of question you might get in an exam (including some real exam questions). There is no attempt at model answers as such, because individual styles can legitimately differ widely, but instead each section considers what an examiner might be looking for. Exam questions (if well set) are drafted with a specific purpose in mind, and if you are to succeed you must appreciate what that purpose is.

In trusts, as I have already observed, the exam is still, I believe, the main form of assessment, so there is little change in this edition on that account. Modularisation almost certainly will make a difference, but it is difficult to predict how this will affect the subject, as I suspect that there will be little consistency among law schools. It would probably be true to say, however, that few courses will expand, and that many will contract around the central core of the subject. All are likely to comply with the Law Society requirements, which include the relationship between equity and common law, and the nature and scope of equitable rights and equitable remedies, but not perpetuities.

I have therefore decided reluctantly to abandon coverage of perpetuities, and have therefore replaced the last chapter with a new chapter on equitable remedies. Chapter 3 is almost entirely new, dealing with the nature of equitable rights, and the distinction between trusts and common law concepts which can be used to achieve similar ends. The chapter on matrimonial property and charities has also been significantly reworked.

Paul Todd
University of Wales College of Cardiff

slapnt@cf.ac.uk
100433.2016@compuserve.com

TABLE OF CASES

1 PREPARING FOR EXAMS

Two common myths which it is necessary immediately to dispel are that there are right and wrong answers in law, and that success in examinations depends primarily on memory. These two myths in fact have a common basis, which is that to succeed in law you have to acquire a great deal of knowledge and regurgitate it. This is also untrue.

It is probably not surprising that students do not believe lecturers who tell them that there are no right and wrong answers in law. You have heard that before, have you not, and you probably did not believe it? The reality, of course, is that a lot of lecturers do not believe it themselves. After all, a common exam rubric is 'Answer four questions', not 'Give your views on four questions' or 'Comment on four questions'. How often do tutors say 'Can anyone answer this question'? They do not believe what they are saying, so why should you? The reason is that law is fundamentally uncertain. There really are no right answers, and those who argue otherwise are wrong.

This is not the place to pursue extensive jurisprudential analysis, but it is possible to describe legal analysis in predictive terms, at any rate in areas of law which are heavily case-based. Suppose, for example, you were presented with a set of facts, and asked to predict what the outcome would be if the matter came before a court; or, if presented with an essay question, you were asked to predict whether the courts would be likely to accept it as a proposition of law. Not only is that quite a good description of legal analysis, but it is also quite a useful one. A barrister arguing a point of law in the higher courts will need to have some idea which propositions are likely to be accepted, and which are not. A solicitor advising a client, for example whether to continue or discontinue a dispute, ought to consider, at least as one factor, the likelihood of success at trial. A High Court judge who is required to decide upon a new proposition of law, and give reasons, is well-advised to consider the arguments that may be considered relevant by the Court of Appeal.

There is no reason why you should take my word for this. Far greater minds than mine have come to the same conclusion. Oliver Wendell Holmes, an American academic in the late 19th and early 20th centuries, who (according to *Grolier's American Academic Encyclopaedia*, accessed on-line via Compuserve) 'was a justice of the U.S. Supreme Court so well known for the eloquence, pungency, and abundance of his dissenting opinions that he was called the "Great Dissenter"', said, in *The Path of Law*, 10 Harv L Rev 457 at p. 461:

> The prophesies of what the courts will do in fact, and nothing more pretentious, are what I mean by law.

There are no doubt those who would object to this view, pointing out that it is too narrow. It does not, for example, tell you who makes the law, or how the courts are constituted in the first place. A constitutional lawyer probably would not care for this definition; nor, perhaps, would a teacher of an area of law that is heavily statute-based, who might also include within the definition of law the interrelationship between the statutes, or sections of them, or regulations made under them. However, trusts is a case law subject, and we are not concerned with constitutional issues. I would strongly suggest that, at any rate for the purposes of the law of trusts, Oliver Wendell Holmes has provided an adequate working definition of law.

If this description of legal analysis appeals to you, or seems to you to be useful, you might observe that you are no longer dealing in certainties but in probabilities, since you cannot predict with certainty what might happen in the future. You should not therefore expect definite answers, but merely an analysis of what may or may not occur. A second observation is that you cannot, as a lawyer, back away merely because no certain answer exists. A barrister arguing a point of law cannot withdraw, still less can the judge refuse to decide the point, merely because the argument becomes difficult. It may be that one of the reasons why the top barristers are able to command the substantial incomes they undoubtedly enjoy is that they are treading in murky waters.

It is noteworthy that if you had chosen medicine as your profession, there are computer programs (expert systems) available to assist in diagnosis, and these are not state of the art: one such program, MYCIN, was written as long ago as 1972. Since as early as 1965, chemists have been able to use an expert system (DENDRAL) to analyse the chemical structure of substances. Geologists can use PROSPECTOR to find oil. Yet in law, computer programs have been developed for only the most trivial tasks, and hardly at all for case law analysis. A conclusion that you may care to draw is that case law analysis is not particularly amenable to the deterministic reasoning appropriate for computer programs. This is actually rather unfair on the expert systems, which are in fact quite good at dealing with uncertainty. Given the cost of lawyers and legal advisers, it would certainly be worthwhile for large companies to develop legal expert systems if it were practical. That they have not done so suggests that there is something especially non-deterministic about case law analysis; for all but the dullest questions there are no right answers, and you need to think in terms of probabilities rather than certainties.

Where will you find the material to enable you to do this? The answer is, primarily in the cases themselves (after all, that is where the main principles of the subject are in fact analysed, and applied to a real-life situation). If you wish to predict the outcome of a committee, let us say considering a planning application, or to predict the arguments that stand any chance of success before such a committee, you could do a lot worse than study what the committee has done in the past. Case law analysis is not that different. Like committees, courts tend to do what they have done before, but the prediction process is made easier by the fact that they have been operating for a long time, have fuller reports of their proceedings than most committees, and have made an attempt to formalise their system of precedent.

Quite a number of students are rather poor at using cases. Lecturers, some textbook writers, and, indeed, some judges occasionally cite cases as examples. This is probably acceptable when attempting merely to describe how an area of law works, perhaps, as a teacher, in order to explain it, but it is unlikely that, as a student, you will be required to do this. You should get into the habit of using cases to *establish* propositions of law, rather than merely to illustrate them. After all, the propositions of law are not self-evident (as appears from some old-fashioned textbooks), merely awaiting litigants willing to come along and illustrate them. The propositions are established only by the cases themselves.

The reality is, of course, that litigation, especially in the higher courts, is expensive and (presumably) stressful, and people do not litigate in order to illustrate self-evident propositions of law. Typically, the case involves a contest between two parties, each of whom before the decision believes that he or she has a good chance of winning. Only one does win, of course, and, hence, the case establishes, as authority and not for purposes of illustrating, which party's arguments are to be regarded as correct. Your job is to decide whether the case would be likely to be followed were a similar issue to arise again, and, if so, the extent to which the reasoning in it might be extended to cover other situations. In order to do this, you must know in which court the case was decided (students are often lamentably bad at this), whether, if there was more than one judge, they all spoke with the same voice, how the case fits in with other authorities, and what has been said about the case, either in other courts or in the academic journals. You also need to form some view of the validity (in terms, for example, of logic and internal coherence) of the judgment or judgments in the case. This is case law analysis, and in chapter 7 I attempt to give an example of what I mean.

That is not to say that you should never use cases as examples. If you are unfortunate enough to be asked merely to describe how the law operates, then you may have no choice but to do so. Another situation is where it is really impracticable to trace a doctrine right back to its origins, perhaps because the doctrine is very old (e.g., the equitable notice doctrine). Generally speaking, however, whenever you find yourself writing, 'For example, in' such-and-such case, consider whether you might not be better using that case (or a different case) to establish a proposition which supports the argument you wish to advance.

Yet given that it is the obvious place to start, I have often been surprised, during nearly 20 years of teaching, how reluctant students are to read cases. If I suggest to a student that a case should really be read, the student will almost invariably respond by asking me to summarise it, or to repeat what I said about it in my lectures, or where he or she can find it in a textbook, or whether it is acceptable merely to read the headnote. Almost anything, it seems, is preferable to reading the case itself. And these are not first-year students, since trusts at Cardiff is exclusively taught as a final-year subject. Yet once you know what you are looking for, cases are no more difficult to read than lecture notes or textbooks (and they are usually far more interesting). And the plain fact is, that in order to do really well in trusts exams, you need to read the *judgments* of the most important cases (and there are not that many really important cases), and think hard about them. Reading of cases will be further discussed in chapter 2.

So there are no right and wrong answers in law, and it should also be becoming obvious why law exams are not primarily a test of memory. Of course, you need to acquire (and retain) some knowledge to be able to advance legal arguments, but it is certainly not the ultimate goal. Knowledge acquisition is really only the first base. Application and analysis are far more important, at any rate for the higher marks (e.g., upper second and above, at which nearly all students — rightly — aim these days).

Recently (after teaching law for 18 years) I was sent on a course to teach me how to do it. Not before time, you might think. I was introduced to *Bloom's Taxonomy of Educational Objectives*. Bloom was a professor at Chicago about 40 years ago who specialised in cognitive learning (as distinguished, for example, from teaching of skills). The taxonomy, which is in the shape of a pyramid, sets out seven objectives, with knowledge as the bottom level, and with higher degrees of attainment above it. Some of these higher levels are probably inappropriate to a trusts course, but application and analysis are both placed higher on the pyramid than knowledge.

Application, I would say, is one of the skills required for a problem question, where you are asked to apply legal principles to a set of facts. Analysis is case law analysis, which, as I have suggested, is essentially predictive, and is placed higher than both knowledge and application. I attempt a demonstration of case law analysis in chapter 7. The important point, however, is that rote learning, or acquisition of knowledge *per se*, is far less important than many students think. Do not spend too much time on knowledge-acquisition, at the expense of developing your abilities at application and analytical skills.

Bearing all this in mind, it is time to look at the assessment process itself. Only by appreciating the skills which are being examined by the process can you hope to succeed at it.

THE ASSESSMENT PROCESS

Although most assessment in trusts is still by traditional examination, the remarks in this section would apply equally to an assessed essay.

Since trusts is unlikely to be studied in your first year, I will not reiterate the importance of keeping to deadlines for assessed essays, and, in exams, reading and observing the rubric, including, in particular, attempting (not answering, note) the correct number of questions. These things are very important, but you already know that.

There is one point, however, which is worth emphasising. Your performance in the exam may have been adversely affected by illness or some domestic difficulty. Exam boards vary as to the extent these are taken into account, but many boards take a sympathetic view, at least if you are on a borderline. But no board can act in the absence of knowledge, so if you are ill get a medical certificate, and if there are other difficulties make sure the faculty or department office (or whoever is the appropriate person) is informed, so that they can be taken into account as appropriate.

Let us concentrate instead on the substance of the exam (or other assessment). Always bear in mind that it is more important for you to demonstrate skills at application and analysis than mere acquisition of knowledge. Therefore the organisation of the answer is more important than the total amount of material contained in it. The most important attribute is the ability to reason logically, and above all clearly. It is a good idea, therefore, to structure your answer in rough before you start, making a note of important points and cases in case you forget them later. Make full use of short paragraphs (perhaps three to a page), each of which make a distinct point, and make it clear where each paragraph begins and ends, even to the extent of leaving a line between paragraphs. Shoulder headings and diagrams can also be useful, but some examiners do not like these, so try to find out what your examiner's prejudices are if you can.

Of course a first-class script will include a great deal of material (none of it repetitive) in addition to being well organised. A surprising number of good-second scripts, however, are quite short, relying on clarity of presentation and cogency of argument. Conversely, huge quantities of repetitive and unconnected waffle will be penalised. Once you have a sound structure you can build on it, but the structure itself must take top priority.

Problem questions in exams will usually contain more points than any candidate will spot, and indeed even the exmainer may not have appreciated all the ramifications, so do not despair simply because you think you may have overlooked something. A far more serious (but very common) mistake with this type of question is where a candidate sees the central point of the problem but avoids it. Commonly this will be a murky area of law, where there is quite simply no clear answer. The candidate writes something like 'The law in this area is very confused', and then moves on.

I still find it difficult to believe that so many people commit this error year after year. A typical problem is set with a handful of important cases in mind, where though the decisions themselves may be clear enough, the extent to which the reasoning applies is not. The facts of the problem will be deliberately chosen so that no authority clearly applies, though the reasoning of a number might. The *whole point* of such a problem is to test your ability to handle legal arguments, and application of principles and authorities, where the law itself is uncertain. The conclusion you reach is far less important than the quality of the argument. After all, there *is* no correct answer, though you should generally express a preference. A great number of marks will be allocated to this particular test, so you *must* have a go at it. The student who avoids the issue in the way described above is throwing marks away, and the most frustrating part about it is that often he or she knows of the authorities in question.

I give an example of the sort of question I mean, and how you should tackle it, in chapter 7.

One final point. Suppose you have run yourself short of time towards the end. One of the skills for which you are being tested is your ability to argue in English prose, and indeed it is difficult to advance legal arguments fully in any other form, but as a last resort note form is better than nothing. So long as you do this only towards the end of the final question you will probably not lose too many marks (but avoid at all costs the temptation to write 'short of time' in the second question and to carry on in note form from there on).

To succeed at assessment at university level is to beat a system. You cannot beat a system without understanding what the system is trying to do. If you understand the system, then all you have to do is to keep that understanding in the forefront of your mind, and keep your nerve. At all costs, do not allow yourself to be panicked into writing down everything you know, with scant regard for relevance and organisation. You will demonstrate your knowledge-acquisition admirably by doing that, but as I hope I have by now persuaded you, that is not what it is all about.

REVISING

There are some general observations that need to be made about revising. First, in chapter 2 I discuss the importance of organising your time in a sane manner, and what is an optimum amount of work. None of that changes just because exams are looming. Do not be tempted to throw away your balanced lifestyle, to give up weekends, or to lose sleep. Acquisition of knowledge is not what it is about, and you need to keep your wits about you if you are going to demonstrate your skills at application and analysis.

Secondly, avoid the mistake of thinking that the course is finished and that it is too late to do new work. You know the structure of the subject by now, and this is just the time to read or re-read the latest cases, articles or notes. They will help you remember the course far better than re-reading your notes will. Another advantage of reading (and thinking about) new material is that it will be much more interesting, and boredom can be a real problem during revision.

The most important point, however, is always work towards the exam. That is the entire purpose of revision. Immerse yourself thoroughly in past papers, perhaps even to the extent of practising answering some of them under simulated exam conditions. Whether or not this is worthwhile depends on the time available as it is a time-consuming exercise, but at the very least consider how you would structure an answer on the types of question you think most likely to arise, or on the areas in which you are most interested. Consider also what the examiner is looking for in the question, especially in problem questions.

Should you try to spot questions? There are pros and cons. The advantage is that by reducing breadth of coverage (assuming there will be a reasonable choice of questions) you can increase depth of coverage, and develop a real expertise on some parts of the course.

The disadvantage of question spotting is obvious, that there is an element of risk involved. The predicted questions may not come up. Also, questions often contain issues from more than one area. For example, take the following question:

'Equity will not permit a statute to be used as a cloak for fraud.' Discuss.

This question does not confine itself conveniently to any self-contained area of the course, and shows up well the penalties of concentrating too narrowly during exam revision. This question encompasses a number of separate areas, certainly at least secret trusts (chapter 8), part performance (chapter 6) and some of the material considered in chapter 7, so it would be unwise to attempt it unless you are reasonably confident about a substantial proportion of the syllabus.

Alternatively, you may be faced with a question involving an imaginary will containing various dispositions, all of which may be invalid, but for a variety of reasons. One disposition may infringe the rule against perpetuities, another may attempt to create a charitable trust which for some reason fails, another may attempt to create a private purpose trust, or make a gift to an uncertain class of objects, and so on.

A number of examples of problems which cover a number of areas can be found in chapter 9, and questions of this type may possibly defeat the question spotter. On the other hand, some areas pretty well always appear, and some areas are more likely to go together in the same question than others. For example, a question primarily on private purpose trusts often also involves points on unincorporated associations, charities, or certainty of objects, but would be unlikely to include anything on trustees' duties to invest, or accumulation of income. So a limited degree of question spotting is probably advisable, but with caution.

Suppose you have to answer four questions out of 10. It would be very foolish to pick on only four areas, but probably quite sensible to concentrate your efforts on a little over half the course. At least that way you should be able to achieve one or two really good answers. But concentration on one half should never be to the total exclusion of the other half. In the first place, you should have a sufficient smattering of the entire course to be able to spot if an area you have neglected arises as part of a question. Then it might be advisable to avoid that question (e.g., if a perpetuity point arises incidentally, and you have largely neglected that area). Secondly, if your predictions have gone awry, and you are unable to pick four questions on your expert areas, at least you have a fall-back position. It would be surprising if this did not occur in at least one exam at finals, but you would be unlucky if you had to compromise on more than one question.

Remember also three other points about the exams. First, they are, as has been explained, not primarily a memory test, but a test of understanding. Secondly, they will require a good deal of thought actually during the exam itself, so it is important to be fresh on the day. Thirdly, at any rate for the problems, a thorough knowledge of the most important cases is required. This must include both the decision itself and the reasoning, and such criticisms as there may be of that reasoning.

Lastly, of course, you need the best of luck!

FURTHER READING

Bloom, B. S., (ed.), *Taxonomy of Educational Objectives: The Classification of Educational Goals*, Handbook 1, Cognitive Domain (1956).

2   WORKING DURING THE COURSE

Since I would recommend that you regard revision as a continuation of coursework rather than as a wholly separate enterprise, it follows that such considerations as apply to revision also apply in general to your coursework. In particular, you should always work towards the exam, and the greatest enemy is probably boredom. Also, given that lectures and tutorials are not only time-consuming themselves, but also force you to work at a particular rate, you will need to organise your work so as to use your time as efficiently as possible. This final consideration should dictate especially the order in which you study materials, and this is considered later in the chapter.

HOW MUCH WORK?

It is a common misconception that the harder you work the better you are likely to do in exams, but if all you do is acquire more and more knowledge, you will never achieve very high marks. As was explained in chapter 1, to achieve high marks you need application and analysis. Analysis in particular is very difficult, and you will find that you cannot do much of it in a day. Another feature of analysis is that it requires thought, but not necessarily sitting in front of books or notes acquiring more and more information.

If you cast your eye around your fellow students, it will probably strike you that the real sloggers, the people who are always in the library when you arrive in the morning and are still there when you leave later in the day, rarely come out at the top of the class. It is true that they rarely fail or do very badly either, but given the hours of dedicated study they put in, they generally perform less well than might be expected. You would expect this, since they are likely to concentrate on the knowledge element of learning, which will get you a lower second, but nothing more.

The sloggers would do better by working less hard, but more effectively. Effective work requires thought, not just transcription, or photocopying reams of material, or learning by rote. Quality of work counts more than quantity. Mere acquisition of knowledge is no substitute for real thought.

Thinking is very interesting, but also extremely hard work. Indeed, it is one of the hardest forms of work there is. No doubt there are plenty of people who will scoff at this. It is fashionable to hold intellect in contempt these days. A moment's reflection will confirm the truth of this statement, however.

Consider, for example, how many people (even 'successful' people) hold prejudices which are indefensible in the face of rational argument. Consider how many (even intelligent people) are deliberately innumerate, and proud of it. How many are terrified of, and feel threatened by, ideas which are different from their own? Probably the majority, *even among students and academics themselves*. Indeed, the overwhelming majority of people seem to organise their lives specifically in order to have to think as little as possible. This is by no means irrational, because thinking is very difficult.

In fact you cannot work effectively more than a few hours each day, and if you try to do so, you will end up achieving less, not more. On the other hand, effective work in short bursts not only achieves more, but makes the subject much more interesting.

I would have thought that four hours a day for a six-day week or five hours a day over a five-day week is about the limit, and you may find that even less obtains better results. A 25-hour week may not sound much, but do not forget that study at this level is much more intensive than most other forms of work.

There are two other reasons for not attempting to extend your working day beyond a reasonable limit. First, your mind must remain active, and it is important not to become stale. Secondly, opportunities to gain many of the experiences available at university will not recur in later life. Do not work so hard that you waste them.

But this should by no means be taken as a justification for laziness. To acquire the skills described in the previous chapter requires you to immerse yourself in the subject, to have it in the back of your mind constantly. So, do not try to get away with very much less than the four or five hours a day suggested above. One of the advantages of working at a steady, rather than insane pace, is that it can be continued over many months. So do not waste the Christmas or Easter vacations. Of course you should take a short break over those periods, but four weeks for each is ridiculous. Sustained work over many weeks is better than trying to go at an insane pace until you are burned out, and certainly better than having to sprint in the few weeks immediately preceding the exam.

There are usually each year, it is true, a small proportion of candidates who appear to do very little during the year, but by getting things together a few weeks before the exam, obtain apparently respectable results (perhaps a good lower or even poor upper second). They are nearly always highly intelligent (otherwise they would fail), and undoubtedly it is possible for some people to do reasonably well on very little work. But in reality these candidates are letting themselves down badly. Had they worked steadily throughout the year, their intelligence would have reaped far greater rewards. In effect, candidates who are capable of obtaining high seconds or even firsts settle for a much lower class of degree.

Laziness has another, less obvious, penalty. A lot of law courses are not at first sight very interesting, and trusts does not, on first acquaintance, arouse great enthusiasm among undergraduate students. It is very conceptual, and abstract concepts tend to be uninteresting at first glance. Even on a factual level, since much of the subject (but by no means all) is about how to hang on to your wealth, it can be rather boring to students who rarely have much wealth to worry about. Nor is everybody intrinsically interested about law which has developed around Victorian family arrangements.

On the other hand, it becomes both easier and more interesting as one progresses through it. Once you have a reasonable grasp of the whole subject everything seems to fall into place. Also, you begin to appreciate how concepts, though developed from Victorian family arrangements, are also utilised in today's commercial world, and that many aspects of the subject have relevance for ordinary transactions, such as buying a house. Students who were thoroughly disillusioned with the subject initially can end up finding it quite interesting.

In other words, a minimum level of attainment is required before the subject becomes interesting. Thereafter, however, it becomes more interesting as one goes on. A lot of students, both in trusts and other subjects, never seem to do enough work to get over the boredom threshold. Therefore they remain bored throughout their whole period of study. A bored student can never study effectively, and cannot therefore do himself or herself justice in the examinations.

LECTURES

A significant change that has occurred since I graduated in 1975 is that today, in nearly all subjects, and certainly in trusts, textbooks are available at almost every level, from the very superficial to the very detailed. It is difficult to justify the lecture, therefore, simply as a means of transmitting knowledge. The books provide a better and more efficient method of doing that.

So, what is the point of a lecture? Good lecturers, I would suggest, will transmit their enthusiasm for the subject, and make suggestions for you to consider which probably you would otherwise overlook.

I observed in chapter 1 that in 1994, after I had been teaching law for 18 years, I was sent on a course to teach me how to do it. I was unenthusiastic about the course, and would not have attended it had it not been compulsory. The same is probably true of most students of the law of trusts. When the professor taking the course was asked what his own qualifications were, he replied that he had been teaching on such courses for 10 years. Yet, my 18 years' experience were not, apparently, sufficient to qualify me to teach law. At this stage, as you can imagine, I was not exactly positive about the course; again, not unlike many students in the first trusts lecture.

Yet this professor was a very good teacher. I found that I enjoyed the course, learnt quite a lot that turned out to be useful, and was sufficiently interested to attend other similar courses on a voluntary basis. In other words, he succeeded in enthusing me when I was in a wholly unreceptive frame of mind. Trusts is an interesting subject, although many students do not realise this when they embark upon it, and I would say that a really good trusts lecturer ought to be able to enthuse you as students, to persuade you to look at areas in a way that may not previously have occurred to you, and, ideally, to enjoy the subject sufficiently that you want to pursue it further. I do not claim to be a particularly good trusts lecturer, but I am always pleased when students at the end of the course (as some do every year) tell me that they enjoyed the subject far more than they thought they would. The best reward of all is when a student expresses a desire to continue the study of trusts at postgraduate level; but, unfortunately, this occurs only rarely. Maybe if I were a better teacher it would occur more often.

On most courses today lectures are voluntary, and although most students seem to be fairly regular attenders this is by no means necessary, and it is perfectly possible to succeed without attending any lectures at all. It is probably best not to adopt an inflexible policy, but to judge on the basis of each lecture course whether the time spent attending the lecture could be more profitably spent in the library, or elsewhere.

Two types of lecture course are nearly always worthwhile. The first is where the lecturer really is an expert, who is perhaps preparing material which will eventually be published. You will not be able to find the content of these lectures anywhere else, so you really should attend. The second is the revision or updating lecture near the end of the course. These will nearly always contain new and original material, on which little will yet have been published, and will pull together various strands of the course.

In deciding whether a course of lectures is worth attending, remember that the first lecture is rarely representative. Often it will include little more than handing out materials and recommending books. Even the second lecture will often be only introductory. The third or fourth is likely to be more representative, however, and this is probably the stage at which to judge how good the lecture course as a whole is likely to be. And of course, if you can discover which topics are likely to be covered when, you may decide to attend only for particular areas, rather than the entire course.

Another possible function of a course of lectures is to provide an overview, or general structure of the subject. You may well say that you can get this elsewhere, for example in a textbook. This is a perfectly reasonable approach to take, as long as you get a basic structure from somewhere. The structure need not, of course, be set in stone. You will find it useful at the start of the course, but if later it gets in the way, or is obviously inadequate, do not be afraid to dump it.

This leads to two other points about lectures. The first is not to rely too heavily on them. The introductory lecture is just that, and once you have become even remotely expert at the subject you will probably not find continued reference to your lecture notes of much use. After all, you only need to acquire the general structure once. A possible analogy might be starting a car. Unlike steam and electric engines, petrol and diesel engines do not start of their own accord; however hard you press the accelerator, the car will not go anywere until you have activated the starter. You need to turn the engine over to get the four-stroke cycle under way. However, once the engine has fired, it will carry on running without further assistance, and there is nothing to be gained by keeping the starter engaged (indeed, it is inadvisable to do so). Similarly, with the introductory lecture; it will get you started, but once you are under way, do not rely too heavily on it.

The final point to note about lectures is that the lecturer's words are not to be construed like statutes. If the lectures provide the general structure, the lecturer will probably try to make the subject as simple as possible. If he or she were to qualify every statement with all the possible counter-arguments and exceptions the lecture would be very dull and difficult to follow. Just because an unqualified and general statement is made in a lecture, therefore, you should not assume that the law is in reality that simple, but should be looking for the counter-arguments and exceptions which inevitably there will be.

TUTORIALS AND SEMINARS

If there is a single article of faith the questioning of which can be guaranteed to bring forth scorn and ridicule upon one's head, it is that small-group teaching is what university education is all about. It is the tutorials that distinguish us from the crammers, that make the British higher education system so eminently worthwhile. Nobody seems seriously to have questioned this; perhaps nobody has been brave enough to do so, for at least 20 years.

The reality, sadly, is often very different. So often I see and hear my colleagues addressing tutorial groups and engaging in demonstrations on the blackboard, just as if they were giving a conventional lecture. When I go into tutorials at the beginning of the year, students pick up their pens and prepare to take notes. Presumably they too are expecting a lecture; perhaps this has been their experience of tutorials in other subjects. I would have no objection to talking throughout the tutorial if that was what was required; after all, I know far more about the law of trusts than I can reasonably expound in 40 hours of lecturing. I would observe, however, that if I am going to give a lecture, it is far more efficient for me to give it once, to a class of 296 (the approximate present size of my trusts class) than 37 times to groups of eight students. Perhaps if staff and students really prefer lectures to tutorials, it is time for universities to recognise this and schedule more lectures, rather than pretend that there is something magic about small-group teaching, when the evidence shows that this is manifestly not the case.

It is also undeniably true (or so at least I have observed from conversations with students) that a lot of students also think that tutorials are a waste of time. However, this is not intended to be a counsel of despair. Tutorials are usually compulsory, and given that you have to go you may as well make the best of them. The suggestions here are intended to help you to do that. You have to realise, though, that the initiative rests with you, but that if you take it others will probably follow, and collectively you may be able significantly to improve the quality of the teaching.

You have to do the assigned work, and be prepared to ask questions, to get anything out of tutorials. Even if the tutorial is very one-way, with the tutor doing most of the talking, it is much easier to interrupt, to ask for elaboration, to test the tutor's reasoning, in a class of eight than it is in a class of 300 or so. I get hardly any questions in my large lectures, but nearly everyone seems happy to speak in tutorials, although I do not require anybody to do so. Another feature of the large lecture is that the lecturer usually has to assume that students do not prepare for them, so the treatment is necessarily rather basic. If in a tutorial you are clearly well-prepared, and if a few others follow your initiative, the tutor has no excuse for making the same assumption, and can talk at a much higher level. Ideally, of course, a tutorial should not be a monologue from the tutor, but should involve a degree of input from every student present, so that at the end of the class you all go away with the benefit of each other's research and ideas. In reality, students all too often decline to participate, and the tutorial degenerates into a mini-lecture. There is not much the tutor can do to force participation, however, so again it really is up to you to provide the input. You must not take a passive attitude towards tutorials, or there is a good chance that they really will be a waste of time. Sometimes students seem embarrassed to express their views, but your opinions are as valuable as those of anyone else in the group, and you are far more likely to gain the respect of your colleagues if you are prepared to test them in debate than if you are not. In any case all lawyers will have to perform publicly to some extent during their careers, and a tutorial is a safe place to practice.

Probably if you take the initiative others in the group will follow, and the tutorial will become much more lively and valuable. If not, and it remains deadly dull, you would be well advised to change to a different group if you can. In summary, then, tutorials can be useful, but too many are not. Whether or not they are depends to a great extent on your own personal effort.

It may be difficult at first to think up questions to ask in tutorials. Past exam papers are not usually much use until well into the course, because they are rarely on self-contained areas. The tutor of course may direct the work towards specific questions, and the casebooks are quite useful. Another good starting-point is to look at the more important cases, as was suggested in chapter 1 for the revision process. Consider how far the facts would have to change before the decision itself would be reversed. This forces you to consider exactly what the case stands for, and where there is more than one judgment, forces you to compare them. Remember also that no case ever reaches a higher court unless both sides have a plausible argument, and another possibility is to consider how you would have argued for the opposite result had you been counsel in the case. Casenotes and articles can assist you in this regard.

You will find, however, that as you go further into the subject questions will occur to you naturally, and study will become more interesting in the process.

In any case discussion should not end with the tutorials. You should try and get to know the other students in your tutorial group and continue the discussion after the tutorial has ended, perhaps over coffee. This should not be frowned upon as not being 'real work'. In fact, informal discussion is one of the best methods of working there is. Almost certainly it will give you ideas to explore during your private study, and will make the study more interesting. It is sadly neglected among many students. It may even be worth actively seeking out people who are prepared to argue over points arising from work on the course.

WRITTEN WORK

Most universities and polytechnics require periodic submission of written work, to which students sometimes object on the grounds that they could spend their time more usefully on other types of work. Nevertheless, essay-writing is useful, because you need to do far more than merely reproduce material. You need also to collect your ideas, work out a line of reasoning that is both coherent and logically consistent, assess contradictory views, and work out a logical order in which to present the material. This is not only time-consuming but also involves a great deal of hard thinking, which no doubt accounts in part for its unpopularity, but for precisely those reasons you are far more likely to remember the area covered.

In reality, of course, the processes required to produce a good essay are essentially the same as those required to attain a genuine understanding of the subject. At the risk of repeating what I have already said in chapter 1, you are being examined primarily on your understanding of the subject, and not merely on your recollection. For this reason, a good essay can be far more valuable than any other form of notes when it comes to revising for the exams, and it may well be a mistake to skimp on essay-writing.

HOW TO WORK

A lot of this has already been covered, because there should be no great difference in emphasis between working on the course and revision for exams, considered in chapter 1.

Try if you can to arrange your days so that your most active study can be accomplished in the part of the day when you are at your freshest, and banish the mundane tasks (e.g., note-taking or photocopying) to some other time. You do not, after all, need to be fresh for the mundane tasks.

There is another factor to bear in mind, which is that your time will certainly be limited, and you may not be able to read everything you wish. I would therefore suggest that the following order of reading materials has the advantage that even if you do not get time to cover them all, you will at least achieve a good basic coverage. This should not be regarded as a rigid order. If questions occur to you as you go along, you may wish to go straight to, e.g., the law reports to answer them, and in that case you should satisfy your curiosity before moving on.

I should perhaps emphasise that these suggestions are intended to apply when you look at a subject for the first time, perhaps for tutorial preparation purposes. Your main priority at this stage is to get a general feel for the area, to see how it fits together, and, possibly, how it fits in with other areas of the course already studied. The nature of law, however, is that it cannot be studied by reading material through once only. When you have got some idea of the general structure, you will need to think about and, almost certainly, re-read some of the material. The order in which you re-read material will probably depend simply on the questions you ask yourself, because you will want to find material that supports or refutes an argument. What follows, therefore, is strictly a first-time through order, the purpose being to provide structure for your later studies.

(a)   The relevant chapter of the textbook. Remember that this is only the first stage, and that textbooks only really cover the basic groundwork, though they can also be useful as triggers when you revise. I believe this to be true even of the very comprehensive textbooks, such as Pettit, *Equity and the Law of Trusts*, or Hanbury and Maudsley, *Modern Equity*. No student should rely on *any* textbook, however detailed, except to provide a starting-point for further study. Though textbooks are often quite good for answering essay-type questions, they are not well-suited to problems, where the examiner is probably looking for a close reading of the cases. Another disadvantage is that they are never right up to date except immediately after publication, and examiners often ask about the most recent developments.

Some students also tend to read textbooks in far too much detail early on in the course. Remember that you can always come back to them later. Your main priority early on is simply to establish some kind of structure. Once you have established the structure, move on to the next stage — you can always return later should your structure need further bolstering.

(b)   Casenotes and articles. Read the most recent first because they will discuss the earlier authorities and articles. Read them before reading the cases, because then you will get some idea of the points you should look for at that next stage. In effect, this is a form of introductory reading, which can enable you to take short cuts when you get to the next stage (i.e., the cases themselves). Also, if you run out of time you will have covered more ground by doing this first.

A number of such recent articles are discussed in the substantive chapters of the book. For example, the article by P. J. Millett on *Quistclose* trusts (1985) 101 LQR 269, mentioned in chapter 3, can give you a good idea what to look for when reading the cases themselves, as can the article by Brian Green (1984) 47 MLR 385, on the formalities cases discussed in chapter 6. Though neither of these articles is particularly easy, reading them at this stage is likely to save you considerable time at the next stage, whereas reading, e.g., the *Vandervell* litigation (chapter 6) without introduction is likely to be confusing in the extreme.

(c)   The cases themselves. Again, read the most recent first, because the earlier authorities will be discussed there. Reading the earlier cases first would have been a lot less efficient in terms of information gained per minute of study.

It is quite common for students in tutorials to claim that they could not read a case in time because too many other students were also trying to get hold of it, and the report was always out. This should rarely be a problem, though. Remember that nearly all cases are reported in several different reports (e.g., QB, All ER and WLR), so if you cannot find (say) the QB reference then *do* check through the indexes of the other reports, rather than leave it altogether.

I have already observed in chapter 1 how reluctant some students are to read cases. This has always genuinely baffled me, because at least 90% of my time is spent reading cases, even for subjects that I am studying for the first time. (Recently I have taken over the teaching of a labour law course, where my knowledge is very rusty, and I have used the textbooks and casebooks only to establish which cases I should read.) As far as I remember I was no different as a student. Perhaps I take this too far, because a criticism that has sometimes been levelled at my publications is that I pay insufficient regard to secondary sources, but the reason I do it is because reading cases is much more interesting. Therefore, why is it that not everybody finds this to be true? I have recently come to the conclusion that a lot of students do not really know how to read cases.

I have sometimes seen students apparently reading cases, or attempting to, from beginning to end. That is not the way to do it, at least not the first time through. As with all aspects of study, you need to work out why you are engaged in the particular activity. You can always read the case again, and you probably will, several times, so do not be too ambitious the first time through. You are trying to gain a general impression, determine where the case fits into the general scheme of things, perhaps discover whether, and if so how, it extended the law, and why it was fought. Some of this information you may already have gleaned from the course handouts, the textbooks and casenotes that you have already read. You may also have found the case in one of the excellent casebooks that are available in this subject. You need not be too ambitious reading the case for the first time. However, there are certainly some things you will want to establish straightaway: in which court the case was decided (I never cease to be astonished how many students overlook this obvious point); whether the decision was unanimous (if there was more than one judge); what the main issues were; and which other cases (if any) were applied, distinguished, or overruled.

When you read a case for a second or subsequent time it will probably be to check something specific. Go straight to it (you can often find from the cross-references in the headnote what you are looking for quite quickly). You can always return to it later, so there is still no need to read it from beginning to end. Maybe you will do this eventually, but you need not do so yet.

Students of trusts are lucky in terms of the quality and range of casebooks: They are useful in three main ways. First, they can be used as introductory reading at stage (b), before reading the cases themselves (indeed, some cases are so well covered that you may not need to read the full report at all). Secondly, they contain questions you can usefully work through. Thirdly, at times when access to the library is difficult (e.g., late at night or during vacations) you can still pursue your studies quite effectively.

You should not expect *never* to need the full reports, and casebooks suffer the same deficiency as textbooks in that they can never cover the most recent material. This is most likely to catch you out if a case has been appealed after publication of the casebook. Nevertheless, a good casebook can save a great deal of time. In fact, given the limited income of most students, there is a good argument that a cheap introductory textbook used in conjunction with one of the casebooks is better value than a single expensive textbook.

Further useful sources, given that examiners sometimes like to concentrate on the most recent material, are the casenotes on the subject in the general journals (e.g., *Law Quarterly Review, Modern Law Review, New Law Journal*) and in *The Conveyancer and Property Lawyer*. Though this last is primarily concerned with land law there is also quite a significant coverage of equity and trusts. Reading these from time to time will allow you to keep abreast of developments in the subject, and the exercise is especially valuable towards the end of the course. Only read the notes which are actually relevant to equity and trusts, of course! There may not be very many. Also, towards the end of the course it may be worth checking through the most recent index of the *All England Law Reports* or *Weekly Law Reports*, to see if there are new developments (and if there are, then reading the cases themselves, of course).

NOTE-TAKING

I am often asked by students about effective note-taking, and until recently I have been diffident in replying. Part of the problem is that I rarely take notes myself, and since I have been teaching trusts for many years, do not really need them. Recently, however, as I have observed, I have taken over a course on labour law, a subject at which I am not particularly expert, and have found myself taking notes again. I would therefore make the following observations, which seem at least to be of help to me.

The most important point, perhaps, is that apart from lectures (where, since the material is transient, it may be natural to try to get down as much as possible), there is little point in taking notes at all unless they are simpler and less detailed than the original material. If necessary, they can be revised to include greater detail later — the source material, after all, will not go away. A student complained to me recently that she had spent about three hours noting up a passage from a textbook, and ended up virtually copying it all out. I would suggest that generally there is probably little point in noting up textbooks at all, but, if you do, then all you need to preserve is the main arguments and outline structure. That will be useful to you at revision time, and you can return to the textbook later if you find you need more detail. Therefore, in general, I would suggest that less-detailed notes are more useful than more-detailed ones.

The same is true of notes of cases and articles, at any rate on a first read-through. In labour law recently, at which as I have observed I am a relative tyro, I have found it easier initially to make short notes on cases, recording the court, the main points at issue, the decision, the differences between judgments (if any), and, perhaps, how it fits in with other case law on the subject. This would amount to perhaps five to 10 lines, depending on the complexity of the case. This helps me fix the case in its proper position in the course. On reading the case on second and subsequent occasions I may spot additional points, and may therefore feel the need to revise my original notes; generally, however, by this stage I am better able to rely on my memory, and may not feel this need.

For articles, I generally find that it is a good idea to note up the main arguments, and references to the sources used to support those arguments (to enable me to check their validity for myself — never assume, incidentally, that the sources cited support the argument advanced, as some writers are uncritical in this regard).

Something I do when I am preparing lectures or writing is to make little notes to myself in the text to do things (e.g., compare Ferguson's view at . . . — is this reconcilable with *Binions v Evans*? — look up). I surround these notes by three exclamation marks so that I can easily search for them (since I generally do not use three exclamation marks in normal writing), and, of course, remove them before submitting the project for publication.

Some people find the need, as the examination approaches, to summarise their own notes. I suspect that this is probably a waste of time, except where these are very short trigger notes which can be looked at just before the exam.

Of course, different methods of study suit different people, but I would hope that this guidance, which is, after all, based on personal experience, is of assistance.

3   FUNDAMENTALS OF A TRUST

It is not possible to progress far in a trusts course without understanding what a trust is. We begin this chapter, therefore, with a broad-brush examination of the trust. Then we consider various aspects of trusts, and requirements for setting one up. The chapter ends with a comparison between the trust and other legal concepts, in particular the contract and the loan.

MAIN FEATURES OF A TRUST

It is necessary to bear in mind the following characteristics of a trust when considering the requirements for setting one up, and when comparing the trusts with other legal concepts, whose effects, seem superficially to be similar:

(a)   An essential feature of a trust is that legal title is vested in the trustee(s) and equitable title is vested in the beneficiary or beneficiaries. This is what is achieved by constituting the trust, and it distinguishes the trust from concepts such as bailment, which does not involve any transfer of title away from the bailor. Only possession is transferred.

(b)   Equitable title can be asserted against anybody except a *bona fide* purchaser of legal title for value without notice, against whom it is lost. This is an application of the equitable maxim 'where there is equal equity, the law shall prevail'. There is equal equity where the acquirer of legal title and the beneficiary are equally 'innocent', which is why the acquirer of legal title must be a *bona fide* purchaser for value without notice. If the acquirer satisfies that test, the law (i.e., the legal title) shall prevail.

By contrast, legal title, which is, of course, retained by a bailor, is in principle good against all the world, but, in reality, can easily be lost through the operation of sale of goods legislation, such as the Factors Act 1889, ss. 2, 8 and 9, or the Sale of Goods Act 1979, ss. 21 to 26.

(c)   Even where legal or equitable title to property is lost, for example where a trustee or bailee sells the property, it may still be possible to trace into the proceeds of sale. Where there is a trust, the equitable tracing rules apply, whereas a bailor is restricted to tracing at common law. This can make a substantial difference where the proceeds are paid into a mixed bank account, into which it is difficult or impossible to trace at law, but where tracing may be possible in equity.

(d)   Equitable title protects the beneficiary against the bankruptcy of trustee. The effect of this is clearly seen in the *Quistclose* trust, discussed later in this chapter.

(e)   A trustee owes duties which are potentially onerous to the beneficiary. By contrast, a donor owes no duties to a donee once the donor has relinquished the property. This is why the courts will not infer a perfect trust (with declaration of self as trustee) from an imperfect gift. There is no reason to infer from an intention to give property away that donor intended to saddle himself/herself with the onerous obligations of trusteeship.

(f)   Once constituted, the trust is irrevocable (unless the settlor has specifically granted himself/herself or someone else a power to revoke the settlement), and the settlor can neither reclaim the trust property nor vary interests granted under the trust. The importance of this can be clearly seen when we consider declaration of self as trustee, later in this chapter. If the declaration is not intended to be irrevocable, then no trust will have been created. It is also one of the differences between granting a third party a benefit under a contract and making that third party a beneficiary under a trust. In the former case the contracting parties can change their minds and vary the contract. In the case of the trust the beneficiary's rights are permanent.

(g)   The beneficiaries have enforceable rights even though they may have given no consideration in return for their benefits under the trust. This is another difference between granting a third party a benefit under a contract and making that third party a beneficiary under a trust. In the former case the third party is given no enforceable rights.

(h)   Only a beneficiary can enforce a non-charitable trust. The settlor has no enforceable rights, because he or she retains no interest in the property (assuming he or she is not a trustee or beneficiary). This is the entire rationale for the existence of the principles of law discussed in chapter 5.

(i)   It is possible to have a trust of any type of property. This was the original meaning of the equitable maxim 'equity follows the law'. Any property interests which are recognised at common law are also capable of existing in equity. Indeed, since the range of legal property interests that can exist in land was restricted by the Law of Property Act 1925, s. 1, equity now recognises a greater range of property interests than the common law. Furthermore, an equitable interest can itself form the subject-matter of a trust. In other words, a beneficiary under a trust may constitute a further trust of his equitable interest, thereby creating a sub-trust. Sub-trusts are common in tax-avoiding settlements. The beneficiary under the sub-trust can himself repeat the process, creating a further sub-trust, and there is no limit to the number of times this process may be repeated.

DISTINCTION BETWEEN LEGAL AND EQUITABLE TITLE

A trust's most important attribute is that legal and equitable title can be vested in different persons. In this section, therefore, we consider how legal and equitable title relate to each other. In the next section we consider how legal and equitable title are separated (in other words, the constitution of trusts), and the related areas of certainty of intention and certainty of subject-matter.

ESSAY QUESTION

The following question appeared on a recent examination paper:

Are equitable rights rights *in personam* or rights *in rem*?

It is not, I would suggest, a very good question, since it appears to presuppose a black or white answer, and I therefore propose that instead we examine the following question:

To what extent, if at all, is it accurate to describe equitable rights as rights *in personam*? To what extent, if at all, is it accurate to describe them as rights *in rem*?

This question more clearly invites you to consider grey areas, and indeed, it will become apparent that it is inappropriate to describe equitable interests entirely in terms of either rights *in rem* or rights *in personam*.

Equity acts *in personam* is a well known maxim of equity. The original use derived from the discretion of the medieval Chancellor to issue royal writs, and to make orders against individuals. These individuals would often have been those with legal title to the property, and it is still a feature of equitable jurisdiction that it is exercised against specific persons, usually trustees. Just as in the case of the use the remedy was personal against the feoffee to uses, who held the legal estate in the land so in a modern trust the action is against the owner of the legal estate in land, or the legal owner of money or goods.

Nevertheless, as equity developed it acted not only against the original legal owner of the property, but also against subsequent owners in certain circumstances. This development blossomed into what later became the notice doctrine, which was most clearly seen in the development of interests in land. As a result it became reasonable to describe certain equitable rights as property rights, and to talk about equitable title to land, and equitable ownership of goods. It is also the case that various statutory provisions, and, in particular, the 1925 property legislation and some taxation legislation, treat equitable interests as property interests. Thus, s. 53(1)(c) of the Law of Property Act 1925 provides:

[A] disposition of an equitable interest or trust subsisting at the time of the disposition must be in writing signed by the person disposing of the same, or by his agent thereunto lawfully authorised by writing or by will.

This clearly suggests the existence of equitable interests, which are presumably property interests, and which therefore have the characteristics of rights *in rem*.

The courts have also accepted that some equitable rights can have the characteristics of rights *in rem*. In *Baker* v *Archer-Shee* [1927] AC 844, a beneficiary was considered to be the owner of dividends for tax purposes. In *National Provincial Bank Ltd* v *Ainsworth* [1965] AC 1175, the House of Lords distinguished between equitable interests in land, which were full property rights capable of binding third parties as overriding interests under s. 70(1)(g) of the Land Registration Act 1925, and 'mere equities', which were not capable of binding third parties at all.

In *Tinsley* v *Milligan* [1994] 1 AC 340, Stella Tinsley and Kathleen Milligan jointly purchased a home which was registered in Tinsley's name alone. On the principles set out in chapter 7, the beneficial interest would have been shared between Tinsley and Milligan in equal shares; however, to both Tinsley's and Milligan's knowledge, the home was registered in Tinsley's name alone to enable Milligan to make false claims to the Department of Social Security for benefits. After a quarrel Tinsley moved out, and claimed possession from Milligan. Milligan counterclaimed, seeking a declaration that the house was held by Tinsley on trust for both of them in equal shares. Tinsley argued that Milligan's claim was barred by the common law doctrine *ex turpi causa non oritur actio* and by the principle that 'he who comes to equity must come with clean hands'.

The House of Lords held (Lord Keith and Lord Goff dissenting) that because the presumption of resulting trust applied, Milligan could establish her equitable interest without relying on the illegal transaction, and was therefore entitled to succeed. The case supports the argument, I would suggest, that Milligan's resulting trust interest was a property interest in its own right, which had an existence that was independent of the precise arrangement between the couple. Had it been no more than merely a collection of personal rights against Tinsley, Milligan would surely have failed, since she would have been unable to assert those rights without disclosing the fraud. Lord Browne-Wilkinson went so far as to say:

> More than 100 years have elapsed since the fusion of the administration of law and equity. The reality of the matter is that, in 1993, English law has one single law of property made up of legal and equitable interests. Although for historical reasons legal estates and equitable estates have differing incidents, the person owning either type of estate has a right of property, a right *in rem* not merely a right *in personam*. If the law is that a party is entitled to enforce a property right acquired under an illegal transaction, in my judgment the same rule ought to apply to any property right so acquired, whether such right is legal or equitable.

Even if (as I would suggest) this statement goes too far, it is clear at the very least that some equitable rights also have the characteristics of rights *in rem*. However, it is also still true to say that they have some of the characteristics of rights *in personam*. Indeed, some equitable rights, such as the 'mere equities' considered by the House of Lords in *National Provincial Bank Ltd* v *Ainsworth* (above), do not have the characteristics of rights *in rem* at all.

In *Richard West and Partners (Inverness) Ltd* v *Dick* [1969] 2 Ch 424, the Court of Appeal held that the English courts had jurisdiction to grant a decree of specific performance of a contract for the sale of land abroad (in Scotland). The defendant was within the jurisdiction, and Harman LJ observed:

> ... that the Court of Chancery, acting as it does *in personam*, is well able to grant specific performance of a contract to buy or sell foreign land, provided the defendant is domiciled within its jurisdiction.

In this case, however, the personal rights are presumably additional to any real rights created. If the land were in England, beneficial interests in it would surely not be defeated merely because the trustee was abroad.

However, there may be situations where the beneficiary's rights are limited by the personal nature of the action. It is also often the trustee, not the beneficiary, who takes action against a third party in respect of the trust property. For example, where property is leased it is the trustee who sues for rent: *Shalit* v *Joseph Nadler Ltd* [1933] 2 KB 79. Of course, the trustee is accountable to the beneficiary, and can be required by the beneficiary to sue, but the beneficiary cannot sue the third party directly. This is a case where the trustee's rights are right *in rem*, whereas those of the beneficiary are limited to a personal action against the trustee.

Students of the law of tort will know that, generally speaking, only the owner of property at the time that it is damaged can sue in negligence. It is probable that an equitable owner does not count for these purposes, and that only the legal owner can sue. Again, of course, the equitable owner can require the legal owner to sue. In *Leigh & Sullivan Ltd* v *Aliakmon Shipping Co. Ltd, The Aliakmon* [1986] AC 785, buyers of a quantity of steel coils failed in a negligence action against the shipowners who had badly stowed the cargo abroad *The Aliakmon*, as a result of which it suffered damage, because property in the cargo had not passed to them by the time the damage occurred. The buyers alternatively claimed that they were equitable owners of the cargo (on the grounds that equity treats as done that which ought to be done, and that property ought to pass to them). However, Lord Brandon thought that even if they were equitable owners, that would not give them the right to sue in negligence:

> My Lords, under this head Mr Clarke [for the buyers] put forward two propositions of law. The first proposition was that a person who has the equitable ownership of goods is entitled to sue in tort for negligence anyone who by want of care causes them to be lost or damaged without joining the legal owner as a party to the action. . . .
>
> In my view, the first proposition cannot be supported. . . . If . . . the person is the equitable owner of the goods and no more, then he must join the legal owner as a party to the action, either as co-plaintiff if he is willing or as co-defendant if he is not. This had always been the law in the field of equitable ownership of land and I see no reason why it should not also be so in the field of equitable ownership of goods.

He also held that the buyers in fact had no equitable ownership, so that these remarks are technically *obiter dicta*, but I would suggest that there is no reason to doubt their correctness.

I would suggest, therefore, that although for many purposes equitable rights have the characteristics of rights *in rem*, vestiges of their personal origins still remain.

CONSTITUTION OF A TRUST, AND ATTENDANT CONSEQUENCES

In order for a valid private trust to come into existence, these two elements are both necessary and sufficient.

(a)   There must be a manifest intention on the part of the settlor to create a trust (and not to effect some other kind of transaction, such as making an outright gift or loan). As a corollary to this proposition, we might add that the intention must be expressed in a way which complies with the certainty requirements (see chapter 5).

(b)   A trust involves a division of the ownership of property. The trustees become owners at common law, and are given control of the property. The beneficiaries become owners in equity, and in effect it is they who may enjoy the property. The property must therefore be properly vested in trustees who hold it in that capacity on behalf of the beneficiaries.

Two Methods of Constituting a Trust

The leading authority on constitution of trusts is often taken to be *Milroy* v *Lord* (1862) 4 De G F & J 264.

In that case the settlor had executed a voluntary deed, purporting to transfer shares to a trustee on trust for the plaintiffs. The voluntary deed was incapable of transferring legal title, however, since that could only be achieved by registering the name of the transferee in the books of the bank.

The Court of Appeal in Chancery held that no trust had been constituted, Turner LJ stating the law as follows:

> ... in order to render a voluntary settlement valid and effectual, the settlor must have done everything which, according to the nature of the property comprised in the settlement, was necessary to be done in order to transfer the property and render the settlement binding upon him. He may of course do this by actually transferring the property to the persons for whom he intends to provide, and the provision will then be effectual, and it will be equally effectual if he transfers the property to a trustee for the purposes of the settlement, or declares that he himself holds it on trust for those purposes; ... but, in order to render the settlement binding, one or other of these modes must ... be resorted to, for there is no equity in this Court to perfect an imperfect gift. The cases I think go further to this extent, that if the settlement is intended to be effectuated by one of the modes to which I have referred, the Court will not give effect to it by applying another of those modes. If it is intended to take effect by transfer, the Court will not hold the intended transfer to operate as a declaration of trust, for then every imperfect instrument would be made effectual by being converted into a perfect trust.

In this passage, Turner LJ envisages two possible methods of constituting a trust: transfer of property to a trustee, and declaration of self as trustee. It is also clear from the last part of the passage, however, that if the intention is to constitute the trust by transfer to a trustee, and for some reason the transfer cannot take effect, the court will not attempt to give effect to the transaction by inferring a declaration of self as trustee. This aspect of the case is discussed further below, but I would suggest that it can be justified on the principle that trusteeship involves onerous obligations, and there is no reason to suppose that somebody who attempts to give property away manifests any intention to be bound by such obligations.

Transfer to Trustees

Usually, the property will be transferred to third parties as trustees. This is also the stage at which problems may arise in examination problems, e.g., if the settlor fails to observe the proper formalities of the transfer — or if, having agreed to transfer the property, he omits to do so.

PROBLEM QUESTION

Alpha has shares, and a controlling interest, in a company in the newly recognised state of Aquarius.

Alpha has an illegitimate son, Gamma, to whom he intends to transfer the shares. Alpha does everything he can to transfer the shares to Gamma, but Aquarian Government consent is required before title can be transferred. In 999 cases in every thousand this is a formality, but the Aquarian Government reserves the right to ask for further and better particulars, and the right to refuse consent.

The Aquarian Government requires further and better particulars, but by this time Alpha has fallen out with Gamma, and refuses to provide them (so that the Government refuses consent to the transfer), or to take any further steps to transfer the shares. Alpha is so angry with Gamma that he fails even to manage the company effectively, so that the shares fall dramatically in value.

Advise Gamma.

This is based on a problem in a recent examination paper, but is actually a slightly shortened version of it, since the original problem question also contained a covenant to settle point (on which see chapter 4).

Generally speaking, the legal title must actually be transferred to the trustees, but in the passage from *Milroy* v *Lord* (above), Turner LJ required the settlor to do no more than everything which was necessary to be done in order to transfer the property. This suggests that the trust can come into existence prior to the actual transfer of property, as long as the settlor has not, as in *Milroy* v *Lord* itself, used a method which is incapable of effecting a transfer at all. However, where the settlor has done all that is within his power to constitute the trust by transferring the property to a trustee, but has been thwarted by formalities which are outside his control, equity regards the trust as constituted by the last act of the settlor.

This principle was applied in *Re Rose* [1952] Ch 449 (CA), where the settlor intended to transfer shares, but where the directors of the company had an effective veto over any transfer. The Court of Appeal held that the date of constitution of the trust was when the settlor had done all he could (March 1943), not when the directors consented to and registered the transfer (June 1943). The precise date was important for the purposes of assessing estate duty.

Evershed MR noted: 'In this case, as I understand it, the testator had done everything in his power to divest himself of the shares in question . . .', and it is clear that the case turns on this. In *Re Fry* [1946] 1 Ch 312, by contrast, more may have been required from the testator effectively to transfer legal title to the shares. The reason in this case that the shares could not be registered was because Treasury consent had not been obtained, as required by the Defence (Finance) Regulations 1939, and the shares could not be registered until Treasury consent had been obtained. Although all the requisite forms had been filled in by the donor, the required Treasury consent had not been obtained before he died.

This may appear, at first sight, to be similar to *Rose*, but, as Romer J explained (at p. 317):

> Now I should have thought it was difficult to say that the testator had done everything that was required to be done by him at the time of his death, for it was necessary for him to obtain permission from the Treasury for the assignment and he had not obtained it. Moreover, the Treasury might in any case have required further information of the kind referred to in the questionnaire submitted to him, or answers supplemental to those which he had given in reply to it; and, if so approached, he might have refused to concern himself with the matter further, in which case I do not know how anyone else could have compelled him to do so.

In this case, therefore, the testator may not have done all that was required, so the principles later elaborated in *Re Rose* could not apply.

As we saw at the beginning of the chapter, a trust is, in principle, irrevocable, so that if, as in *Fry*, the settlor has the opportunity later to change his mind, the courts should not hold that a trust has been created. The problem is that it may be difficult to know whether or not the settlor will be required to do anything else. In the problem question, we are told that in 999 cases in every thousand Aquarian Government consent is a formality, but the Aquarian Government reserves the right to ask for further and better particulars, and it does so in this case. You are being asked to consider whether this case is analogous to *Rose* or *Fry*. If you consider that there has been no effective transfer here, you should also consider exactly what requirements are necessary before the *Rose* principle operates. Would it be necessary, for example, for the recipient to be under a legal obligation to consent?

If there is a trust, you are also asked to consider the effect of Alpha's mismanagement of the company. After all, legal title has, in fact, remained in Alpha throughout, so Gamma's title, if any, is equitable, in which case Alpha is necessarily a trustee. On normal principles of trusteeship, therefore, Alpha will be liable to Gamma for the fall in value of the shares. However, whatever else Alpha intended, he never intended, nor manifested any intention, to take on the onerous obligations of trusteeship of these shares. Surely it is quite unreasonable, therefore, to require him to be bound by these obligations.

Re Rose itself is silent on this issue, but one way around the problem would be for this to take effect as a constructive trust, in which case Alpha's obligations may be lower than those of an express trustee. It is possible to argue that the trust is imposed by law, simply because although Alpha undoubtedly has legal title, he has retained no beneficial title in the shares. This is similar to Jenkins LJ's reasoning in *Re Rose*.

Further support for the constructive trust view can be found from the Court of Appeal decision in *Mascall* v *Mascall* (1984) 50 P & CR 119, where *Re Rose* was applied to a transfer of registered land. The transferor had executed a transfer and sent it to the Inland Revenue; he had also handed the land certificate to the transferee. At this stage, before the transfer and land certificate had been sent to the Land Registry for registration of the transferee as proprietor, the transferor changed his mind, after a quarrel with the transferee. The Court of Appeal held the transfer effective, since it was for the transferee to apply to the Land Registry for registration as proprietor, and the transferor had done everything he had to do to complete the transfer.

The relevance of *Mascall* v *Mascall* to the present discussion is that declarations of trusteeship in land must be in writing by virtue of s. 53(1)(b) of the Law of Property Act 1925, but a constructive trust is exempted from this requirement by s. 53(2). Therefore, although there is no discussion of this point in the Court of Appeal, it is probably reasonable to assume that this was a constructive trust. If *Rose* trusts are constructive trusts then that has implications for Alpha's liability in the problem.

Declaration of Self as Trustee

Another possibility is for the settlor to declare himself trustee of the trust property, in which case no transfer of the legal title is necessary. We have already seen that the courts will not infer this intention from a failed gift, and that the rationale for the principle is that the obligations of a trustee are onerous, whereas a donor's responsibilities end from the date of the gift. There is no reason, therefore, to infer from a failed gift that the intended donor is prepared to accept the onerous obligations of trusteeship.

Thus, in *Jones* v *Lock* (1865) LR 1 Ch App 25, the father of a baby boy handed a cheque to his nine-month old son, uttering words which made it clear that he meant the child to have the sum represented by the cheque, although he immediately removed the cheque from the baby for safe-keeping. He died some days later, without having endorsed the cheque, which would have been necessary to pass title in it to the child. The court refused to construe his actions as amounting to a declaration of trust, with himself as trustee, in favour of the child.

Lord Cranworth LC did not think that an irrevocable intention to part with the property had been manifested. There was an intention to make an outright gift, but no gift had actually been made. It was not, therefore, a declaration of trust.

A similar result obtained in *Richards* v *Delbridge* (1874) LR Eq 11. Delbridge wished to give his infant grandson, Richards, the lease he had on his place of business as a bone manure merchant. He indorsed on the lease: 'This deed and all thereto belonging I give to Edward Benetto Richards from this time forth, with all the stock-in-trade'. He gave the lease to Richards' mother to hold for Richards, but died before the lease was actually delivered to Richards himself. It was held that there had been no transfer of the lease to Richards, nor a declaration of trust in his favour. Sir George Jessel MR refused to infer a declaration of trust from the failed gift:

> ... the legal owner of the property may ... declare that he will hold it from that time forward on trust for the other person. It is true that he need not use the words, 'I declare myself a trustee', but he must do something which is equivalent to it, and use expressions which have that meaning ... for a man to make himself trustee there must be an expression of intention to become a trustee, whereas words of present gift shew an intention to give over property to another, and not to retain it in the donor's own hands for any purpose, fiduciary or otherwise.

This passage emphasises the difference between gift and trust, that the donor retains no interest after the property has been transferred, whereas a trustee's fiduciary obligations continue. It is no surprise, therefore, that the courts will not infer a declaration of trusteeship from a failed gift.

In the above passage, however, Jessel MR observed that the settlor need not use the words, 'I declare myself a trustee', but he must do something which is equivalent to it. It is possible to infer declaration of trusteeship from conduct, or from words which can be construed as equivalent to a declaration of trusteeship, or from a mixture of the two. In *Paul* v *Constance* [1977] 1 WLR 527, Constance was injured at work, and obtained £950 in damages, which he put into a bank account in his name alone. The evidence suggested, however, that the money was intended for himself and Mrs Paul, with whom he was living, but he was not married to Mrs Paul, and the reason for not opening a joint account was to save her embarrassment (this was apparently on the instigation of the bank manager).

Subsequent additions were made to the account, in particular from bingo winnings which Constance and Paul played as a joint venture. One withdrawal of £150 was also made, which was divided equally between them.

Constance died, and the question at issue was whether Mrs Paul could claim any share of the fund. If the money in the account had belonged solely to Constance, then his wife, Mrs Constance, from whom he had parted, would be entitled to it on his death.

The Court of Appeal held that Constance held the money on trust for Mrs Paul. No words of trust were used, but regard was had to the unsophisticated character of Constance, and the nature of his relationship with Mrs Paul. Scarman LJ said:

> ... there must be clear evidence from what is said or done of an intention to create a trust ... 'an intention to dispose of property or a fund so that somebody else to the exclusion of the disponent acquires a beneficial interest in it.' ...
>
> When one looks at the detailed evidence to see whether it goes as far as that — and I think that the evidence does go as far as that — one finds that from the time that the deceased received his damages right up to his death he was saying, on occasions, that the money was as much the plaintiff's as his. When they discussed the damages, how to invest them or what to do with them and when they discussed the bank account, he would say to her: 'The money is as much yours as mine'....
>
> It might, however, be thought that this was a borderline case, since it is not easy to pinpoint a specific moment of declaration, ...

There are two further points to make regarding *Paul* v *Constance*. First, in addition to Constance's conduct, there are his words: 'The money is as much yours as mine'. These may not obviously seem equivalent to a declaration of trusteeship, but surely what he is really saying is that although (because the bank manager advised it) legal title to the money would be vested in Constance, the money in fact belonged to both of them. Since Constance had legal title, it could only be the equitable title that was shared, so, in fact, these words are exactly appropriate for a declaration of trusteeship. We discuss similar informal words of declaration in chapter 7.

The second point is that Scarman LJ thought it difficult to pinpoint a specific moment of declaration. If it had been impossible to do so, I would suggest that there ought to have been no trust. Trusts are, in principle, irrevocable, and there must be a moment at which the irrevocable commitment is made. Before that moment, Constance could have changed his mind. Afterwards, he could not. That is essential to the nature of a trust, although in the case itself it was difficult to pinpoint exactly which moment this was.

PROBLEM QUESTION

The following question appeared on a recent examination paper:

> Omega is a raver who frequents acid-house parties, where a substance known as 'Z' is regularly consumed, because of the euphoric effects it induces in the consumers. He is also a manufacturer of, and dealer in 'Z'. 'Z' is a newly invented substance, the legality of which has not been determined.
>
> Omega is also the owner of an enormous Stilton cheese. He is unusually ecstatic because of a big 'Z' deal which he has just satisfactorily concluded. In celebration, he takes centre stage at the acid-house party he is attending, and to the accompaniment of the laser light show announces to everyone present: 'I'm definitely and irrevocably giving away my Stilton cheese. All you ravers out there on 'Z' who like Stilton are entitled to an equal share'.
>
> There are about 2,000 people at the acid-house party, most but not all of whom have consumed various quantities of 'Z'. No record is kept of the identity of those present. On the assumption that there is enough Stilton for 2,000 people, is there a trust of the Stilton? If not, could Omega have created a trust of the cheese by using different wording, and, if so, what wording would have sufficed?

Although the main part of this question raises issues of certainty of object considered in chapter 5, there is also the additional question whether the words that Omega uses are sufficient to constitute a declaration of trusteeship by him of the cheese. You may prefer to regard this as a question of certainty of intention, but whether it should be regarded as a certainty or constitution issue is not really important; it is, in any, case probably a mistake to attempt to classify everything too precisely.

We have seen earlier in the chapter that it is possible to declare oneself trustee of property even in the absence of words of trust. In *Re Kayford* [1975] 1 WLR 279, a mail order company was in financial difficulties. In order to protect customers in event of insolvency, the company considered setting up a separate bank account, called the 'Customers' Trust Deposit Account', to hold the customers' deposits and payments until their goods were delivered, the intention of the company being that this money should be kept separate from the company's general funds. However, the company took the advice of the bank and, instead of opening a new account, used a dormant account (with a small credit balance) in the company's name. On the winding-up of the company, Megarry J held that the money in the account (apart from small credit balance) was held on trust for the customers. The company was held to have declared itself trustee of the money for its customers. Hence, the customers were not mere creditors of the company but beneficial owners of

FUNDAMENTALS OF A TRUST

the moneys which they had paid until such time as their goods were delivered. Megarry J observed that:

... it is well settled that a trust can be created without using the words 'trust' or 'confidence' or the like: the question is whether a sufficient intention to create a trust has been manifested.

There are no words of trust here, so the question is whether a sufficient intention to create a trust has been manifested. *Re Kayford* was applied by the Court of Appeal in *Re Chelsea Cloisters Ltd* (1980) 41 P & CR 98, where a 'tenants' deposit account' was set up to hold deposits against damage and breakages. However, there must be evidence of an intention to create a trust, which it must be remembered is an irrevocable step, depriving the settlor of all beneficial interest in the money. The requisite intention was not present in *Re Multi Guarantee Co. Ltd* [1987] BCLC 257, where the Court of Appeal distinguished the two previous cases. It had not been finally decided what to do with the money in the account, so an irrevocable intention was not established. (These cases have been criticised recently by Professor Michael Bridge (1992) 12 OJLS 333, at pp. 355–7.)

There is no particular problem here about irrevocability, since Omega claims to be 'definitely and irrevocably giving away my Stilton cheese'. The only problem is that he talks in terms of gift rather than trust, and, as we have seen, the courts do not regard gifts as equivalent. This may not necessarily be fatal, but you are asked whether, if there is no trust, Omega could have used different wording and, if so, what wording would have sufficed. Obviously, it is better to use words of trust rather than words of gift.

Further Points to Note on Declaration of Trusteeship

In chapter 7, we examine declaration of trusteeship in a different context, so we tie off this section by noting aspects of declaration of trusteeship which are also relevant to the discussion in that chapter. The irrevocable and immediate effect of trusteeship has been noted: a mere statement of future intention, for example, would clearly not constitute a declaration of trusteeship.

I would also suggest that in determining whether someone has declared himself trustee, the courts are not concerned to ascertain his intention as such, but, instead, to adopt the position of a reasonable observer. Thus, in *Richards v Delbridge* (1874) LR Eq 11, Sir George Jessel MR concentrates on the words used, observing that 'however anxious the Court may be to carry out a man's intention, it is not at liberty to construe words otherwise than according to their proper meaning'. This suggests that the man's actual intention is irrelevant. In *Re Kayford* [1975] 1 WLR 279, Megarry J, at p. 282A, talks in terms of an intention being manifested, rather than merely held. The emphasis is again on the manifestation — the effect on the reasonable observer — rather than on the actual subjective intention of the company.

As we will see in chapter 4, it is also necessary that the property must be existing property: (*Re Ellenborough* [1903] 1 Ch 697); that is to say that, at the time of the declaration, legal title must be vested in the settlor. It is not possible to declare oneself trustee of property to which one might become entitled at some future time. This is usually regarded as an aspect of certainty of subject-matter (see below).

Finally, a trust creates full beneficial interests in the beneficiary, which (subject to the proviso at the beginning of the chapter) are capable of binding third parties.

CERTAINTY OF SUBJECT-MATTER

To be valid, a trust must satisfy the three certainty requirements, certainty of intention, certainty of subject-matter and certainty of object. Certainty of intention is really no more than the requisite intention that needs to be shown to set up a trust, and was essentially covered in the last section. Certainty of object is discussed (because it fits in there better) in chapter 5. It is also necessary, however, that the subject-matter be defined with reasonable certainty.

To satisfy the test it appears to be necessary that the trust property be defined in objective rather than subjective terms, or, in other words, so as not to be a matter on which opinions may reasonably differ. In *Palmer* v *Simmonds* (1854) 2 Drew 221 a testatrix left on trust 'the bulk' of her residuary estate, and Kindersley V-C, after consulting a dictionary, concluded that the word 'bulk' was inadequate to specify any portion of the property as trust property:

What is the meaning then of bulk? The appropriate meaning, according to its derivation, is something which bulges out ... Its popular meaning we all know. When a person is said to have given the bulk of his property, what is meant is not the whole but the greater part, and that is in fact consistent with its classical meaning. When, therefore, the testatrix uses that term, can I say that she has used a term expressing a definite, clear, certain part of her estate, or the whole of her estate? I am bound to say that she has not designated the subject as to which she expresses her confidence; and I am therefore of opinion that there is no trust created; that [the residuary legatee] took absolutely, and those claiming under him now take.

A similar approach was adopted in *Re Kolb's WT* [1962] Ch 531, where the testator referred, in an investment clause in his will, to 'blue-chip' securities, a term generally used to designate shares in large public companies which are considered an entirely safe investment. The term has no technical or objective meaning, however, and Cross J held that its meaning in the context must depend on the standard applied by the testator, which could not be determined with sufficient certainty to enable the clause to be upheld. The case was considered in a different context in *Trustees of the British Museum* v *Attorney-General* [1984] 1 All ER 337, which is discussed in chapter 10.

In *Re Golay's WT* [1965] 1 WLR 969, the testator had directed his trustees to allow 'Totty' to 'enjoy one of my flats during her lifetime and to receive a reasonable income from my other properties'. Ungoed-Thomas J felt able to uphold the gift, as the trustees could select a flat, and the income to be received by Totty could be quantified objectively by the court. If, on the other hand, Totty had been entitled to receive what the testator or a specified person considered to be reasonable, then the trust would fail, since the test would be subjective.

The judgment in *Re Golay's WT* is very short, and the case appears to be out of line with the others considered. The test cannot simply be whether the income could be objectively quantified by the court, since a court could equally well quantify 'the bulk' or 'blue-chip securities'. Can it really be supposed that a court, faced with a statutory provision which applied to 'blue-chip securities' would be unable to apply the provision? The courts can define the reasonable man. Surely they would not be defeated by 'blue-chip securities'.

I would suggest that in *Re Golay's WT*, Ungoed-Thomas J misunderstood the function of a certainty test (further elaboration upon which can be found in chapter 5). It is not, I would suggest, to make life easier for courts, but to ensure that the trustees can administer the trust. That is why precise objective definitions are required, so that the trustees know exactly which property is subject to the trust, and which property is not. A 'reasonable income' would not seem sufficiently certain to satisfy that criterion, unless the view were taken that the trustees should forever be coming to court to obtain directions.

In *Hunter* v *Moss* [1994] 1 WLR 452 (followed in *Re Lewis's of Leicester Ltd* [1995] 1 BCLC 428), an oral declaration of trusteeship of 50 shares of a company's issued share capital of 1,000 shares succeeded, even though the particular shares were not ascertained or identified. However, the company was precisely identified, all the shares in that company were identical, and the quantification (50 shares) was obviously precise. Moreover, as long as the trustee retained all 1,000 shares there would be no point in identifying which 50 shares were subject to the trust. However, if I were an examiner looking to set a problem based on *Hunter* v *Moss*, the trustee would have sold the shares and invested (say) half the proceeds in fund A and half in fund B. One fund would have performed very badly and the other very well, and the question would be, in which fund are the trust shares?

I would suggest that this problem would not arise if the settlement had been of 5% of the issued share capital, since then it would be clear that the trust owned 5% of fund A and 5% of fund B. I would also suggest that this should be the starting point here also, but would tentatively advance the following additional suggestions, which are not based on authority (there is none), but are consistent with authorities on tracing into mixed funds (an area which raises similar issues).

(a)   The trustee might have expressly identified the fund into which the trust shares were to be placed. This would be sensible, for example, if the powers of investment under the trust allowed investment in fund A but not fund B, or *vice versa*. Such an identification ought to be conclusive, since the trustee ought to be entitled to separate out his or her own shares and invest them wherever he or she pleased. If, however, the trust investment had performed badly, the trustee might, on the principles enunciated in *Speight* v *Gaunt* (1883) 9 App Cas 1, become liable to reimburse the trust.

(b)   If there had been no identification of the fund into which the trust shares were to be placed, and investment in fund A (but not fund B) would be a breach of trust, either because it exceeded the investment powers or because, in respect of the fund A investment, the trustee had fallen below the *Speight* v *Gaunt* standard, the trustee ought not later to be able to plead his own breach of trust, so as to claim that any of the trust money had been invested in fund A. Therefore, if fund A had performed badly all the trust moneys would be in fund B. However, if fund A had performed well, the beneficiaries would be able to ratify the unlawful investment and claim a 5% share of fund A. This is consistent with the principles enunciated in *Re Hallett's Estate* (1880) 13 Ch D 696, one of the leading cases on tracing into mixed funds. It is doubtful, however, that the trust could claim that all its moneys had been invested in fund A, since there would be nothing unlawful in the trustee claiming that 95% of fund A was made up of the proceeds attributable to his shares, rather than those of the trust. The trustee could not insist on 100%, however, without previously having expressly divided the funds.

TRUSTS COMPARED WITH CONTRACT

One way for A to provide for X is for A to transfer property to B on trust for X. In keeping with the principles discussed at the start of this chapter, the setting up of the trust would give X, and only X, enforceable rights against B, and the arrangement would be permanent. Neither A nor B, nor indeed A and B acting together, could later vary the arrangement to X's detriment.

Another method is for A and B to make a contract, under which B agrees to make provision for X. This is an entirely different type of arrangement, however. If B were to default, only A could sue, X, as a third party to the contract, having no enforceable rights. Furthermore, no permanent arrangement would have been set up. The contracting parties could later consensually vary the contract so as to exclude X, but A could not unilaterally vary it (which is why the trustee in bankruptcy failed in *Re Schebsman* [1944] Ch 83, although X failed to persuade the Court of Appeal that A had contracted as trustee).

All of the above is clear from *Beswick* v *Beswick* [1968] AC 58, where A, but not X, could sue B, and in that case A was able to obtain specific performance. However, specific performance is not available for all contracts (see, further, chapter 11), in which case A is limited to a damages claim. The problem is that A has suffered no loss (although X has), and in *Woodar Investment Developments Ltd* v *Wimpey Construction (UK) Ltd* [1980] 1 WLR 277, the House of Lords held that if A has not contracted as trustee for X, A cannot claim damages to compensate A for X's loss. A's damages will compensate for A's loss only, which, of course, is nothing.

In *Lloyd's* v *Harper* (1880) 16 ChD 290, the Court of Appeal held that A can claim damages covering X's loss, holding for X (note that Lush LJ's wider views in the case can no longer be regarded as good law). So why not use this device routinely to avoid the damages problems in *Woodar*? Again, we need to refer to the principles enunciated at the start of this chapter. A trust is permanent, and gives X enforceable rights, so that if A has contracted as trustee there is no possibility of A later varying the arrangement and, indeed, X can force A to sue on the contract. In *Lloyd's* v *Harper* itself, the Court of Appeal was content not to disturb Fry J's finding of fact at first instance that A contracted as trustee, but usually very clear evidence is required that A has bound himself in this irrevocable manner (see, e.g., *Re Schebsman* [1944] Ch 83).

A comparison between trusts and contracts benefiting third parties therefore provides a good illustration of some of the most important features of a trust.

TRUSTS AND LOANS

Usually, when A loans money to B, B becomes a debtor, not a trustee, and A becomes a creditor, not a beneficiary. Since A has retained no property in the loaned money, if the debtor goes bankrupt he is merely one among many unsecured creditors, and is unlikely to see the return of much, if any, of his money.

A loan can also constitute a trust, however, so that if A can retain a beneficial interest in the money loaned, this protects him in the event of the B's bankruptcy. This is often done expressly, but is also the rationale of *Quistclose* trusts, which can exist even in the absence of any words of trust being used.

QUISTCLOSE TRUSTS

Quistclose trusts are becoming increasingly important in practice, and help to emphasise the role of trusts in a commercial context. A surprising number of people tend to group trusts and land law together, but although there is undoubtedly an overlap between those two subjects, and although the law of trusts had its origin (a very long time ago) in dealings in land, trusts today are every bit as relevant to personal as they are to real property.

This is a relatively self-contained area which is not quite as easy as it may appear at first sight.

Problem Question

The following question appeared on a recent examination paper:

A is worried that his son, B, who is a law student, is spending all his money unwisely, and is not eating properly. He accordingly arranges with B that he will give B jewellery worth £500. The arrangement is subject to B agreeing to sell the jewellery, and to put the proceeds of sale into a separate account, part of the money to be used to pay off his debt (£250) to C Sausage Co., and the balance to be used solely to purchase further sausages from C. (Note that A is concerned that C's debt is paid only because he fears that if it is not, C will not supply B with any more sausages.)

B agrees to the arrangement; A gives the jewellery to B, and B sells it. He does not, however, place the £500 proceeds of sale into a separate account, but pays it instead into his general account. B does not pay any money to C, but continues to lead a profligate and degenerate life until he is declared bankrupt a month later. Two weeks after that B dies of starvation.

A claims £500 from the trustee in bankruptcy on *Quistclose* principles. C claims £500, also arguing from *Quistclose*, but on the ground that the primary trust can still be carried out. The trustee in bankruptcy is resisting both claims.

Discuss.

This is a relatively straightforward question on *Quistclose* trusts. Essentially, for either A or C to succeed they have to be able to show that there is a *Quistclose* trust. If there is, A will succeed if he can show either that the primary trust has failed, i.e., that this is on all fours with *Quistclose* itself, or that even if the primary trust has not failed, he rather than C is entitled to enforce it (adopting the arguments of P. J. Millett QC, as he then was, in (1985) 101 LQR 269, at pp. 290-91). C needs to show that the primary trust has not failed, and that he is the beneficiary under the primary trust (adopting the views of Peter Gibson J in *Carreras Rothmans Ltd* v *Freeman Mathews Treasure Ltd* [1985] Ch 207). The trustee in bankruptcy will win if he can show that no *Quistclose* trust has been established.

Quistclose Trusts in General

The leading authority for the *Quistclose* variety of trust is the House of Lords' decision in *Barclays Bank Ltd* v *Quistclose Investments Ltd* [1970] AC 567. The case revolved around Rolls Razor Ltd, who were in serious financial difficulties, and had an overdraft with Barclays Bank of some £484,000, against a permitted limit of £250,000. If Rolls Razor were to stay in business, it was essential for them to obtain a loan of around £210,000 in order to pay dividends which they had declared on their ordinary shares, and which in the absence of such a loan they were unable to pay. They succeeded in obtaining the loan from Quistclose Investments Ltd, who agreed to make the loan on the condition 'that it is used to pay the forthcoming dividend due on July 24, next'. The sum was paid into a special account with Barclays Bank, on the condition (agreed with the bank) that the account would 'only be used to meet the dividend due on July 24, 1964'.

Rolls Razor went into voluntary liquidation on 27 August, without having paid the dividend. Barclays wanted to count the money in the special account against Rolls Razor's overdraft, but the House of Lords held that Barclays held the money on trust for Quistclose, so that Quistclose was able to claim back the entire sum. Lord Wilberforce stated, at p. 580:

> The mutual intention of the respondents [Quistclose] and of Rolls Razor Ltd, and the essence of the bargain, was that the sum advanced should not become part of the assets of Rolls Razor Ltd, but should be used exclusively for payment of a particular class of creditors, namely, those entitled to the dividend. A necessary consequence of this, simply by process of interpretation, must be that, if for any reason, the dividend could not be paid, the money was to be returned to the respondents: the word 'only' or 'exclusively' can have no other meaning or effect.
>
> That arrangements of this character for the payment of a person's creditors by a third person, give rise to a relationship of a fiduciary character or trust, in favour, as a primary trust, of the creditors, and secondarily, if the primary trust fails, of the third person, has been recognised in a series of cases over some 150 years.

The effect of the decision, of course, was that the money loaned by Quistclose was secured from the consequences of Rolls Razor's bankruptcy, since it never became part of Rolls Razor's general assets.

The decision seems to depend on the fact that the money was to be used for a specific purpose, that that purpose was known to the recipient, and that the money was paid into a special account, which could be used for no other purpose. The last requirement, for a special account, may not be absolutely rigid, but at the very least the money must be earmarked for the particular purpose *and no other*, in order to negative the inference that the payments are to be included in the general assets of the company. In the absence of such a requirement, a prospective purchaser through a car import company, for example, who pays a deposit of £1,000 for the purpose of importing a car, would be able to reclaim that £1,000 in the event of the car import company going into liquidation before the car is obtained. The payment, after all, is made for a particular purpose, which is known to the recipient (the company), but except in the unlikely event that the company can use that money for *no purpose other* than obtaining the car, the prospective purchaser is not protected on *Quistclose* principles. The position is somewhat similar to cases where money has been paid to a company for the purpose of obtaining an allotment of shares, but no trust has been held to have been created. Commenting on those cases, Lord Wilberforce said (at p. 581):

> I do not think it necessary to examine these cases in detail, nor to comment on them, for I am satisfied that they do not effect the principle on which this appeal should be decided. They are merely examples which show that, in the absence of some special arrangement creating a trust ..., payments of this kind are made on the basis that they are to be included in the company's assets. They do not negative the proposition that a trust may exist where the mutual intention is that they should not.

The setting up of a special fund negates the inference that the payments are to be included in the company's assets, but so long as that inference is negated, it may be that a special fund is not absolutely necessary. In *Re EVTR* [1987] BCLC 646, the appellant, Barber, who had just won £240,000 on premium bonds, agreed to assist a company for whom he had worked in purchasing new equipment. He accordingly deposited £60,000 with the solicitors to the company, and authorised them to release it 'for the sole purpose of buying new equipment'. The money was not paid into a special fund, but was paid out by the company in pursuit of the purpose. Before the new equipment was delivered EVTR went into receivership. The Court of Appeal held that Barber was entitled to recover his money (or at any rate, the balance of £48,536, after agreed deductions) on *Quistclose* principles. Dillon LJ also thought (at p. 649):

> in the light of *Quistclose*, that if the company had gone into liquidation, or the receivers had been appointed, and the scheme had become abortive before the £60,000 had been disbursed by the company, the appellant would have been entitled to recover his full £60,000, as between himself and the company, on the footing that it was impliedly held by the company on a resulting trust for him as the particular purpose of the loan had failed.

At this stage, however, the money would not have been held in a special account, but the inference that it was intended to be included as part of the general assets would have been negated by other factors. The existence of a special account does not appear, then, to be absolutely essential, so long as the inference that the payments are to be included in the company's assets is negated.

There are other cases where *Quistclose* (or at any rate similar) trusts have been held to exist without any requirement of a separate account. Mention may perhaps be made of *Guardian Ocean Cargoes Ltd* v *Banco do Brasil SA, The Golden Med* [1991] 2 Lloyd's Rep 68, and *Neste Oy* v *Lloyds Bank plc, The Tiiskeri* [1983] 2 Lloyd's Rep 658, although this last case may not be, on proper analysis, a true *Quistclose* trust.

Is there a Quistclose Trust Here?

In this problem it is clear that the jewellery is to be used for a specific purpose, and that that particular jewellery is earmarked for that specific purpose. Now it is true that B did not pay the proceeds of sale into a separate account, but in the light of the previous section that may not matter unduly. In any case, on the assumption that B was never intended to take the jewellery beneficially, the trust (if any) must have come into existence when the jewellery was handed to B. B's subsequent actions (and in particular, his failure to put the money into a separate account) cannot have made any difference to his trusteeship, since otherwise anybody could avoid the obligations of trusteeship by simply not keeping to the terms of the trust.

The reality is, however, that *Quistclose* trusts are used, as here, when the trustee is in liquidation. Merely to have a personal action against the trustee is therefore useless; it is essential for the lender to be able to point to a fund of money held by the trustee and say 'that money is my property'. To be able to do this it is necessary to be able to identify the money, and this is clearly easiest where the money has been paid into a special account. It is not essential, however, so long as the money can be traced in equity. In *Re Kayford Ltd* [1975] 1 WLR 279 (see above), where it was held that a trust fund had been set up for customers of an insolvent company, Megarry J did not think it fatal that the money had been mixed with small amounts of other money. The case was not decided on *Quistclose* principles, but it was essential to be able to establish that the money belonged in equity to the customers; a personal action against the company would have availed them nothing. The money in *Kayford* was clearly traceable, however, so there was no problem even though there were other small sums in the account.

We are not told enough here to be able to decide whether the £500 proceeds of sale from the jewellery are traceable in equity, presumably because the examiner did not want issues of equitable tracing examined in detail. It is only necessary for you to observe, therefore, that for A or C to succeed they must be able to identify the trust property, without writing a detailed essay on the rules of equitable tracing.

Has the Primary Trust Failed?

In both *Quistclose* and *EVTR*, the provider of the money was able to claim it back, the primary purpose of the trust having failed. A may try to claim that here, but there is a difficulty that if A's purpose is to be taken literally, it can still be carried out, since C's debt can be paid, and further sausages can still be supplied by C. A will no doubt argue that his real purpose was to keep B alive, and that the primary trust has failed although its precise terms can still be carried out. C would have to argue that it is the precise terms that count, that a trust fails only when it becomes either illegal or impossible to perform, that the primary trust has therefore not failed here, and that C is the beneficiary under the secondary trust.

C's main problem is with *Quistclose* itself, since Lord Wilberforce's analysis clearly presupposes that the primary trust there had failed. But it can be argued that the dividends could still be paid, in which case the House must have inferred some other primary purpose, such as keeping the company alive. C might then argue that since the only basis for the *Quistclose* trust was that the money had been paid for a specific purpose, it would be illogical for the courts, in determining the primary trust, to ignore the stated purpose that is the very basis of the trust. He would also observe that it is very doubtful whether if the money had been paid for the purpose of keeping the company alive, the courts would have construed a *Quistclose* trust at all. C will further argue that the real reason for the failure of the primary trust in *Quistclose* was that it is illegal for a company which is in liquidation to pay out dividends, so you do not need to look beyond the specific purpose. Indeed, in the Court of Appeal ([1968] 1 Ch 540), Harman LJ's judgment begins (at p. 548):

> ... The money was deposited with the respondent bank, and accepted on the footing that it should only be used for payment of the dividend. That purpose was, however, frustrated by the liquidation of Rolls Razor on the following August 27 before the dividend had been paid, thus making its payment illegal.

However, Russell LJ (at p. 557) talked only of the purpose ceasing to be feasible, and Sachs LJ thought (at p. 566) that the primary trust would remain in being unless 'there was not the slightest chance of the money being thus applied' (for the specific purpose of paying the dividend). In the House of Lords, Lord Wilberforce assumes without argument that the primary trust has failed. However, since on the reasoning in the case the money never belonged beneficially to Rolls Razor it is difficult to see why there should have been any restrictions on the purposes to which it could be put. It was never company money, so it could reasonably be argued that there would have been no illegality, whatever it had been used for.

If it is indeed the case that the primary trust may fail even when (as perhaps in *Quistclose* itself) the specific purpose can still technically be carried out, then A is likely to succeed here. This raises interesting issues, which might well amuse examiners in the future, as to what the position might be if A's purpose is known only to himself, and could not easily be guessed at. Suppose, for example, A is an eccentric millionaire who delights in the name Mondeo, and is very pleased, now that Ford have produced a car by that name, that the streets are going to be full of cars called Mondeo. Suppose also that in a few years time, A believes (rightly or wrongly) that Ford is in financial difficulty, and that if they do not pay their dividends due on 1 July, their backers will pull out and there will be no more Mondeos. He therefore pays Ford £5 million for the specific purpose of paying the dividends due on 1 July. On 30 June, Ford (which is actually in a position to, and fully intends to pay the dividends) drops the Mondeo from its range of cars. If A's motive is to be taken into account in deciding whether the primary trust has failed, A can presumably move for an injunction to prevent his money being used to pay the dividends, and can claim it back on *Quistclose* principles. The conclusion seems absurd, but illustrates the problems that can arise once the courts look behind the stated purpose, and try to guess at the motivation of the provider of the money.

Can A Win even if the Primary Trust has not Failed?

The analysis in *Quistclose*, in both the Court of Appeal and the House of Lords, is clearly in terms of a primary trust in favour of the shareholders, and a secondary trust in favour of Quistclose. The natural inference is that the shareholders can enforce the primary trust, as beneficiaries.

This question has never actually been decided, since in both *Quistclose* and *EVTR*, the provider of the money was able to claim it back, the primary purpose of the trust having failed. In *Carreras Rothmans Ltd v Freeman Mathews Treasure Ltd* [1985] Ch 207, the primary trust could still be carried out, and an order was made to that effect. Peter Gibson J thought (at p. 223) that the third-party creditors might themselves have had enforceable rights. However, support can be found from *Quistclose* itself (at p. 581) that it is the provider of the money who can enforce the trust, that:

> the lender acquires an equitable right to see that [the money advanced] is applied for the primary designated purpose ... if the primary purpose cannot be carried out, the question arises if a secondary purpose (i.e.,

repayment to the lender) has been agreed, expressly or by implication: if it
has, the remedies of equity may be invoked to give effect to it ...

This suggests that even if the primary trust has not failed, only A (and not C)
can enforce it. It is also the view of P. J. Millett QC (as he then was), counsel
for Carreras Rothmans in *Carreras Rothmans Ltd* v *Freeman Mathews Treasure
Ltd*, that the provider of the moneys, and only he, can usually enforce a
Quistclose trust: ((1985) 101 LQR 269, at pp. 290-91). You may well take the
view that if the primary trust has not failed there is little point in A attempting
to enforce it, because C rather than A will benefit, but if C cannot enforce, A
may be able to negotiate with him to enforce on certain terms, which could
(obviously) be to A's advantage.

In order to make progress on this issue we need to consider *Carreras
Rothman Ltd* v *Freeman Mathews Treasure Ltd* in more detail.

The plaintiff (cigarette manufacturers) engaged the defendant advertising
agency. The defendant contracted as principal with production agencies and
advertising media. The arrangement was that CR paid a monthly fee to FMT,
which was used:

(a)   as payment in arrears for FMT's services, and
(b)   to enable FMT to pay debts incurred to agency and media creditors

The defendant (FMT) got into financial difficulties, but needed funds to pay
its production agencies and advertising media, if it was to carry on acting for
the plaintiff.

Carreras Rothmans also knew that if FMT went into liquidation still owing
money to media creditors, the media creditors would have sufficient
commercial power to compel CR to pay, and therefore (although they were
not legally obliged to do so) they would in practice have to pay twice over.
An agreement was therefore made between CR and FMT whereby the
plaintiffs would pay a monthly sum into a special account at the defendant's
bank, the money to be used 'only for the purposes of meeting the accounts of
the media and production fees of third parties directly attributable to CR's
involvement with the agency'. The first payment (of just under £600,000) was
made at the end of July, covering debts incurred in June. Unlike the position
in the cases discussed above, however, this was money which CR owed to
FMT in any event.

The defendant went into liquidation before the debts were cleared. CR
immediately found another advertising agency, and so that its advertising
campaign would not be jeopardised, paid the debts of the media creditors,
taking assignments of those debts. Of the money in the special account, Peter
Gibson J held that it was held by FMT (and hence by the liquidator) on trust,
since it had been paid for a specific purpose, and he made an order requiring

the liquidator to carry out that purpose (i.e., payment to the third parties). He did not think (at pp. 221-2) it relevant that CR was under a contractual obligation to pay the money to FMT in any event, noting (at p. 222C-E) that:

> if the common intention is that property is transferred for a specific purpose and not so as to become the property of the transferee, the transferee cannot keep the property if for any reason that purpose cannot be fulfilled. I am left in no doubt that the provider of the moneys in the present case was the plaintiff. True it is that its own witnesses said that if the defendant had not agreed to the terms of the contract letter, the plaintiff would not have broken its contract but would have paid its debt to the defendant, but the fact remains that the plaintiff made its payment on the terms of that letter and the defendant received the moneys only for the stipulated purpose. That purpose was expressed to relate only to the moneys in the account. In my judgment therefore the plaintiff can be equated with the lender in the *Quistclose* case as having an enforceable right to compel the carrying out of the primary trust.

This is again consistent with A, rather than C, having the right to enforce the primary trust, and indeed at the end of the day it was CR, as provider of the money, who was able to apply for the order. Elsewhere in his judgment, however, Peter Gibson J thought that the third-party creditors could enforce the primary trust.

One may well wonder why, since they had after all paid off the media creditors, CR did not simply attempt to claim the money back from FMT, following *Quistclose* directly by enforcing the secondary trust. They may well have been able to argue that the primary trust had failed, and this would surely have been more logical than getting an order to pay the third parties, whom they had themselves already paid? The problem was that they were contractually liable to pay this money to FMT, and if they had simply claimed it back themselves, the liquidator would almost certainly have been able to sue for it in contract (as indeed he did for the £780,000 that was due a month later, and had never been paid by CR). That probably explains why CR chose instead to argue that the primary trust was still alive. It is necesssary then to explain why CR, rather than the third-party creditors, were able to obtain the order. They had taken assignments of the third-party creditors' debts, and one might argue that they were suing as assignees. The problem with this view is that debt actions against a company which is in liquidation are valueless, and (at least as far as it is possible to tell from the report) CR had not taken assignments of any other rights the third-party creditors might have.

To return to the problem, C will probably argue that if the third-party creditors were the beneficiaries under, and hence able to enforce, the primary trust, the actual decision in *Carreras Rothmans* (that CR could enforce it) is wrong. That is also a tenable view; after all, it is a first instance decision which has not been followed, where the decision appears inconsistent with the reasoning in the judgment. A will argue that *Carreras Rothmans* is correct, that the decision is consistent with the views in the above passage from *Quistclose* that *the lender* acquires an equitable right to see that the money advanced is applied for the primary designated purpose, and that the views advanced by Millett in the LQR article are correct.

Yet another possible view is that the primary trust in *Quistclose* cases is a pure purpose without true beneficiaries at all. This view was taken by Megarry J in *Re Northern Developments (Holdings) Ltd*, unreported, 6 October 1978, but considered in *Carreras Rothmans* and discussed by P. J. Millett QC in the article referred to above. It is subject to the criticisms advanced in chapter 5.

SUGGESTED ADDITIONAL READING

For *Quistclose* trusts it is essential that you read:
• Millett QC, (1985) 101 LQR 269.

See also, on *Kayford* and *Quistclose* trusts:
• Professor Michael Bridge (1992) 12 OJLS 333.

4 COVENANTS TO SETTLE

As we saw in the last chapter, it is not possible to constitute an immediate trust of future property. There is no reason, however, why one should not covenant to settle the property when it is obtained. This chapter considers the position of the covenantor, and those intended to benefit from the covenant. Usually, for some reason, there will be no valid trust of the property that is intended to be settled.

This is a ripe area for examination problems, for although, in real-life, cases which raise these issues are very unlikely to arise today, the topic calls for a good grasp of basic principles and an ability to apply them logically.

FACTUAL SITUATIONS IN WHICH THE CASES ARISE

Nearly all the cases are of essentially the same type, and it is worth briefly examining the factual nature of the situation in order to explain the issues which have arisen.

Nearly all the cases have concerned marriage settlements, and the agreements to settle are therefore usually made in consideration of marriage. The parties may also enter into a deed of covenant, to which trustees, or intended trustees, may also be a party. A typical arrangement might be where the husband-to-be agrees to settle not only the property he owns now, but also *property yet to be acquired* (for example, an expected inheritance yet to be received), on the terms of the settlement. Under the terms of the settlement, the beneficiaries will usually include the issue of the marriage, and in default of such issue, the next of kin of the wife.

The first point to note is that the settlement usually covers not only existing, but also after-acquired property. The courts have held, e.g., in *Re Ellenborough* [1903] 1 Ch 697, that future property, or expectancies, cannot form the subject matter of a trust, because there is insufficient certainty of subject matter. There is not usually, therefore, a failure by the settlor properly to constitute the trust: the trust *cannot* be properly constituted since the trust property does not yet exist.

The second point to note is that the agreement is made, not in consideration of money or money's worth, as with most contracts, but in consideration of marriage. The relevance of marriage consideration (which means that the marriage must actually constitute consideration, and must therefore be a future marriage) is that it enables not only the parties to the contract to sue on it, but any issue *of that marriage* can also sue. This is usually regarded today as a narrow and anomalous exception to the rule that equity will not assist a volunteer. Historically, it appears to have been a device to impose upon the conscience of the husband (forcing him to settle the property he had agreed to settle) at a time (before the Married Women's Property Act 1882) when the wife herself had no economic independence (and could not sue in her own right).

It is clear, however, that only the issue of the marriage can sue, and not, for example, in the event of failure of issue, the next-of-kin of the wife, who will typically be the intended beneficiaries in that event (see *Re Plumptre's Marriage Settlement* [1910] 1 Ch 609, below). Furthermore, the policy behind marriage consideration would probably not go beyond providing an action against the husband, and indeed there is no authority on whether the issue of the marriage, who though parties to the marriage consideration are otherwise volunteers, can sue anyone *apart* from the husband.

It is sometimes argued that others, apart from the issue of the marriage, can sue on the marriage consideration, for example step-children, but Buckley J made it clear that it is indeed limited to the issue of the marriage in *Re Cook's Settlement Trusts* [1965] 1 Ch 902.

The third point to note is that the parties may also have entered into a deed of covenant, to which, indeed, the intended trustees may also be party. At common law, parties to a deed can sue on it even in the absence of consideration, but they are limited to common-law remedies (i.e., damages), and cannot obtain specific performance of the covenant. This is made clear by *Re Ellenborough* itself. Emily Towry Law had covenanted to settle after-acquired property and sought a summons, when she became entitled to it, to decide whether she could refuse to transfer it to the trustees. Buckley J held that she could, because a court of equity would not enforce a voluntary covenant (i.e., a covenant unsupported by consideration) by compelling her to do what she had not yet done (the case is however silent on the attitude taken by the common law to voluntary deeds of covenant). It is in any case very unlikely that the intended *beneficiaries* will be party to the covenant, at any rate if they are the issue of the marriage, since at the time of the covenant they will not have been born. For an unusual example, where a beneficiary *was* party, see *Cannon* v *Hartley* [1949] Ch 213, below.

The final point to note is that although the cases usually arise because a trust has not been constituted, the intended trustees under the settlement are often actually trustees of other family property. Another possibility is that trusts of the settlement *have* been constituted, but not of the particular property in dispute. It is likely that although no trusts had been constituted of the property in dispute, the decisions in *Kay* and *Pryce*, below, may well have been influenced by the fact that the intended trustees of the settlement were actually trustees of other property.

PROBLEM QUESTION

Occasionally examiners will raise the issue in the form of an essay question, but as the same rules apply, and since a problem question will provide a convenient illustration of the difficulties, let us begin with one of those. There is, of course, no reason why examiners should base their problem questions, even remotely, on fact situations similar to those which have been considered in the cases themselves:

Alpha covenants with Beta that he will settle existing property on Beta as trustee for Gamma. Only Alpha and Beta are party to the deed, and no consideration moves from either Beta or Gamma. Alpha later refuses to settle the property.

ANSWER ALL PARTS:

(i)   Can Gamma require Beta to sue Alpha on the covenant?

(ii)   Will Beta be allowed to sue Alpha on the covenant?

(iii)   If Beta can sue, what will his remedy be? If he obtains damages, on what basis will they be assessed, and will he be allowed to keep them for himself?

Would any of your answers be different if valuable consideration had moved from Beta?

Would any of your answers be different if Beta was trustee of the promise for Gamma? In determining whether he is trustee of the promise, is his intention relevant? Is Alpha's?

This is a fairly typical question, in that although Alpha has covenanted to settle property, there is as yet no trust. The missing element, as is typical in problems of this type, is the actual vesting of the property in the trustee. Alpha, having agreed to transfer property, omits to do so. The problem therefore breaks down into a very simple issue. Alpha (the would-be settlor — WS for short) has made a covenant (a contract, in other words) with Beta, the would-be trustee (WT) to confer a benefit upon Gamma, the would-be beneficiary (WB).

If you get a problem of this type in your exam paper, there is a lot to be said for drawing a diagram using these symbols, making clear what role each of these parties is playing, and the relationship between them. Examples can be found in *Textbook on Trusts*, at pp. 69–70.

The question in effect is whether, as between these three people — WS, WT and WB — there exists any relationship which the courts will enforce. You will need to consider both contract and trust possibilities.

Before we embark upon the contractual analyses, however, we need first perhaps to consider whether there really is no trust here. No doubt, Alpha has not transferred the property to the trustee, but this is existing property, so the problems of *Re Ellenborough*, considered in the previous section, do not apply. Why can we not say that Alpha, by entering into the covenant, can be taken to be declaring himself trustee of the property for Gamma? In *Re Ralli's Will Trusts* [1964] Ch 288, considered further below, Buckley J thought that the trust had become fully constituted by the accident of the trustee obtaining legal title to the property by other means; but in the alternative he thought that, by entering into the marriage settlement, Helen could be regarded as declaring herself trustee of that property (which was existing and not future property) from that moment. In general, however, there must be a difference between entering into a contract, which is in principle revocable (should both parties to the contract so agree) and declaring oneself trustee, which is not. In *Re Ralli's Will Trusts*, the case turned upon the precise wording of clause 8 of the covenant, which (in Buckley J's view) indicated an irrevocable intention on Helen's part:

> ... it being the intention of these presents and of the said parties hereto that by virtue and under the operation of the said covenants all the property comprised within the terms of such covenants shall become subject in equity to the settlement hereby covenanted to be made thereof.

Buckley J interpreted this as indicating that Helen, as WS, declared herself trustee of the property pending its transfer to the trustees. In this question there is no equivalent evidence, and we should proceed on the assumption that there has been no declaration of trust by Alpha.

In addition to tackling the problem itself, the following discussion will be interspersed with the basic principles relevant to the topic. It is important to note, though, that not only is there no need to do this in an examination, but many examiners actively dislike answers which are, in effect, an essay on the topic, with a mere paragraph or so actually directed at the problem tacked on at the end. The general propositions in the following discussion may be useful for your revision, or if the topic comes up in the form of a general essay, but if you get a problem then on no account attempt to answer it by writing down all you know about the topic. A problem is intended to test your ability to sort out the relevant from the irrelevant, and to apply your knowledge of an area to a particular fact situation. It is not simply a memory test.

COVENANTS TO SETTLE IN GENERAL

'Incompletely constituted trusts' are situations where WS, having undertaken to transfer property to trustees, does not do so. There is thus no trust, and for that reason it is misleading to continue to speak of 'settlors', 'trustees' and 'beneficiaries' as though a trust actually existed. Indeed, this practice is probably the major cause of the difficulties people have with this area.

In this book, therefore, I prefer to use 'would-be settlor' (WS), 'would-be trustee' (WT), and 'would-be beneficiary' (WB). It sounds horrible and clumsy, but once we start to use these terms any difficulties caused by textbooks, and even judges, speaking of the parties as though there was a fully constituted trust, disappear.

The whole point at issue, of course, is whether any of the parties can compel the would-be settlor to carry out his promise, and actually to constitute the trust. Let us consider the parties in turn, still in general terms.

Can WB Compel WS to Transfer the Property to WT?

The answer to this depends upon whether there is an enforceable contract between WB and WS. No one has the right to demand that someone should gratuitously create a trust in his favour (although the courts have statutory powers to compel the creation of a trust in certain cases, e.g., under s. 25 of the Matrimonial Causes Act 1973 — see chapter 6), but if WS has bound himself by a contract enforceable at the instance of WB, then the court may compel him to carry it out.

A contract between WB and WS, made for conventional consideration in the form of money or money's worth, would be rather unusual, though not of course impossible. People sometimes 'buy' a benefit in this way, for example, in certain types of commercial transactions, and if WB has indeed provided consideration, then there is no difficulty in the way of his obtaining a remedy. At common law, he can simply sue on the contract and obtain compensation for his lost benefit by way of damages. Alternatively, he may be able to obtain an order of specific performance to compel this settlor actually to carry out the terms of his promise. Since specific performance is an equitable remedy its award is discretionary, rather than as of right, and certain conditions have to be satisfied before the court will grant it, but the court may award damages under the Chancery Amendment Act 1858.

There are two complications concerning this type of contract. The first is that the common law recognises contracts made under seal, such as a deed of covenant, as enforceable even though no consideration moves from the promisee. Equity does not, however. So, if WB is a party to the deed executed by WS, but otherwise gives no consideration for the promised benefit, he will be unable to obtain the equitable remedy of specific performance, though he can still get common law damages, which may be perfectly adequate.

As has already been explained, it would be unusual under the conventional form of marriage settlement for the intended beneficiaries to be party to the deed, but an unusual case, where an intended beneficiary was party, was *Cannon* v *Hartley* [1949] Ch 213, where on the breakdown of a marriage, a father (WS) covenanted to make provision for a daughter (WB) by settling on her property expected later to be acquired under the will of his parents. When he received the property he refused to settle it on the agreed terms. The daughter was not of course within the marriage consideration, as the covenant itself was not made prior to or in consideration of marriage. But as a party to the deed, she could enforce the contract at common law, and obtain substantial damages.

The second complication is that marriage consideration is recognised only by equity, and where the beneficiary relies on this form of consideration, he must seek an equitable remedy: specific performance or damages in lieu. As stated above these remedies are discretionary, though this causes no difficulty in a straightforward case.

Thus in *Pullan* v *Koe* [1913] 1 Ch 9 the children of WS, being within the marriage consideration, could obtain specific performance. More remote kin, however, not being within the consideration, would be volunteers in the eyes of equity unless they had provided other consideration of value.

If on the other hand WB is neither a party to the covenant nor within any marriage consideration, and has given no other consideration, then there is no remedy, by virtue of the maxim that 'equity will not assist a volunteer'.

Authority for this proposition can be found in *Re Plumptre's Marriage Settlement* [1910] 1 Ch 609, where the WBs were the next of kin of the wife, this being a settlement of the conventional type and there having been a failure of issue, and so not within the marriage consideration. The only way they could benefit from the covenant would be if there were beneficiaries who were not volunteers, such as the children of the marriage, on whose behalf the trustees could enforce, as in *Pullen* v *Koe*, or if they were themselves parties to the covenant.

Let us return to the particular problem.

Can WB (Gamma) Compel WS (Alpha) to Transfer the Property to WT?

In our problem WB is neither a party to the covenant nor within any marriage consideration, and has given no other consideration. This is similar to *Re Plumptre's Marriage Settlement*. Our conclusion on this part of our problem will therefore be that Gamma has no right either at law or in equity to compel Alpha to perfect the trust in his favour.

We now have to consider whether Beta, WT, may have a remedy for Alpha's failure to transfer the property as promised.

Can WT Enforce WS's Promise?

If he can obtain specific performance of their agreement, he will of course hold the shares on the terms of the trust, and thus in a roundabout way, he could compel Alpha to perfect the trust in Gamma's favour. Gamma himself cannot compel Beta to take any steps on his behalf, because unless and until the property is transferred to him, there is no trust of which Beta could be a trustee, or Gamma a beneficiary. The initiative lies with Beta.

From Gamma's viewpoint, the most desirable remedy which Beta might claim is of course specific performance, but in the main part of the problem the bar to this is the fact that Beta has provided no consideration recognised by equity: a bare promise, even when supported by a seal, will not do.

You are also asked whether any of your answers would be different if valuable consideration had moved from Beta. One reason for asking this, of course, is that specific performance may now be at least theoretically possible.

In *Beswick* v *Beswick* [1968] AC 58, a case you may recall from contract days, old Mr Beswick transferred his coal business to his nephew in return for the nephew's promise to pay Mr Beswick a consultant's fee during his life, and a small annuity to his widow after his death. When Mr Beswick died, the nephew refused to make payments to Mrs Beswick.

Though this is not a covenant to settle, the nephew can be regarded as equivalent to WS, old Mr Beswick to WT and Mrs Beswick as WB.

As a mere third party to the agreement, Mrs Beswick as WB could claim no remedy on her own account, but as the personal representative of Mr Beswick she could maintain an action on behalf of his estate (in her other capacity, as WT). Since Mr Beswick himself suffered no loss, one would expect any damages in such an action to be nominal, the very real benefit to Mrs Beswick being quite irrelevant in calculating those damages.

Partly because damages would be an inadequate remedy, the House of Lords granted specific performance to Mr Beswick's estate (WT). This reasoning has been criticised, for the basis of equitable remedies is the inadequacy of the common law remedy, and from the standpoint of Mr Beswick, the legal remedy was quite adequate. Nonetheless, it would seem that where a WT has provided consideration, he may be able to obtain specific performance as against a recalcitrant WS, provided always that the other conditions for the grant of this remedy are satisfied.

It should be noted that the remedy depends in general upon the mutuality requirement being satisfied, that is to say that the same contract would also have been specifically enforceable by WS against WT. The mutuality requirement was satisfied in *Beswick* v *Beswick*, because old Mr Beswick had promised to transfer the goodwill of a business, but it will by no means always be so. In particular, the mutuality requirement is unlikely to be satisfied where the consideration moving from WT is money alone. Nor is it satisfied in the problem, because Beta's obligations would have required supervision, and would not therefore have been specifically enforceable.

For the sake of completeness, even if WT cannot obtain specific perform-ance, if WS does not perform the bargain at all, then WT can get back any consideration provided by him (if he has transferred property or money to WS) on the ground of a total failure of consideration by WS. But this is of no direct benefit to WB. It also depends on the nature of the consideration provided by WT: obviously, if WT has provided a service, there is no way that this can be returned.

But — and here we arrive at the core of our problem — the courts appear to have laid down a principle that even if WT has a useful remedy, he may not sue in this situation. Students are apt to take this as an absolute rule (so are some academic writers), but for a good answer, you ought to explore the issue further.

The chief stumbling-block to the WT is *Re Kay's Settlement* [1939] Ch 329, where the WTs (though they were actually trustees of other property) were parties to a covenant under seal to settle after-acquired property. Note that the 'would-be' terminology is continued even though there was a properly constituted trust of other property, because no issue arose regarding that other property. No consideration moved from the WTs, however. The WBs were not party to the covenant, nor were they within the marriage consideration, so were therefore volunteers. On a request for directions as to whether the WTs could sue to enforce the covenant or recover damages, Simonds J, following Eve J in *Re Pryce* [1917] 1 Ch 234 said:

> [I]t appears to me that ... I must direct the trustees not to take any steps either to compel performance of the covenant or to recover damages through [the settlor's] failure to implement it.

This dictum was followed by Buckley J in *Re Cook's ST* [1965] Ch 902, a case in which, as part of a resettlement of family capital, a son covenanted with his father, who provided consideration, and with WTs (who were also actual trustees of other property) who did not, to settle the proceeds of sale of some paintings which he owned absolutely. One painting, which he had given to one of his numerous wives, was eventually sold by her after her divorce from him, and the issue arose as to whether the WTs were obliged to take steps to enforce the covenant. Buckley J thought not, which on the facts is perhaps not surprising, on the basis that the *Re Pryce* and *Re Kay's Settlement* line of authority was a bar to an action by the WTs. The case is not a particularly strong authority on this point, however. Buckley J did not decide that the trustees had no remedy, but only that they could not be compelled to do so by the WBs. However, the actual order was in similar terms to that in *Re Pryce* and *Re Kay's Settlement*.

On the face of it, the dictum of Simonds J in *Re Kay's Settlement* seems extraordinary, and deserves close scrutiny. It appears to deprive a plaintiff of an otherwise perfectly valid personal right to sue on a contract, for which very good reasons would have to be found. One wonders whether the answer might have been different if the facts of the case had been closer to our own problem (varied so that Beta had a useful remedy), however.

In *Re Pryce* and *Re Kay's Settlement* (and *Re Cook's ST*) the personal nature of the WT's right was in fact obscured. The facts were that WS refused to add, to an already constituted trust, further property which was yet to be acquired. The WTs were therefore already trustees of a perfect trust (of other property), and the question seems to have been regarded as one in which they were contemplating taking steps to get in property which is owed to a trust, as of course they should. The court appeared to regard them as acting on behalf of the trust, thereby obscuring the status of their personal rights as parties to the covenant. If, as in our own problem, there is as yet no trust at all, those rights are thrown into clearer relief.

There is also the point that the cases were in the form of a summons for directions. Had the WTs been told to go ahead and sue, the cost of the suit would presumably have fallen on the trust fund (this is one reason why trustees seek directions before suing in the first place: if they obey the court, they are not personally liable for costs in an action which goes against the trust). With the outcome so uncertain, it would have been arguably inapposite for a court to direct trustees to engage in speculative litigation. But if Beta wants to spend his own money in an attempt to perfect the trust on Gamma's behalf, there seems no good reason in principle to stop him.

Perhaps, then, Simonds J did not decide that a WT is prohibited from bringing an action, but only that the court would not direct them to sue, and force upon them the onerous burdens of trusteeship, in favour of volunteers. Professor Elliott (1960) 76 LQR 100 has argued that the WTs should have been directed that they need not sue, not that they ought not to sue. It would indeed be perfectly proper for the court to leave the decision as to whether to exercise one's rights to the private individual, just as in any other case where a person has a right of action.

On the other hand, this apparently gives trustees a discretion as to whether or not to enforce the trust, and it is arguable that this is inconsistent with the mandatory nature of a trust. Since the court will not force the WTs to act in favour of a volunteer, it can only prohibit them from suing. Though this argument has a superficial plausibility, remember that they are not yet trustees, so objections based on giving them discretion should not be relevant. The choice given to a WT is not whether to carry out his or her duties under a trust — there is no trust — but whether or not to become a trustee at all. This is a perfectly proper choice which anyone faced with a request to become a trustee is entitled to make.

Another argument is that, at any rate where the covenant is voluntary, it is for the settlor voluntarily to constitute the trust, by some form of deliberate action. There may be good policy reasons for taking this approach, especially when it is remembered that the covenants are usually entered into when the would-be settlor is young and the property covered often includes much of what he or she will acquire over an entire lifetime. Where the contract is for consideration, then arguably different considerations apply.

One problem with this view is that there is little, if any, authority for the proposition that it is for the settlor voluntarily to constitute the trust (I think it derives from a reading of *Re Ellenborough*, consider above, where the court would not compel Emily Towry Law to carry out the terms of a voluntary deed of covenant and constitute the trust, but it is a misreading of the case as *Ellenborough* is silent as to the attitude taken by the common law to a voluntary covenant). There is, however, what may well be contrary authority in *Re Ralli's WT* [1964] Ch 288 (see below). Another problem is that a different position ought to obtain where the contract is for consideration, but the cases do not seem to distinguish. Certainly, *Re Kay* concerns what appears to be a genuine voluntary settlement by a spinster, who married only much later. There was no marriage consideration, and hence the children of the marriage were volunteer beneficiaries. The covenant in *Re Pryce* also appears at first sight to have been voluntary, but closer examination shows that it actually formed part of a marriage settlement, with consideration moving from both husband and wife (but admittedly none from the trustees). There was no issue and the beneficiaries in default of issue were volunteers (the facts are actually very similar to those in *Re Plumptre's Marriage Settlement*, although the issues were different). There was consideration in *Re Cook*, but again none moving from the trustees. It does not seem that the cases distinguish between voluntary covenants and covenants for consideration, although whether consideration moving from the trustees themselves would make any difference has not been tested.

I would suggest, therefore, that this argument, supposedly based on some fundamental principle that it is for the settlor voluntarily to constitute a trust, is wrong. You should be very suspicious of 'fundamental principles'. The law of trusts was not laid down by God, but by incremental development through the authorities. The problem is that the authorities really do not support the existence of this fundamental principle.

It may be more fruitful to consider the question of remedies (indeed, we are specifically asked to do this in part (iii) of the problem). Let us first suppose that specific performance is, in principle, available. The action for specific performance would have the effect of constituting the trust. Arguably, the equitable remedy would be being used to assist the volunteers, and that could be an argument for equity refusing to grant the remedy. On the other hand, it is by no means clear that the principle that equity will not assist a volunteer implies that it will act positively to prevent assistance. Why should the WBs be any worse off than Mrs Beswick, who (in her personal capacity) was a volunteer, but in whose favour the House of Lords was prepared to grant specific performance? In any case, the principle that equity will not assist a volunteer would not be an argument for interfering with the common law remedy for damages.

Where the covenant is voluntary, damages are in the case the only available remedy. Damages compensate for loss suffered, and since it is the WB who is intended to receive the benefit, arguably the WT personally suffers no loss if the trust is not constituted. Indeed, if the duties under the putative trust are of an onerous nature, as they will often be, the WT may actually be seen as gaining from the settlor's breach (by virtue of being relieved of an onerous obligation). On this argument the damages will be nominal.

However, Goddard argues ([1988] Conv 19) that this situation is not comparable with *Beswick v Beswick* [1968] AC 58, above, where damages would have been nominal, since here the WS has covenanted to transfer property to the WT, whereas in *Beswick v Beswick* the contract was to transfer money directly to the third party, without any intermediate transmission to the other contracting party. Arguably, therefore, the breach has deprived the WT of property to which he or she is entitled, and damages should compensate for that. No doubt, the WT is not intended to obtain the benefit of that property, but rather to hold it on trust, rendering the WT's loss nugatory, but this is irrelevant as far as the common law is concerned (the common law would take no account of equitable title). Goddard notes that there are pre-Judicature Act authorities that the common law would grant substantial damages, and ignore equitable obligations. It seems unlikely that the Judicature Acts altered the substantive position on damages taken by the common law.

If this analysis is correct the next question is whether the WT holds the damages as trustee. If equity requires him or her to hold them on the trusts of the covenant (Goddard's solution, but argued from principle rather than authority), equity will be assisting a volunteer, so this seems an unlikely solution. If the WT has given consideration it is difficult to see why he should not keep the damages. After all, he has given value for the contract, and if the WS were to object that the WT was never intended to benefit personally from the contract, and that if he had known that the WT would benefit he would never have entered into it, the answer must be that the WS has the choice of performing the contract and constituting the trust. If, however, the covenant is made under seal and unsupported by consideration, the WT should clearly not be entitled to keep the damages beneficially, since that was never intended and he has not given any value. Equity would surely impose on his conscience and require him to hold them on trust (perhaps adopting a principle similar to that in *Neste Oy* v *Lloyds Bank plc, The Tiiskeri* [1983] 2 Lloyd's Rep 658, where in a rather different situation the recipient of money could not in all conscience hold on to it, and was required to hold it on constructive trust). But on trust for whom? If equity is not to assist the volunteer, the only possible solution would be to require him or her to hold the damages on resulting trust for the settlor.

The conclusion that I would draw is that whatever *Pryce, Kay* and *Cook* decide, it does not necessarily follow that a WT would have a useful remedy even were he or she allowed to sue.

Whether or not you find this argument convincing, it serves to illustrate that nothing in law should be accepted without contention, especially where, as here, you are confronted with a line of decisions at first instance only.

Returning to the problem, even where Beta has provided consideration he may not be permitted to bring an action, and even if he can, he may be unable to obtain a remedy which is of any value to Gamma. But that is not entirely the end of the matter, for we are also asked whether any of our answers would be different if Beta was trustee of the promise for Gamma.

A TRUST OF THE PROMISE?

There is no reason in principle why a covenant to settle property should not of itself form the subject matter of a trust. Such a covenant, giving the other party a right to sue on it, is itself a form of property: a chose in action. If a settlor so wishes, he can settle (i.e., create a fully constituted trust of) that chose in action in just the same way as he could settle land, shares or the proceeds of betting on a fast greyhound. All he has to do is to transfer that property — the benefit of the covenant — to the intended trustees. This will perfect the trust, and the beneficiaries can now enforce that trust just as if the subject matter were land or cash.

Nevertheless, transferring the benefit of a covenant is not the most obvious option open to would-be settlors, and the courts are reluctant to place this interpretation on a transaction. One such case, however, was *Fletcher* v *Fletcher* (1844) 4 Hare 67. Ellis Fletcher covenanted by deed to pay £60,000 to his trustees, on trust for his illegitimate sons, who were outside the marriage consideration, and were thus volunteers. The surviving son, Jacob, was able to compel the trustees (note that the term is here correctly used) to enforce the covenant on his behalf. Though the *money* was never settled, Wigram V-C held that the *covenant* was held on a fully constituted trust for Jacob. Thus Jacob could enforce it in his own right, despite being a volunteer. Substantial damages were recoverable, amounting to the promised £60,000.

This was in spite of the fact that the trustees knew nothing of the covenant until the death of the settlor, Ellis Fletcher, and even then were most reluctant to sue upon it. However, the ignorance of the trustees, or their unwillingness to accept the trust, should not be a bar to a finding that Fletcher meant to give his trustees a chose in action rather than the money itself, so creating a valid trust. The relevant intention is that of the settlor, not of the trustees. Reluctant trustees can always be replaced by the court (see Feltham (1982) 98 LQR 17).

Nevertheless, the later case of *Re Schebsman* [1944] Ch 83 suggests that the courts today would demand much more conclusive evidence before construing that the settlor really did intend to settle the benefit of the covenant, and it seems likely that were the same facts as in *Fletcher* v *Fletcher* to arise today, no such intention would be construed.

Accepting that the relevant intention is that of settlor, however, we still have to ask who this is. After all, this is a trust of the promise, not of the property to be settled. It is arguably the WT of the property who owns the contractual cause of action, since he can enforce it, so surely he rather than the WS of the property is settlor of the contract. Indeed, on this view the WT of the property is both settlor and trustee of the promise, declaring himself trustee of it.

Now there is no doubt that the WT of the property is the legal owner of the contract, but who owns it in equity? The covenant in *Fletcher* was voluntary, and on the argument in the previous section the WT is not intended to take the benefit beneficially, and cannot therefore be the owner in equity of the covenant. Surely the position is that if the settlor of the property contracts with the WT as trustee of the promise, then the WBs of the property under the settlement are *true* beneficiaries of the promise. There is a fully constituted trust of the promise. But if the WS of the property enters into a voluntary covenant with the WT *otherwise* than as trustee of the promise, the position is exactly as in *Pryce*, *Kay* and *Cook*. The WBs under the settlement are clearly not in that case beneficiaries of the promise, nor is the WT. The only possible beneficial owner of the promise is the WS himself. In other words, in the absence of a declaration of a trust of the promise in favour of the volunteer beneficiaries, *the WTs hold the chose in action on resulting trust for the WS.*

It would seem to follow, therefore, that although the WT is legal owner of the promise, the WS is beneficial owner unless it (the promise) is settled in trust. It is therefore for the WS to create the trust of the promise, and his intention is the relevant intention. Were it otherwise the WTs in *Pryce*, *Kay* and *Cook* could at any time declare themselves trustees of their promise, thereby significantly improving the position of the volunteers.

If the argument in the previous section is correct, however, the WT would be both legal and beneficial owner of the promise if he had provided consideration, and therefore his intention, not that of the WS would be relevant. It is difficult to see that any injustice would be caused by this result.

A NOTE ON AFTER-ACQUIRED PROPERTY

In *Fletcher* v *Fletcher* itself, the £60,000 was real, existing property, and the trustees were able to recover substantial damages for the failure to transfer it to them, even though they had personally suffered no loss. The same principle probably applies to covenants to settle existing property other than money, presently owned by the settlor, and authority can be found in the judgment of Younger J in *Re Cavendish Browne's ST* [1916] WN 341. There seems no reason not to apply it also to property to which I have a contractual right, but have not yet received, such as the royalties I may hope to receive from a book.

In our problem, we are concerned only with existing property, but obviously it could easily have involved future property as well, and you need to be prepared for questions of that sort. It has been held (in *Re Ellenborough* [1903] 1 Ch 697) that such future property cannot form the subject matter of a trust, and there is also doubt about whether a covenant to settle such property can itself form the subject matter of a trust. Buckley J thought that it could not in *Re Cook's ST* [1965] Ch 905, already referred to:

> Counsel for the second and third defendants have contended that on the true view of the facts there was an immediate settlement of the obligation created by the covenant, and not merely a covenant to settle something in the future ... He relied on *Fletcher* v *Fletcher* (1844) 4 Hare 67 ... I am not able to accept this argument. The covenant with which I am concerned did not, in my opinion, create a debt enforceable at law, that is to say, a property right, which, although to bear fruit only in the future and upon a contingency, was capable of being made the subject of an immediate trust, as was held to be the case in *Fletcher* v *Fletcher*. Nor is this covenant associated with property which was the subject of an immediate trust ... Nor did the covenant relate to property which then belonged to the covenantor ... In contrast to all these cases, this covenant upon its true construction is, in my opinion, an executory contract to settle a particular fund or particular funds of money which at the date of the covenant did not exist and which might never come into existence. It is analogous to a covenant to settle an expectation or to settle after-acquired property. The case, in my judgment, involves the law of contract, not the law of trusts.

The view that a covenant to settle after-acquired property cannot form the subject matter of a trust has also been taken by Lee (1969) 85 LQR 213, and Barton (1975) 91 LQR 236, but this reasoning has been criticised: e.g., Meagher and Lehane (1976) 92 LQR 427. Perhaps this is the explanation for no trust of a promise being constituted in *Re Kay*, which concerned after-acquired property.

Nevertheless, it is by no means obvious why a *contract* to settle after-acquired cannot form the subject matter of a trust, even though it is impossible to create an immediate trust of after-acquired property. The contract after all is existing not future property. The reasoning in *Re Ellenborough* [1903] 1 Ch 697 does not apply to it. There may be a remedies problem, however. We saw above that a party who contracts as trustee for another can claim substantial damages to hold on trust for that other, and where the contract is to settle existing property (or an existing sum of money as in *Fletcher* itself) there is no difficulty in calculating those damages. In *Re Cavendish Browne's ST* [1916] WN 341, Catherine Cavendish Browne made a voluntary settlement containing a covenant to 'convey and transfer to the trustees all the property, both real and personal, to which she was absolutely entitled by virtue of the joint operation of the wills of' two named persons. She died without having settled property to which she was so entitled in trust. Younger J, 'without delivering a final judgment, held ... that the trustees were entitled to recover [from Catherine's administrators] substantial damages for breach of the covenant ..., and that the measure of damages was the value of the property which would have come into the hands of the trustees if the covenant had been duly performed'. Although it is not entirely clear, it appears that Catherine was *already* entitled to the property at the time that the contract was made.

In the above passage from *Cook*, Buckley J talks of the covenant in *Fletcher* creating a debt enforceable at law, and the same is presumably true in *Re Cavendish Browne's ST*: see also Friend [1982] Conv 280. The trust of the promise constituted the settlor as debtor of the trustees. This reasoning may not be possible where the covenant is to settle after-acquired property, however, since it will be difficult or impossible to assess damages based on the value of property which has not yet been acquired, may never be acquired, and indeed need not even yet exist. Perhaps this is the real reason for limiting the principle in *Fletcher* v *Fletcher* to covenants for existing property (but see the contrary argument by Meagher and Lehane (1976) 92 LQR 427).

PROBLEM QUESTION

The following problem question recently appeared on a university examination paper:

Alpha expects to receive a valuable diamond in his grandfather's will and covenants with Beta that he will settle it on Beta as trustee for Gamma when he receives it. Only Alpha and Beta are party to the deed, and no consideration moves from either Beta or Gamma. Alpha later inherits the diamond and refuses to settle it.

Advise Beta and Gamma.

Would your answer be different if Beta had paid Alpha £100,000 by way of consideration, and had physically appropriated the diamond from Alpha's mansion while Alpha was out shopping?

Most of the issues in this problem are similar to those in the previous one, but notice that here we are dealing with future rather than existing property. The last part of the problem addresses a different issue, which is what happens if the WT obtains the property otherwise than by voluntary constitution by the WS. There is some authority, based on *Re Ralli's WT* [1964] Ch 288, that the trust can be fully constituted if the property comes into the trustee's hands in some capacity other than that of trustee.

Helen's father left his residue on trust for his wife for her life, thence to his two daughters, Helen and Irene. Helen, by her marriage settlement, covenanted with trustees of whom the plaintiff (Irene's husband) was one, to settle all her existing and after-acquired property on Irene's children.

On Helen's death, in 1956, the plaintiff, who was the sole surviving trustee under the marriage settlement, was also appointed a trustee under Helen's father's will, and hence obtained title to Helen's residuary estate under her father's will, on the death of Helen's mother (in 1961). He brought an action to determine whether he held the property on the terms of Helen's will, or on the trusts of Helen's marriage settlement.

Buckley J held that the trust of the after-acquired property in the marriage settlement was completely constituted, since the plaintiff held the property under Helen's father's will. It was irrelevant that the plaintiff came by the property under Helen's father's will, rather than under Helen's marriage settlement itself:

In my judgment the circumstance that the plaintiff holds the fund because he was appointed a trustee of the will is irrelevant. He is at law the owner of the fund, and the means by which he became so have no effect upon the quality of his legal ownership.

It is also true that, if it were necessary to enforce performance of the covenant, equity would not assist the beneficiaries under the settlement, because they are mere volunteers; and that for the same reason the plaintiff, as trustee of the settlement, would not be bound to enforce the covenant and would not be constrained by the court to do so, and indeed, it seems, might be constrained by the court not to do so. As matters stand, however, there is no occasion to invoke the assistance of equity to enforce performance of the covenant.

One of the arguments considered above was that it is for the settlor under a voluntary settlement voluntarily to settle the property. Yet clearly in *Re Ralli's WT* Helen took no steps at all to settle the property, yet a fully constituted trust was held to have been created. If *Re Ralli's WT* is correct, and this is the true explanation of it, a trust can be constituted without any action at all by the settlor.

So is *Re Ralli's WT* correct, and is this the true explanation of the case? Rather surprisingly, *Re Brooks* [1939] Ch 993 was not cited, Buckley J reasoning instead from *Re James* [1935] Ch 449, a *Strong* v *Bird* (1874) LR 18 Eq 315 authority which is not on all fours since that doctrine requires an intention on the part of the transferor, continuing until death, to transfer. By contrast, *Re Ralli's WT* required no intention of any kind on Helen's part. It is, however, very difficult to reconcile *Re Ralli's WT* with *Re Brooks*, which is pretty well on all fours with *Re Ralli's WT*. *Re Brooks* concerned the property of a mother and her son, and in particular a voluntary settlement of after-acquired property by the son. Lloyds Bank were the trustees under this voluntary settlement. Later, because of the exercise by his mother of a power of appointment in his favour, the son acquired property, which should have been caught by the voluntary settlement. The power of appointment had been granted to his mother under her marriage settlement. But Lloyds Bank were also trustees under the marriage settlement, and hence already had legal title to this property. The issue was whether Lloyds Bank held the property for the son, or on the trusts in the son's voluntary settlement. It was held that they held the property for the son. The main issue was whether this property was existing or after-acquired property at the time the son's voluntary settlement was made. It was held that it was after-acquired property until the appointment was actually made in his favour. It could therefore not form the subject matter of a trust. *Re Ellenborough* was followed.

The problem is that Lloyds Bank's position was exactly analogous with that of the plaintiff in *Re Ralli's WT*; they had acquired the property which was subject to the son's voluntary settlement otherwise than in their capacity as trustees under that settlement. Yet the opposite decision was reached to that in *Re Ralli's WT*. Both sets of reasoning cannot be correct.

There is only one way of reconciling the cases. In *Re Ralli's WT* Helen settled a reversionary interest, which counts as existing property, even though enjoyment of it was postponed until after her mother's death. Existing property is not subject to *Re Ellenborough*, and the alternative view adopted by Buckley J was that Helen had declared herself trustee of it from the moment of her marriage settlement. If this is right there is no need to treat *Re Ralli's WT* as an authority on covenants to settle at all. It was simply an immediate declaration of trust of existing property. Trusts do have to be constituted by some act of the settlor. Of course, one would have to regard the covenants reasoning in *Re Ralli's WT* as wrong.

It is more likely, however, that *Re Brooks* is wrong. Bennett J reached a conclusion similar to that in *Ralli*, with after-acquired property, in *Re Bowden* [1936] 1 Ch 71. Unfortunately, *Bowden* was not considered in *Brooks*, and *Brooks* was not considered in *Ralli*; and given that all these decisions are at first instance only, it is not possible to reach a clear conclusion.

Let us suppose that the covenants reasoning in *Re Ralli's WT* is correct, in which case *Re Brooks* is presumably wrong. The logic of *Re Ralli's WT* extends to all cases where the trustee acquires legal title, and so long as he does so the method of acquisiton is irrelevant. Thus, the principle ought still to apply if, for example, he comes by his legal title not as his executor, but as the settlor's trustee in bankruptcy, or even as a judgment creditor, or where the settlor has mortgaged his property to the would-be trustee and the would-be trustee forecloses. However, it seems that transfer of legal title is required, and not merely physical possession. On the facts of this problem Beta probably does not obtain legal title, but if the property had been money rather than a diamond then he might have. It is difficult to believe that equity would encourage what amounts to theft by WTs, however, so *Ralli* would probably not assist here in any event.

SUGGESTED ADDITIONAL READING

On covenants to settle:

- Elliott (1960) 76 LQR 100;
- Hornby (1962) 78 LQR 228;
- Lee (1969) 85 LQR 213;
- Goddard [1988] Conv 19.

On trusts of promises:

- Lee (1969) 85 LQR 213;
- Barton (1975) 91 LQR 236;
- Meagher and Lehane (1976) 92 LQR 427;
- Friend [1982] Conv 280.

5 CERTAINTY OF OBJECT, PRIVATE PURPOSE TRUSTS AND UNINCORPORATED ASSOCIATIONS

Certainty of object, private purpose trusts and unincorporated associations may appear at first sight to be a motley collection of unrelated subjects, but in fact they are all interrelated, and it is by no means unlikely that a single exam question will include elements of more than one of these areas. They are also central to the law of trusts, so it would be a very odd paper that did not cover any of them.

If question spotting, you should also bear in mind that any question about whether a trust is charitable will, in all probability, invite you to consider the alternative possibility of a valid private purpose trust. These two areas should also be considered together, therefore. Charities are dealt with in chapter 9.

The connection between the areas discussed in this chapter is (in general terms) as follows. Certainty of object problems are (at least in part) about identifying the human beings who, as possible beneficiaries (who are also referred to as 'objects'), can enforce a trust (or power). If they cannot be identified in accordance with the test to be applied, the trust (or power) will fail.

One of the problems presented by private purpose trusts is precisely that they usually fall foul of certainty of object requirements. They may not be for the benefit of human beings at all (for example animal trusts), and even if they are there may be no human beneficiaries in the full sense (i.e., having a full beneficial interest). There are also sometimes perpetuity difficulties with purpose trusts.

Unincorporated associations usually exist to further a purpose, so the problems of private purpose trusts would also apply to them, except that it is usually possible to construe gifts to them so as to avoid the problems of a trusts analysis altogether.

If a purpose trust is charitable, or if an unincorporated association exists to further a charitable purpose, the above problems do not apply. Because the Attorney-General can always enforce a charitable trust they are exempt from certainty of object requirements, and they are also exempt from the perpetuity rules.

CERTAINTY OF OBJECT

The most difficult part of certainty of object probably lies in the actual method of application of the *McPhail* v *Doulton* test, discussed later in this section, especially in the light of the decision of the Court of Appeal in *Re Baden's Deed Trusts (No. 2)* [1973] Ch 9. A problem question will be discussed later in the chapter, which will examine this particular difficulty, but first it is necessary to consider certainty of object in general terms.

What are the Rules For?

Certainty of object rules apply to both trusts and powers, and serve two main functions. The certainty tests have been developed to further (to a greater or lesser extent) these two functions, and virtually all the discussion that follows can be related to them. So it is of the utmost importance that you know what they are.

First, if a trustee, or donee of a power fails to carry out his duties, or exercises such discretion as he may have, in an improper manner, it is important to be able to ascertain who has *locus standi* to come to court to remedy the situation. Note that throughout this chapter 'he' includes 'she'.

You may think at first sight that the settlor would be the appropriate person, but in fact he drops out of the picture once a settlement has been made, and ceases to have any interest in the property. The settlor, therefore, cannot enforce the trust, so the courts have always been very concerned that someone who benefits in equity (i.e., an object) is able to enforce the trust or power. People with a full beneficial interest certainly have sufficient interest to enforce it (whether the same can be said of people with lesser interests is considered in the discussion of purpose trusts, below). The certainty requirements must allow these people to be identified. If certainty of object tests are not satisfied the property will be held on resulting trust for the settlor, because otherwise there would be nothing to stop the trustees keeping it for themselves.

The stringency of the test required depends on how the courts ultimately enforce the trust or power. This varies depending on whether they are faced with a fixed trust, discretionary trust or power, and so will be discussed separately for each variety of disposition. The minimum requirement, applicable to any disposition, is first that there must be human beneficiaries capable of enforcing the trust (or power), and secondly, that if one of them comes to court it must be possible to show that he has *locus standi*. This minimum requirement is satisfied by the individual ascertainability test, discussed in detail below. Note that it is enough to show of any individual that he is or is not an object: it is unnecessary to be able to draw up a list of all the objects.

The second reason for certainty rules is to enable trusts or powers to be administered. A trustee, or donee of a power, may have to be able to ascertain who the objects are in order to be able to exercise any discretion he may have in a proper manner. Again the precise requirement will vary depending on the nature of the disposition, but often a stricter test is required for the second function than for the first. For example, if a trustee or donee of a power has to get an impression of the size or composition of the entire class of objects in order to carry out his duties, it may be necessary to draw up a list of all or at any rate most of the objects, in effect to ascertain the entire class, or most of it. This requirement is satisfied by the class ascertainability test, discussed below.

The Rules Themselves

Powers
Whereas trustees under a discretionary trust must distribute the trust property, albeit that they have a discretion as to how, the donees of a power have a discretion not only as to *how* to distribute the property, but also as to *whether* to distribute it. They are under no obligation to appoint at all. In other words, whereas a trust is imperative, because the trustees have to appoint, a power is discretionary, because the donees of a power need not appoint at all — the choice is theirs.

There may be limited exceptions to this position. In *Klug v Klug* [1918] 2 Ch 67, a mother who disapproved of her daughter's marriage without her consent capriciously refused to exercise a power in her favour. On application by the public trustee, the court ordered that the power should be exercised. This case was relied on in *Mettoy Pension Trustees v Evans* [1991] 2 All ER 513, noted [1991] Conv 364, where Warner J held that the court could enforce a fiduciary power in the same manner as a discretionary trust. The case is unusual, however, in that there was nobody else who was capable of exercising the power. Assuming that these cases are correct, they create limited exceptions where non-exercise of a power is capricious, and where there is nobody available to exercise a power. The cases do not affect the general principle that where donees of a power make a *bona fide* decision not to exercise it, the courts will not compel them to do so.

If the donees of a power do not appoint, a gift or trust over may have been provided for in default of appointment. A gift or trust over is a gift or trust which takes effect where the property has not otherwise been fully disposed of. It must be provided for in the original trust instrument, and if it has been, it will take effect. If not, the property goes on resulting trust to the settlor.

If there is a gift over in default of appointment, the disposition must take effect as a power, not a trust, since the existence of the gift over is obviously inconsistent with an imperative duty to appoint. The absence of a gift over in default is not necessarily indicative of a trust, however, since the alternative construction, of a power with a resulting trust in favour of the settlor in the absence of appointment, is also possible. It will all depend on the words used in the instrument.

In the case of mere powers i.e., a power not given to a fiduciary), the donee's discretion seems to be unfettered except in so far that he must not dispose of the property otherwise than in accordance with the terms of the power. The objects can come to court to enforce the power, therefore, only to the limited extent that the court will restrain disposal of the property otherwise than in accordance with the terms of the power.

This limited negative duty can be carried out and enforced so long as 'it can be said with certainty that any given individual is or is not a member of the class'. No more stringent test of certainty than the individual ascertainability test is required.

It is probably more common for powers of appointment to be given to trustees, in which case the donees of the power will not enjoy an unfettered discretion. Sir Robert Megarry V-C took the view in Re Hay's ST [1982] 1 WLR 1202, that the extent of the duty to consider both whether or not a power should be exercised, and how it should be exercised, is stronger when the power is given to someone who is also a trustee, than when a mere power is exercised. For example, it is not sufficient simply to appoint to the objects who happen to be at hand, whereas the donee of a mere power can do this. It seems that it is necessary periodically to consider whether or not to exercise the power, and at least to appreciate the width of the field of objects, even if it is not possible to compile a list of all the objects, or ascertain accurately their number. Also, individual appointments need to be considered on their merits:

> The trustee must not simply proceed to exercise the power in favour of such of the objects as happen to be at hand or claim his attention. He must first consider what person or classes of persons are objects of the power within the definition in the settlement or will. In doing this, there is no need to compile a complete list of the objects, or even to make an accurate assessment of the number of them: what is needed is an appreciation of the width of the field, and thus whether a selection is to be made merely from a dozen, or instead, from thousands or millions ...

Nevertheless, if at the end of the day the donees of the power refuse to exercise it, that is a choice that they are entitled to make, and there is no reason why the courts should be required to distribute on their behalf. It is still necessary to be able to ascertain of any given individual whether or not he or she is an object of the power, since only objects of the power will have *locus standi* to enforce it, even to the limited extent of preventing the donees acting otherwise than in accordance with its terms. It is also necessary for the objects to be defined so that the donees can, as required by Sir Robert Megarry V-C above, get a feel for the width of the class.

Despite this, the duty to consider is not so stringent as to require the donees, in order to carry it out, to draw up a list of the entire class of potential beneficiaries, and there is therefore no reason in principle to apply the class ascertainability test to powers.

In *Re Gestetner's Settlement* [1953] 1 Ch 672, Harman J had to consider the validity of a power given to trustees to distribute among a very wide class, including directors and employees or former employees of a large number of companies, with a gift over in default. Since membership of the class constantly fluctuated, it was impossible to draw up a list of the entire class at any one time. He held that it was not necessary to know all the objects in order to appoint, and that it was not fatal that the entire class could not be ascertained.

In *Re Gulbenkian's Settlements* [1970] AC 508, trustees were given a power to apply income from the trust fund to maintain, among others, any person in whose house or in whose company or in whose care Gulbenkian may from time to time be residing, and there was a gift over in default of appointment. In upholding the power, the House of Lords held that the individual ascertainability test was the applicable test for powers: a power would be valid if it could be said with certainty whether any given individual was *or was not* a member of the class, and would not fail simply because it was impossible to ascertain every member of the class.

Note that the dispositions in both *Gestetner* and *Gulbenkian* must have been powers, as in each case there was a gift over in default of appointment. A gift over would be inappropriate in a discretionary trust, since the trustees are obliged to appoint.

There are two points specifically to note about the *Gulbenkian* test. First, the italicised words, *or was not*, are important. Secondly the House of Lords expressly rejected Lord Denning MR's test in the Court of Appeal in *Gulbenkian* [1968] Ch 126, at pp. 132-4. On the basis that a power would be held void for uncertainty only if it was impossible to carry it out, he had taken the view that it should be necessary only to be able to identify one single beneficiary as being clearly within the class. The House of Lords disagreed, primarily because this test took no account of the trustee's duty to carry out the power in a fiduciary manner. The Denning test would only really be appropriate were the trustees at liberty to distribute to the first person who came to hand, and as we have seen that is not the case. The Denning test is, in any case, no good for enforcement purposes, where the donees of the power propose to appoint somebody who is not an object of the power. Anybody coming to court for an injunction will have to show that he is an object, and also that the person in whose favour it is proposed to appoint is not. That requires the ability to determine of anybody whether or not he is within the class. It is not sufficient to be able to say of one person alone, whether that is the case.

The importance of these two points will become apparent later in the chapter.

Discretionary trusts

Whereas a court will never be called upon ultimately to enforce a power, if the donees refuse to distribute, if no distribution is made by trustees under a discretionary trust, the court may, as a last resort, be called upon to effect a distribution itself. The certainty test for discretionary trusts has largely depended on the nature of their ultimate enforcement, and the courts' view of this has changed recently. At one time they took the view that the court could not exercise any discretion on behalf of recalcitrant trustees (see, e.g., the view of Jenkins LJ in *Inland Revenue Commissioners* v *Broadway Cottages Trust* [1955] Ch 678). It could remove the trustees and appoint others in their place, but in theory it could be impossible to find any other trustees prepared to execute the trust. It followed that, however unlikely this eventuality may be, at the end of the day a court had to be prepared to carry out the trust itself. Since it refused to exercise any discretion it could only divide the property equally among all the objects.

Though there is a logic to this conclusion, given the premises, equality of distribution will often not implement the intentions of the settlor, and indeed is quite likely to frustrate them. It seems that the equality principle originated in 19th-century family settlements (e.g., *Burrough* v *Philcox* (1840) 4 My & Cr 72), where it may have been the most reliable method of carrying out the settlor's intention. It is much less likely to be appropriate, however, in modern settlements, for example, dividing proceeds among employees of a company.

Nevertheless, equality of distribution was the rule, and of course it could only be done if it was possible to draw up a list of all the objects. For this reason, *Inland Revenue Commissioners* v *Broadway Cottages Trust* applied class ascertainability test to discretionary trusts.

The class in *Broadway* was undoubtedly extremely wide, consisting mostly of remote issue, as well as a number of charities. Two charities (Broadway Cottages Trust and Sunnylands Trust) had received income under the settlement, and claimed an income tax exemption on it, but in order to do so they had to show that the settlement was valid. The class was never held to be unascertainable, since the charities conceded the point (perhaps unwisely, since it was conceptually certain, and only evidential difficulties prevented drawing up an entire list of objects: see further, the discussion on fixed trusts, below). The Crown for its part conceded that the individual ascertainability test was satisfied. On the basis of these concessions, the Court of Appeal held that the trust failed: *Gestetner* did not apply, since here there was no gift over, there was an obligation to distribute, and the whole range of objects had to be ascertainable.

Jenkins LJ took the view that if the court was called upon to enforce the trust: 'It could not mend the invalidity of the trust by imposing an arbitrary distribution amongst some only of the whole unascertainable class.' The Court could only effect a distribution to all the objects equally. The irony of this is that, given that some of the objects were charities and others people, equality of distribution was probably the last thing the settlor would have wanted.

One result of this case was that the test for certainty was much more stringent for discretionary trusts than for powers (on which, see above). This had two main consequences: first, many perfectly reasonable trusts failed; secondly, the courts were at pains to construe doubtful dispositions as powers, rather than discretionary trusts.

In *McPhail* v *Doulton* [1971] AC 424, however, the House of Lords decisively rejected the principle of equality of distribution, in a case where equal distribution would have made a nonsense of the settlor's intention. The House accepted that even in the final analysis, assuming in other words that no trustee could be found who was prepared to execute the trust, it could exercise the necessary discretion itself. Therefore, at least so far as ultimate enforcement is concerned a less rigid certainty test should be sufficient. All that is required is for it to be possible to tell, with certainty, whether any individual coming to court to enforce a trust or power has sufficient interest to do so: in other words, whether or not he is within the class of objects. This requirement is of course satisfied by the individual ascertainability test.

The *ratio* of *McPhail* v *Doulton* is that the test for certainty for discretionary trusts is essentially the same as that for powers, the individual ascertainability test, not the class ascertainability test. *Inland Revenue Commissioners* v *Broadway Cottages Trust* was overruled.

Lord Wilberforce also made the point that in applying the test the courts are concerned only with conceptual uncertainty. A trust will not fail merely because there are evidential difficulties in ascertaining whether or not someone is within the class, as the court is never defeated by evidential uncertainty, and can deal with problems of proof when an application for enforcement arises:

I desire to emphasise the distinction clearly made ... between linguistic or semantic uncertainty which, if unresolved by the court, renders the gift void, and the difficulty of ascertaining the existence or whereabouts of members of the class, a matter with which the court can appropriately deal on an application for directions.

Thus, a discretionary trust in favour of the first 20 people who crossed Clifton suspension bridge in 1991 should be enforceable: the class is conceptually certain even though proof may be difficult. A trust in favour of 'all my friends' is different, however. It is conceptually uncertain, because 'all my friends' is not a phrase capable of precise definition. Such a trust ought therefore to fail even on the *McPhail* v *Doulton* test.

A major problem is that the change in *McPhail* v *Doulton* was consequential on the court changing its views about ultimate enforcement. Unfortunately, the relaxation may lead to difficulties over administration. Unlike donees of mere powers (see last section), the trustees' discretion is not absolute. In considering its exercise, they must, according to Lord Wilberforce in *McPhail* v *Doulton* itself, make a survey of the entire field of objects, and consider each individual case responsibly, on its merits. This ought to require a more rigorous certainty test than individual ascertainability. For example, the Clifton suspension bridge example should fail (assuming no central record is kept of people walking over Clifton bridge), because the trustees could not possibly survey the entire field.

Since under the new test trustees may be unable to discover the identities of all the possible beneficiaries, they will sometimes be unable to carry out their duties. Some discretionary trusts could be very difficult to administer were the trustees unable to survey the entire field of possible beneficiaries. An example might be a discretionary trust to distribute property 'according to the age and ability of the potential beneficiaries'.

Lord Wilberforce himself suggested a way out of the difficulty. He thought that dispositions might fail if the class is so widely drawn as to be administratively unworkable, even if they otherwise satisfy the new test. An example he gave was a gift to 'all the residents of Greater London', but the acceptable width of the class presumably depends on the exact nature of the trustees' duties, and whether they must actually survey the entire field.

Another possible solution is that if the terms of a trust negative any sensible intention on the part of the settlor, it may fail on the grounds of capriciousness. This was suggested *obiter* by Templeman J in *Re Manisty's Settlement* [1974] Ch 17. The same applies, incidentally, to powers, and indeed *Re Manisty's Settlement* actually concerned a valid power.

Perhaps these qualifications are sufficient to give the trustees the protection they require, though at the expense of the vagueness inherent in tests of this nature. Further discussion of this problem follows in consideration of the problem, below.

Another problem with the new certainty test is how, if at all, the doctrine in *Saunders* v *Vautier* (1841) 4 Beav 115 applies. Under this doctrine, all the beneficiaries, collectively entitled, can (so long as they are adult and *sui juris*) terminate the trust and distribute or resettle the trust property. It is difficult to see how this doctrine can operate if the entire class of beneficiaries cannot be ascertained.

One possible answer is that *Saunders* v *Vautier* applies only to fixed trusts, on the grounds that the objects of a discretionary trust do not have full beneficial interests unless and until the trustees' discretion is exercised in their favour, but Lord Upjohn in *Gulbenkian* suggests otherwise. The other possible answer is that the courts would use a device similar to the *Benjamin* order discussed below (in the section on fixed trusts).

The settlement in *McPhail* v *Doulton* was further litigated as to the application of the new test in *Re Baden's Deed Trusts (No. 2)* [1973] Ch 9. This is a very difficult case, and will be considered in detail in discussing the problem, below.

Fixed trusts
It is usually argued that, since it is the essence of a fixed trust that the property is to be divided among all the beneficiaries in fixed proportions (e.g., in equal shares), it can only be workable if the entire class of beneficiaries is known; the conventional view, therefore, is that the test of certainty is the class ascertainability test.

This was certainly the view of Jenkins LJ in *Broadway* (at p. 29): 'There can be no division in equal shares amongst a class of persons unless all the members of the class are known.' In other words, a complete list of objects must be able to be drawn up. From the fact that, in *McPhail* v *Doulton*, the House of Lords was concerned only to assimilate discretionary trusts and powers, the implication usually drawn is that the reasoning was not intended also to apply to fixed trusts.

However, there are fairly convincing contrary arguments (see, e.g., *Matthews* [1984] Conv 22). The orthodox view presupposes that *Broadway* still stands in so far that later cases have not directly detracted from it, but it is arguable that even when it was decided, *Broadway* was wholly out of line with other authorities, in which case there is no reason for it still to be regarded as authority for anything at all.

The central issue, I would suggest, is the basis upon which the trust property is distributed by the trustees, or if the issue becomes one of ultimate enforcement, by the courts. It is often assumed that distribution is impossible unless the entire class can be ascertained, but this need not be the case, and even if it is, application of the class ascertainability test may not necessarily resolve the difficulty.

Suppose, for example, that in 1986 Michael settled property upon trustees with directions in 1991 that the property was to be sold, and that the proceeds of sale were to be distributed equally, in favour of those of his three sons, Paul, Quentin and Richard, who are still then living. Assuming that in 1986 all three of the settlor's sons were known to be alive, it is obvious that this is a fixed trust, and that it satisfies the class ascertainability test.

Suppose now that at some time after 1986 Richard went on an Antarctic expedition, from which by 1991 he has not returned. He is thought (but not known definitely) to have perished on the expedition. The trustees sell the property, and wish to distribute it in accordance with their directions. Despite the fact that the class ascertainability test was clearly satisfied, and that the trust did not fail for want of certainty, it is obvious that they have a problem.

If at this point the trustees asked for directions, it is likely that the court would resolve the difficulty by making a *Benjamin* order (based on *Re Benjamin* [1902] 1 Ch 723). The trustees would be directed to distribute on the basis that Richard was dead. If Richard later turned up alive, he would still have an interest in the proceeds of sale, which he would be able to claim from Paul and Quentin if it were still traceable, and assuming that his claim was not barred by limitation. The trustees personally would be protected from any action, however.

It is clear, then, that evidential difficulties, even in the distribution of fixed trusts, can be resolved by the courts. Is there any reason of logic or principle why the position should be any different if by the time of the settlement in 1986, Richard had already embarked upon the expedition, and it was not known even then whether he was alive or dead? In those circumstances it would not after all, be possible at the date of the settlement, to draw up a list of all the objects, since it would not be possible to say with certainty whether Richard should be included or not. The question is one upon which you must form your own views, but a strong argument can be made that there is no need to apply the class ascertainability test, even to fixed trusts.

As we saw in the last section, in applying the individual ascertainability test, Lord Wilberforce distinguished between evidential and conceptual uncertainty, on the ground that the courts are never defeated by evidential uncertainty. Another interesting question is whether, if the class ascertainability test does still apply to fixed trusts, the same distinction also applies. If it does, it leads to some interesting consequences.

It may be remembered that in *Broadway*, although the class was very large, it was not conceptually uncertain. There was no problem over defining the class conceptually, and *it was conceded* in *Broadway*, rather than concluded from rational argument, that the class could not be ascertained. Perhaps the concession was wrongly made, and that in reality, even in *Broadway* itself, the class ascertainability test was satisfied. *Broadway* was indeed criticised in *Gulbenkian* (in particular, by Lords Reid and Upjohn), and by Lord Wilberforce in *McPhail* v *Doulton*, on the grounds that the Court of Appeal had confused conceptual and evidential uncertainty.

If, however, the distinction between conceptual and evidential uncertainty applies equally to the class as to the individual ascertainability test, it is difficult to see any difference between the two tests. If it can be said of any individual that he or she falls outside the class, then there can be no conceptual difficulty in defining the class as a whole. Indeed, there is no *conceptual* difficulty in defining the class in the above example, merely an evidential difficulty in ascertaining whether Richard is a member. In principle, however, evidential difficulties, as in *Broadway* and the example, are capable of resolution by the courts.

I would suggest, however, that the class ascertainability test has always been an evidential test, and that the distinction between conceptual and evidential uncertainty has only ever been applied to the individual ascertainability test. In the discussion of the problem question, below, I suggest that the distinction between conceptual and evidential uncertainty is, in any case, misconceived. Further, if it is accepted that a function of the certainty of object test is to ensure that the trust is administratively workable, then even if it is accepted that there is no need to apply the class ascertainability test to fixed trusts, it can be argued that a more rigorous test is required than for discretionary trusts. One way of achieving this is to apply different tests of administrative workability, since it does not follow that merely because a discretionary trust is administratively workable with a given class of objects, a trust with the same class of objects will necessarily be so, if the trustees' discretion is removed. It is probably more satisfactory, however, to have a stricter certainty test for fixed trusts, albeit, perhaps, a test not as strict as the class ascertainability test.

Administrative unworkability is considered in greater detail in the discussion of the problem question.

PROBLEM QUESTION

In recognition of the merger of University College, Cardiff, with its sister institution, UWIST, in September 1988, Jones, a former student, made a will in which he left his residuary estate to University of Wales, College of Cardiff on trust to apply the money as the officers of the College in their absolute discretion see fit for the benefit of the descendants of those ex-students of University College, living at his death, who appeared in the official College photograph of 1910. Jones has now died, and his next of kin wish to challenge the bequest. Discuss.

This question concerns the detailed application of the *McPhail v Doulton* test. Though it looks easy it is a lot more difficult than appears at first sight, and you will need to have a sound knowledge of the post *McPhail v Doulton* cases. It is a likely area for a problem question in an exam.

It looks at first sight like a valid discretionary trust, which satisfies the individual ascertainability test, because any given object should be able to show whether he is within the class. No conceptual uncertainty arises in applying the test. It was Sachs LJ in *Re Baden's Deed Trusts (No. 2)* [1973] Ch 9 who elaborated on the distinction between conceptual and evidential uncertainty. He gave 'someone under a moral obligation' as an example of conceptual uncertainty, and 'first cousins', 'members of the X trade union' and 'those who have served in the Royal Navy' as examples of conceptual certainty where proof might be difficult. This problem falls into the latter category because whether or not you are a descendant of one of a number of people can be answered yes or no. It is not a matter of degree, on which opinions may differ, like for example 'fat middle-aged men'. That would be conceptually uncertain.

So here apparently is a very easy question about a trust which is obviously valid. Not so by any means. Difficulties begin to emerge when one considers the detailed application of the certainty test. This is what the examiner is really looking for, and where the majority of marks will go. There are at least two arguments that this disposition is invalid.

First, it is arguable that the class is so widely drawn as to be administratively unworkable, as in 'all the residents of Greater London' (discussed above), in which case on Lord Wilberforce's own view the disposition should fail.

On the other hand, the trustees are ostensibly given 'absolute discretion', so arguably may not need to survey the entire class to administer the trust. But even 'absolute discretion' must be exercised on equitable principles, so the trustees would be in breach were they to appoint the first objects who happened to be at hand. Indeed, the trustees were ostensibly given 'absolute discretion' in *McPhail* v *Doulton* itself, yet Lord Wilberforce thought that they would need 'to know what is the permissible area of selection and then consider responsibly'.

The question of administrative unworkability was considered in *Re Manisty's Settlement* [1974] Ch 17, where a power given to trustees was upheld where they were able to appoint anyone in the world apart from a small excepted class (a power where the objects are defined only by reference to an *excepted* class is called an intermediate or hybrid power). A similar decision was reached in *Re Hay's ST* [1982] 1 WLR 1202. These decisions suggest that very rarely will a power fail on grounds of administrative unworkability, simply because of the width of the class.

The courts are not concerned with questions of ultimate enforcement with a power, however, and it is arguable that the decisions in *Hay* and *Manisty* ought not to apply directly where, as here, the instrument is drafted as a trust. Indeed, in *Re Hay's ST* [1982] 1 WLR 1202 itself, Sir Robert Megarry V-C noted that: 'The words of Lord Wilberforce [about administrative unworkability] . . . are directed towards trusts, not powers.'

The problem arose directly in the Divisional Court in *R* v *District Auditor, ex parte West Yorkshire Metropolitan County Council* [1986] RVR 24. Prior to the abolition of the Metropolitan County Councils, they were prohibited from incurring expenditure under Local Government Act 1972, s. 137(1), 'which in their opinion is in the interests of their area or any part of it or some or all of its inhabitants,' after 1 April 1985.

When West Yorkshire Metropolitan County Council realised that they were going to have a large surplus on 1 April 1985, they sought to find ways of ensuring that this money could still be spent after the 1 April deadline. In their attempt to achieve this aim, they purported to set up a discretionary trust of £400,000, having a duration of 11 months, 'for the benefit of any or all or some of the inhabitants of the County of West Yorkshire'. The trust also directed the trustees to use the fund specifically:

(a)   To assist economic development in the county in order to relieve unemployment and poverty.
(b)   To assist bodies concerned with youth and community problems.
(c)   To assist and encourage ethnic and other minority groups.
(d)   To inform all interested persons of the consequences of the proposed abolition of the Council (and the other Metropolitan County Councils) and of other programmes affecting local government in the county.

This was held to be administratively unworkable. The inhabitants of the County of West Yorkshire numbered about two and a half million. The range of objects was held to be so hopelessly wide as to be incapable of forming anything like a class.

There are clear statements in the case that trusts may be treated differently from powers in this regard, since a court may be called upon ultimately to execute a trust, whereas it will not, of course, be required to execute a power.

The second argument that can be advanced is that the terms of the trust negative any sensible intention on the part of the settlor, in which case the disposition should fail on another principle discussed in *Re Manisty's Settlement*. The argument is quite plausible here, and indeed Templeman J thought this was the real problem over 'residents of Greater London':

The settlor neither gives the trustees an unlimited power which they can exercise sensibly, nor a power limited to what may be described as a 'sensible' class, but a power limited to a class, membership of which is accidental and irrelevant to any settled purpose or to any method of limiting or selecting beneficiaries.

In addressing these issues the width of the class is not the only factor, since other factors may make clear what the intention of the settlor was. For example, in *Re Hay's ST* [1982] 1 WLR 1202, Sir Robert Megarry V-C said of this passage:

> In *Re Manisty's Settlement* [1974] Ch 17 at 27 Templeman J appears to be suggesting that a power to benefit 'residents in Greater London' is void as being capricious 'because the terms of the power negative any sensible intention of the part of the settlor'. In saying that, I do not think that the judge had in mind a case in which the settlor was, for instance, a former chairman of the Greater London Council, as subsequent words of his on that page indicate.

Alternatively, suppose that trustees were directed to use the fund, in their discretion, to provide library facilities for the residents of Greater London. It might also be perfectly possible to infer a sensible intention on the part of the settlor. On the other hand, fairly precise guidelines were laid down in *R v District Auditor, ex parte West Yorkshire Metropolitan County Council*, but this was still insufficient to save the trust. In any case, in the problem question itself, no guidance is given to the officers of the college, so the trust may fail on this ground.

Even if the disposition does not fall foul of either of the above arguments, there are further difficulties to be resolved in the actual application of the test. It should not be forgotten that the disposition in *McPhail v Doulton* was remitted to the Chancery Division so that the House of Lords test could be applied. Eventually it came again to the Court of Appeal, where differing opinions were given: *Re Baden's Deed Trusts (No. 2)* [1973] Ch 9. By this time some 12 years had passed since Mr Baden's death, the fund was still sterilised by litigation, and a considerable proportion had been dissipated in legal costs. Sachs LJ observed that the situation 'lacks attraction'.

Re Baden's Deed Trusts (No. 2) is a very important case, and must be studied in detail. The disposition was 'to or for the benefit of any of the officers and employees or ex-officers or ex-employees of the company or to any relatives or dependants of any such persons'. It was argued by John Vinelott QC, who was challenging the disposition on behalf of the executors, that it could not be shown that any person definitely is or *is not* within the class (as required by the *Gulbenkian* test). Had this ingenious argument been accepted it would have meant virtually returning to the rejected class-ascertainability test, as Megaw LJ observed. In the disposition in the problem, for example, it would have been necessary to draw up a list of all the objects to show that any given applicant was *not* among them, and the disposition would fail. The Court of Appeal rejected the argument, but not on identical grounds.

Sachs LJ avoided the difficulty by emphasising that the court was concerned only with conceptual certainty, so that it should not be fatal that there might be *evidential* difficulties in drawing up John Vinelott QC's list.

This effectively destroys the Vinelott argument, which was addressed primarily towards *evidential* difficulties in drawing up the class. Sachs LJ also took the view that the courts would place the burden of proof, in effect, on someone claiming to be within the class. This seems acceptable if ultimate enforcement is the issue, and the test is of the *locus standi* of the claimant, but it does not help the administration of the trust. If the test is correct the disposition in the problem satisfies it.

Megaw LJ adopted a different solution, however, requiring that as regards a substantial number of objects, it can be shown with certainty that they fall within the class. This is rather a vague test — clearly it is not enough to be able to show that *one* person is certainly within the class, as this test was rejected in *Gulbenkian* (see the discussion of powers, above). Presumably, the test requires evidential, as well as conceptual, certainty. Maybe Megaw LJ adopted it simply because he could find no other way of rejecting Mr Vinelott's argument without returning either to the rejected *Broadway* test, or to the test which had been rejected in *Gulbenkian*. Indeed, none of the judges in the Court of Appeal was able to find a satisfactory solution to this difficulty. The test may have the merit, however, of ensuring that the trustees will be able to get a feel for the width of the class, which they need properly to be able to exercise their discretion.

Whether the disposition in the problem satisfies Megaw LJ's test is largely a question of fact, depending on how difficult the descendants of these particular students are to ascertain.

Stamp LJ's test is probably the strictest of the three, and he seemed to be quite impressed by the Vinelott argument. He emphasised that it must be possible for the trustees to make a comprehensive survey of the range of objects, but he did not think it would be fatal if, at the end of the survey, it was impossible to draw up a list of every single beneficiary. He would have taken the view that the trust failed, had he not felt compelled to follow an early House of Lords authority, which had held that a discretionary trust for 'relations' was valid, 'relations' being defined narrowly, as 'next of kin'. If Stamp LJ's view is correct, it is very unlikely that the disposition in this problem is valid.

This problem illustrates then what many others also illustrate. First, there are not very many relevant cases, but you have to know them well (all three judgments in *Re Baden's Deed Trusts (No. 2)*). Secondly, you must be fresh *on the day* because you will have to think *in the exam itself* to apply the cases to the particular facts before you. You might also consider whether there is any substance to Mr Vinelott's argument in *Re Baden's Deed Trusts (No. 2)*, and if not how you would have dealt with it had you been sitting in the Court of Appeal.

You should also consider which of the three views advanced in *Re Baden's Deed Trusts (No. 2)* you prefer. You can advance convincing arguments in favour of any of them, but I would tentatively invite you to consider the following:

(a)   The distinction drawn by Sachs LJ between conceptual and evidential uncertainty has its origin in Lord Wilberforce's speech in *McPhail v Doulton*, and, indeed, there are traces of a similar distinction in *Gulbenkian*. The justification is that evidential distinctions can always be resolved by the courts, but as we saw in the discussion of certainty of subject-matter in chapter 3, the courts can also resolve conceptual uncertainties. However, once the *Broadway* equality of distribution principles has been abandoned, the justification for certainty rules is not to assist the courts, but rather the trustees, in administering the trust. Trustees will be defeated just as easily by evidential problems, as they will by conceptual difficulties.

(b)   As we saw in the earlier discussion of fixed trust, if a class is conceptually certain, then the only reason why a list of the entire class cannot be drawn up is evidential. The class ascertainability test, if it was ever meaningful at all, must have been an evidential test; if the test were simply conceptual, then there would be no difference between the individual and class ascertainability tests.

(c)   I would suggest, therefore, that no good basis can be found for the conceptual/evidential distinction. Proponents of Sachs LJ's view would respond that the test of administrative workability is sufficient to ensure that the trust is workable, but in that case it is reasonable to ask why any test is needed at all apart from administrative workability. In any case, evidential issues would now need to be dealt with by the administrative workability test, and it is not obvious that that is an improvement over dealing with them as part of the individual ascertainability test itself.

(d)   Megaw LJ's test is evidential and addresses the problem of making the trust workable for trustees. It is therefore (I would suggest) preferable to Sachs LJ's test.

(e)   Stamp LJ's test is also evidential (indeed, entirely so, since 'next-of-kin' is not itself conceptually certain), but once the *Broadway* equality of distribution principle has been rejected, it is difficult to justify a test as strict as Stamp LJ's, since his test amounts virtually to a return to the class ascertainability test.

This, then, is an argument for preferring Megaw LJ's test, or, at any rate, a test similar to it.

The problem considered in chapter 2 (at p. 34) raises certainty issues, as well as issues as to whether Omega has declared himself trustee. If he has, then the beneficiaries are 'all you ravers out there on "Z" who like Stilton'. The beneficiaries are entitled to an equal share, so that this is a fixed trust. Obviously, if the *Broadway* test still applies to fixed trusts, then the disposition will fail for uncertainty, but the question asks you whether Omega could have created a trust of the cheese by using different wording, and if so, what wording would have sufficed. If he had given himself discretion as to each raver's share, or if the individual ascertainability test is applicable to fixed trusts, then the cases discussed in this section are relevant.

Whether an individual was present at the acid-house party raises no conceptual difficulty, so if everybody had been entitled to a share that would probably have satisfied Sachs LJ's test, but probably not Megaw LJ's and certainly not that of Stamp LJ. The term 'ravers' may not be conceptually certain, and the question whether an individual likes Stilton clearly raises conceptual difficulties. On the other hand, in *Re Barlow's WT* [1979] 1 WLR 278, Browne-Wilkinson J upheld a direction to an executor 'to allow any member of my family and any friends of mine who may wish to do so to purchase any ... pictures'. 'All my friends' would be regarded as conceptually uncertain, because the executor could not have sensibly surveyed the entire class. Friendship is after all a matter of degree on which opinions can differ.

This did not matter in *Barlow* itself, however, because friendship was simply a condition of exercising an option, and there was therefore no need for the purposes of the particular disposition to survey the class at all. It was enough, therefore, to place the burden on each person coming forward to prove that he was a friend, and Browne-Wilkinson J laid down certain minimum qualifications. Had it been necessary for the executor to ascertain who all the friends of the testator were, the gift would have failed as being conceptually uncertain, because he could not have sensibly surveyed the entire class. *Barlow* would not assist in the particular problem, therefore, and Omega would certainly have to strike out the requirement that an object likes Stilton.

PRIVATE PURPOSE TRUSTS

Examiners also like questions on private purpose trusts, and though these are often combined with charities issues (e.g., the problem question alluded to at the beginning of chapter 9), they need not be. A possible essay question might be:

How, if at all, does the beneficiary principle affect the validity of private purpose trusts?

A lack of ascertainable beneficiaries is also a reason why private (non-charitable) purpose trusts are usually struck down, because for that reason they are not enforceable by anyone (trusts for a charitable purpose are valid, but they are enforced by the Attorney-General).

Sometimes humans are not intended to benefit at all, in which case no one can enforce the trust. Dispositions of this nature are generally void. A classic example is *Re Astor's ST* [1952] Ch 534, where trustees were instructed to hold a fund upon various trusts including 'the maintenance of good relations between nations [and] ... the preservation of the independence of newspapers'. The purposes were not charitable, but the settlement was drafted expressly so as to be valid under the perpetuity rules. The trust was held by Roxburgh J to be void, because there were no human beneficiaries capable of enforcing it. Further examples are *Re Shaw* [1957] 1 WLR 729, where Harman J held void on the same principle a trust to research the development of a 40-letter alphabet, and *Re Endacott* [1960] Ch 232, where a gift 'to North Tawton Devon Parish Council for the purpose of providing some useful memorial to myself' was held void by the Court of Appeal.

On the other hand, trusts to erect or maintain tombs and monuments have been upheld, as have trusts for the maintenance of specific animals (e.g., *Re Dean* (1889) 41 ChD 522) and even, in *Re Thompson* [1934] Ch 342, a trust for the promotion and furtherance of fox-hunting. It is difficult to reconcile these with the general principle; on the other hand too much reliance has been placed upon them for them now to be regarded as wrong (except perhaps *Re Thompson*), and they are usually regarded as exceptions (e.g., in *Re Astor's ST*).

Sometimes, on the other hand, humans are intended to benefit, but the gift is nevertheless limited to use for a particular purpose. Here the problem is different. There are people (who must be ascertainable within the certainty tests discussed above) with an interest in enforcing the trust, but none is entitled to a full beneficial interest, because of the limitation to the particular purpose.

It is arguable that these dispositions are also void, on similar principles to those considered above. In *Leahy v Attorney-General for New South Wales* [1959] AC 457, property was to be held on trust for 'such order of nuns of the Catholic Church or the Christian Brothers as my executors and trustees shall select'. The trust was not charitable, and Viscount Simonds in the Privy Council thought that it failed as a private trust on the grounds that though the individual members had an interest in enforcing the trust, they were not granted a full beneficial interest. Since this is invariably the case with purpose trusts of this nature, the reasoning leads to the conclusion that such trusts are never valid.

Leahy v Attorney-General for New South Wales is not an especially strong authority, however, because it is explicable on other grounds. The gift ought also to have failed for perpetuity, except that in any case it was validated by the New South Wales Conveyancing Act, so Viscount Simonds's views are technically *obiter*.

Goff J took what may have been a different view in *Re Denley's Trust Deed* [1969] 1 Ch 373. He thought that the principles of *Re Astor's ST* and *Re Endacott* invalidated only 'abstract or impersonal' purpose trusts. He went on to say that:

> Where, then, the trust, though expressed as a purpose, is directly or indirectly for the benefit of an individual or individuals, it seems to me that it is in general outside the mischief of the beneficiary principle.

This quotation is unfortunately not very clear. One view is that the test is not whether a full beneficial interest is granted, but whether individuals who are ascertainable have *locus standi* to sue. They will have so long as the benefit is not too indirect or intangible. The trust (which was upheld by Goff J) was 'for the purpose of a recreation or sports ground primarily for the benefit of the employees of the company . . .', with a gift over at the end of the perpetuity period, to the General Hospital, Cheltenham.

Another view of *Re Denley's Trust Deed*, however, which is easier to reconcile with Viscount Simonds's views in *Leahy* v *Attorney-General for New South Wales* is that Goff J construed it as a trust for individuals, and not as a purpose trust at all. If this view is correct then the case breaks no new ground, and all private purpose trusts remain void, apart from the anomalous exceptions discussed above. This view was advanced by (among others) Vinelott J in *Re Grant's WT* (considered in the next section) and P. J. Millet QC (1985) 101 LQR 269, 280-2, as part of an analysis of the *Quistclose* and other similar trusts (see chapter 3). He was concerned to reject the view that *Barclays Bank Ltd* v *Quistclose Investments Ltd* [1970] AC 567 concerned a resulting trust arising on the failure of the primary trust (to enable dividends to be paid), that primary trust being a variety of a *Denley*-style purpose trust. I would reiterate what I say in that chapter, that the article is well worth reading.

Given that the trust was enforceable in *Denley*, and that similar trusts will continue to be enforceable, does it matter how the case is analysed? Well, it might. Consider the question of enforcement. If the trustees decided to use the fund to install a kidney machine for the benefit of the patients of the hospital, then that can be relatively easily prevented by injunction. Suppose, however, the trustees do nothing, and no trustees can be found to build and/or maintain the sports ground. Specific performance cannot be awarded, as constant supervision would be required, and an injunction is clearly of no use.

At the end of the day, it is difficult to see what solution can be adopted, apart from distribution of the income from the fund directly to the employees of the company (not the capital, because of the gift over). That puts them into exactly the same position as a beneficiary under an ordinary discretionary (or is it fixed?) trust.

The issue could also arise if the objects of the trust wanted to terminate it on the basis of *Saunders* v *Vautier* (see the discussion of discretionary trusts, above). Presumably, only beneficiaries in the conventional sense can invoke this doctrine, and if the objects of a *Denley*-style purpose have a lesser interest, they will be unable to do so.

UNINCORPORATED ASSOCIATIONS

Consider the following essay question:

Analyse the possible legal bases for a gift to a non-charitable unincorporated association. What difficulties, if any, are posed by the trust solution (or solutions) to this problem, and how are they avoided by a contractual solution?

This question, in effect, asks you to compare contractual and trust solutions to the problem of making a gift to a non-charitable unincorporated association, which is incapable itself of owning property.

On the conventional view, it might be thought that a *Denley*-style purpose trust might be a good method of allowing property to be conveyed to a non-charitable unincorporated association. Such an association (e.g., club or society) would be unable to hold the property itself, and would exist to use the property for a particular purpose.

On this view the property would be held in trust for the members of the association, for the purposes of the association, and it would be necessary only that the identity of those members was sufficiently certain. Unfortunately, however, a gift to members for the time being (i.e., present and future, assuming a fluctuating membership) will usually infringe the perpetuity rules (another difficulty in *Leahy* v *Attorney-General for New South Wales* [1959] AC 457), so the purpose trust solution is not generally appropriate.

It should be noted that in *Re Denley's Trust Deed* [1969] 1 Ch 373 itself the grant was only effective until 21 years from the death of the last survivor of a number of specified persons, so no perpetuity difficulty arose. There are also, of course, no perpetuity difficulties where the association is charitable.

Undoubtedly it is possible for any association, by clever drafting of its rules, also to avoid the perpetuity problem (see, e.g., Warburton [1985] Conv 318, 321), but most existing associations have not in fact drafted their rules so as to allow a purpose trust solution which avoids these difficulties.

The purpose trust solution also depends upon it being generally possible to make gifts for non-charitable purposes, so long only as there exist persons with *locus standi* to enforce the trust, even where they do not have a full beneficial interest. As has already been noted in the previous section, this is by no means certain.

Perpetuity difficulties can be avoided by construing the gift to present members only. The problem is that, if it is construed simply as a gift to them as joint tenants, then a retiring member is perfectly at liberty to sever and sell his or her share. New members could obtain any benefit from association property only by acquiring shares (or part shares) from existing members. No doubt it would be theoretically possible to run an unincorporated association on that basis, but it would be very inconvenient.

For this reason gifts to non-charitable unincorporated associations are usually construed as being to the existing members only, but subject to their contractual duties as members of the society or club. These will be determined by the rules of the association, but usually a member will be prevented from severing his share, and it will accrue to other members on death or resignation. Thus, although present and future members of a fluctuating body will benefit *de facto*, because the gift is construed as one to existing members alone, there is no perpetuity problem.

This was Cross J's analysis in *Neville Estates v Madden* [1962] Ch 832, and a similar approach was taken by Brightman J in *Re Recher's WT* [1972] Ch 526. Both views are technically *obiter*, in *Neville Estates v Madden* because the property was in the event held on charitable trusts, and in *Re Recher's WT* because the society (the London and Provincial Anti-Vivisection Society) had been dissolved at the date of the gift. It had in fact been amalgamated with the National Anti-Vivisection Society, and the gift failed in the end because it could not be construed as a gift to the larger combined society. Thus in neither case was the analysis of unincorporated associations a necessary part of the decision.

The issue arose directly in *Re Lipinski's WT* [1977] Ch 235, however, where Oliver J adopted the same analysis, and in *Re Grant's WT* [1980] 1 WLR 360 a gift failed precisely because it could not be fitted into this analysis. The testator attempted to make a grant to Chertsey and Walton Constituency Labour Party, but it could not be construed as a gift to the members of the CLP; they did not have exclusive control over the CLP rules, because those rules were also subject to the control of the National Labour Party.

In *Conservative & Unionist Central Office v Burrell* [1982] 1 WLR 522, the Court of Appeal held that the Conservative Central Office was not an unincorporated association (and therefore did not come within a statutory tax provision). The problem was not the same as in *Re Grant's WT*, however. Here there were no enforceable mutual understandings between the members, and the court held that members of unincorporated associations must be subject to mutually enforceable obligations. It was assumed (though not clearly held) that these would usually be contractual.

Contract theories lead to a different distribution of property when a club or society is wound up. Since on resignation from a club or society the retiring member gives up any contractual claim on the property of the association, it follows that only existing members have a right to claim any part of the fund.

If the rules provide for the contingency of dissolution of the fund, division will be according to the rules. Often the rules do not so provide, however, and in this event the courts are left to imply terms into the contract of membership.

In accordance with normal contractual doctrine, implication of terms is on the basis of inferred intention, and since this is largely a question of fact, no rigid rules of law can be stated. Nevertheless, generally in the case of members' clubs, the inference is that division is equally among existing members. In mutual benefit or friendly society cases, the prima facie rule also appears to be equal division, though there have also been cases where division has been proportional to total contributions. This is appropriate where the benefit contracted for while the fund subsists is also proportional to total contributions.

As we saw above it is possible in theory (though rare in practice) for club or society funds to be held on the basis of a trust, so long as perpetuity difficulties are overcome. If such a club or society is dissolved, the property will be held on resulting trust for the contributors. The main difference is that *all* contributors, including those who have ceased to contribute (e.g., past members), will be entitled to a share, and division will be in proportion to the *total amount* they have contributed. Thus, assuming everyone pays subscriptions at the same rate, a person who has contributed for 10 years is entitled to twice the share of the proceeds as someone who has contributed for only five.

Such was the basis of division in *Re Hobourn Aero Components Ltd's Air Raid Distress Fund* [1946] Ch 86, affirmed on other grounds [1946] Ch 194. It seems that this fund was limited to known and existing employees of a company who were on war service, to compensate for air raid damage in the Second World War. Since the contributors to the fund fluctuated, it is difficult to see how a trust analysis avoids perpetuity difficulties, although the fund was wound up after only four years, and may have been intended from the start to be of short-term duration. It has been suggested that Cohen J's analysis does not form part of the *ratio* of the case, the inference being that it may be wrong. Whether or not this is so, the case is clearly not of general application, since the duration of most funds is, in principle, unlimited, and fluctuations in contributors are assumed.

Walton J's analysis in *Re Bucks Constabulary Widows' & Orphans' Fund Friendly Society (No. 2)* [1979] 1 WLR 936, will usually be more appropriate. The case involved a fund which was made up of voluntary contributions from its members, for the relief of widows and orphans of deceased members of the Bucks Constabulary. In April 1968 the Bucks Constabulary was amalgamated with other constabularies to form the Thames Valley Constabulary, and in October 1968 the society was wound up. The trustee applied to court to determine how the funds were to be distributed. Walton J thought that the members' rights to share in the fund were governed by their contractual rights and duties *inter se*, and that in the absence of evidence to the contrary, members who resign lose all claim on the fund. Therefore, division should be made among only those who are still members at the time of the dissolution of the fund; and in the absence of evidence to the contrary, they are entitled to an equal share in the fund. Accordingly, he held that the surplus should be held by the trustees for the members at the time of dissolution, in equal shares.

It cannot be assumed, however, that the courts have finally resolved in favour of a contractual basis for the holding of funds. In *Re West Sussex Constabulary's Widows, Children and Benevolent (1930) Fund Trusts* [1971] 1 Ch 1, Goff J held that the proportion of surplus funds attributable to identifiable donations and legacies was held on resulting trust for the donors, and was not owned by the members of the association. Similar reasoning was adopted by Scott J in *Davis v Richards and Wallington Industries Ltd* [1991] 2 All ER 563, where a pension fund was wound up. The *ratio* of the case was that distribution of the assets was by a definitive deed which was executed by the trustees, but Scott J went on to consider the position if he were wrong. There were three main sources of contributions to the fund — employers, employees and money transferred from other funds. Scott J thought that the employers' contributions should be held on resulting trust for them, since they were similar to the legacies in *West Sussex*. There was no reason to rebut the conclusion that there was a resulting trust. But in both these cases the problem is exactly the same as in *Hobourn Aero*. What was the trust upon which the funds were held prior to the winding up of the fund? It must have been a trust for a fluctuating body of individuals. Surely, similar perpetuity problems arise as before, although perhaps in *Davis* the trust could have been saved by the Perpetuities and Accumulations Act 1964, on which see chapter 11.

Re Bucks Constabulary Widows' and Orphans' Fund Friendly Society (No. 2) was not mentioned by Scott J, although according to the report the case was cited, and there was some consideration given to a contractual analysis (at pp. 589-90). No obvious reason was given for its rejection, though. I would suggest, however, that the trust analysis in these cases simply cannot work, and it is greatly to be hoped that the courts adopt the analysis of Walton J in *Re Bucks Constabulary Widows' and Orphans' Fund Friendly Society (No. 2)*.

SUGGESTED ADDITIONAL READING

On certainty, see:

- Williams (1940) 4 MLR 20;
- Harris (1971) 87 LQR 31;
- Hopkins (1971) CLJ 68;
- Watkin (1979) 8 AALR 123;

- Matthews [1984] Conv 22;
- Jill Martin [1984] Conv 304.

On unincorporated associations, see:

Warburton [1985] Conv 318.

6 FORMALITIES

You might get a question of the following nature:

What, in your view, is the policy behind s. 53 of the Law of Property Act 1925? Explain, with the aid of reported decisions, the meaning of 'disposition' for the purposes of s. 53(1)(c). How far do the cases accord with the policy of the legislation?

It may well be that you have not thought much about the policy behind s. 53, or even assumed that there is no coherent policy. By examining what it might be, however, and criticising the cases in terms of that policy, it becomes a great deal easier to remember the details of the subject. Remembering details in a vacuum is difficult, whereas if a structure can be found the task becomes a whole lot easier.

Let us therefore consider what the policy might be, and look in detail at the three main House of Lords' cases, which are the only really important cases in the area, and must be mastered. The whole area was reviewed in an article by Brian Green (1984) 47 MLR 385, which is well worth reading.

Though the bulk of the question concerns s. 53(1)(c) of the Law of Property Act 1925, we are asked to consider the question of policy for the entire section, so s. 53(1)(b) should not be forgotten. It relates specifically to land:

[A] declaration of trust respecting any land or any interest therein must be manifested and proved by some writing signed by some person who is able to declare such trust or by his will.

Land differs from personalty in that even declarations of trust require writing, whereas as far as personalty is concerned, a settlor may create a trust merely by manifesting an intention to create it, and no special formalities are required (except in the case of wills). Only dispositions of equitable interests are caught in the case of personalty.

Presumably one reason why land is subject to special rules is because of its value, but that cannot be the only reason because even personalty of great value may be settled without formality. Another likely reason is that transactions involving land are sufficiently complex for it to be undesirable for them to be taken lightly.

We return to s. 53(1)(b), in a different context, in chapter 7.

But why require formality for dispositions of equitable interests in other property? There are two main reasons. Remember that we are dealing specifically with transactions involving *equitable* interests, which are intangible, so that it may be difficult to trace their movement unless that movement is evidenced by written documents. So, bearing in mind these evidential problems, the primary purpose of a writing requirement is to prevent fraud, to prevent people claiming interests to which they are not entitled. Indeed, the precursor to the 1925 Act was the Statute of Frauds 1677. The secondary purpose is to enable the trustees to ascertain where the equitable interests lie, to enable them to carry out the trusts.

The litigation has borne little relation to these primary and secondary purposes, however, but nearly always results from settlors avoiding taxation, and particularly stamp duty, the *ad valorem* part of which (now abolished on *inter vivos* gifts) was imposed only upon the written instrument by which property was transferred. If writing was not required, *ad valorem* duty was not payable.

It could be argued, then, that the courts should take into account taxation policy in addition to the policy referred to above, and perhaps they do. But in principle I would argue the courts should construe the formalities legislation on its own account, without regard to tax legislation which is parasitic upon it. If the Inland Revenue wishes to close a potential loophole there should be fresh taxation legislation for the purpose.

In my opinion, therefore, it would be wrong to interpret formalities legislation, the main purpose of which is quite unrelated to taxation, in such a way as to ensure a consistent tax position, if to do so would be at the expense of that purpose.

Let us now look at the law in the light of the relevant policy. The question relates specifically to s. 53(1)(c), on dispositions of equitable interests, so a general review of all formalities requirements is not required.

DISPOSITIONS OF EQUITABLE INTERESTS

Section 53(1)(c) of the Law of Property Act 1925 provides:

[A] disposition of an equitable interest or trust subsisting at the time of the disposition, must be in writing signed by the person disposing of the same, or by his agent thereunto lawfully authorised in writing or by will.

This provision covers both land and personalty, and even in the case of land it is much more stringent than s. 53(1)(b). The disposition must *itself* be in writing, not merely manifested and proved by writing, and failure to comply probably renders the disposition void, not merely unenforceable.

If the law were to accord with the policy discussed above, dispositions would be defined to include dealings with the beneficial interest which can be kept secret from the trustees, but to exclude other dealings. After all, the whole reason for treating dispositions of equitable interests differently from other dispositions is precisely because of the difficulties which would ensue were the trustees to be kept unaware of them. The precursor to this section, s. 9 of the Statute of Frauds 1677, caught 'grants and assignments', clearly reflecting this policy, but the term 'disposition' is at least theoretically wider.

Nevertheless, generally speaking the law defines 'dispositions' in accord with the policy described. The creation of a trust, by declaration, is outside the scope of the section. So, in general, it is extinguishment (by merger with the legal interest). If the purpose of formality rules is to prevent hidden transactions which prevent trustees from ascertaining who the beneficiaries are, there is no reason ever to require them where the legal and equitable interests merge. The same ought also to apply to the extinguishment of sub-equitable interests.

The position is not clear from a surrender of an equitable interest. A surrender cannot, of course, be kept secret from the trustees, and on the principles discussed above surrender should probably not be a disposition. The Court of Appeal held in Re Paradise Motor Co. Ltd [1968] 1 WLR 1125 that a *disclaimer* of an equitable interest is not a disposition. Dankwerts LJ commented that 'a disclaimer operates by way of avoidance and not by way of disposition'. A surrender, however, differs from a disclaimer in that surrender requires a transfer of equitable interest, whereas with a disclaimer there is never any movement of the beneficial interest at all. I would suggest that a surrender may well be a disposition, even though this does not accord with the policy described above.

Transfers or assignments of existing equitable interests, on the other hand, normally require writing. They are within the mischief covered by the legislation if the trustees are not party to the arrangement, but not, one would have thought, if the trustees themselves are directed to transfer the interests. Nevertheless, Grey v Inland Revenue Commissioners [1960] AC 1 suggests that writing is required even in this situation, and I would suggest that the decision is not in accordance with the policy described.

GREY v INLAND REVENUE COMMISSIONERS

The usual interpretation of the House of Lords' case of *Grey* v *Inland Revenue Commissioners* is that a transfer of an equitable interest on its own constitutes a disposition, even if the trustees are directed to make it, and therefore must be in writing and attract consequent liability for *ad valorem* stamp duty.

Mr Hunter was beneficial owner of shares, the legal title being held by nominees. In order to transfer his beneficial interest, Mr Hunter orally directed the nominees (one of whom was Grey) to hold the shares on trust for beneficiaries under six settlements (the nominees were also the trustees under these settlements). Later the trustees/nominees executed deeds of declaration to this effect, which were of course in writing.

In effect the whole scheme was a tax-avoidance device, which may account in part for the House of Lords' reasoning (though I argued above that it should not in principle). If the oral direction had transferred the shares no *ad valorem* stamp duty was payable; if the transfer had been effected by the written declaration, however, it was.

It should be noted that stamp duty is imposed, not upon a transaction itself, but upon the written instrument by which property is transferred. The amount of *ad valorem* duty was calculated as a proportion of the value of the interest being transferred. If the value of such interest was nothing, as (for example) where a bare legal estate carrying no right to beneficial enjoyment was transferred, no *ad valorem* duty was payable, but taxpayers obviously preferred to avoid transferring the valuable beneficial interest in writing if they could.

In deciding in favour of the Inland Revenue, the House of Lords held that a direction by a beneficiary to the trustees, to transfer his interest to someone else constituted a disposition and must therefore be in writing. While on a literal interpretation it may be difficult to regard this as being other than a disposition, it does not fall within the mischief of the legislation, as a request to trustees can hardly constitute a secret transaction.

Lord Radcliffe's view was that s. 53(1) did not merely consolidate the earlier Statute of Frauds: this was a disposition, whether or not it was also within the mischief of s. 9 of the earlier statute.

Problem Question

A has equitable title to shares in X Co. and Y Co. and wishes to transfer his interests to B. His shares in X Co. and Y Co. were conveyed by D to C (a nominee) some time ago, on trust for A.

In order to effect the transfer of his equitable title in the shares in X Co. A orally surrenders his interest to C. He tells C that he would like C to hold the share on trust for B, and C does so.

A orally declares himself trustee for B of his equitable interest in the shares in Y Co.

Has A effectively transferred his beneficial interest in the shares to B?

This question, which was recently set as one part of a multi-part question, is intended to get you to examine some variations on *Grey*. If surrenders of equitable interests do not require writing (on which, see above), A's transfer of X Co. would illustrate an easy method of avoiding the consequences of *Grey* v *Inland Revenue Commissioners*. If Mr Hunter had surrendered his interest this would probably not have required writing. But of course the trustees could immediately have declared new trusts, and would presumably have done so had Mr Hunter asked them, these not requiring writing. This therefore allows for an easy way to achieve a *Grey* disposition without attracting stamp duty.

This only works, of course, if surrenders do not require writing, and that is what this part of the problem is about. On this issue, see the discussion above.

On the question of the transfer of Y Co. the issue is this. Suppose a beneficiary declares that he himself will hold his interest on trust for another (rather than directing the trustees to do so), so creating, in effect, a subtrust. A commonly held view is that the issue depends on whether the equitable owner effectively gives away the totality of his interest, so that he, like the trustees who hold the legal title, becomes in turn a merely nominal owner. If so, this is in reality a case of substitution of a new beneficiary, for which on policy grounds formality ought to be required.

If, on the other hand, the equitable owner purports to assume the active role of a trustee of his equitable interest, for example, by declaring discretionary trusts, the case resembles a straightforward subtrust, and should arguably be regarded as a declaration of trust, and not a disposition of an equitable interest at all.

THE VANDERVELL LITIGATION

I have suggested that in principle, the merger of legal and equitable interests, extinguishing rather than disposing of the equitable interest, should not require writing, on the grounds that it is not a hidden transaction of the type which the law would wish to prevent. On the same principle, it should also be possible for an equitable owner orally to direct the trustees to transfer *both* their legal and his equitable interest to a single third party. In this event also, the equitable interest is extinguished, and the transaction cannot be secret from the trustees. The House of Lords came to this conclusion in *Vandervell* v *Inland Revenue Commissioners* [1967] 2 AC 291.

There are two *Vandervell* cases, both arising out of a scheme which was originally intended to transfer money to endow a chair without attracting taxation, in this case surtax.

Vandervell No. 1

Mr Vandervell wished to endow a chair of pharmacology. He was also equitable owner of a substantial number of shares in Vandervell Products Ltd, a private limited liability company which he controlled. The legal interest in Vandervell's shares was held by a bank as nominee.

In order to endow the chair, he arranged with the bank orally (presumably to avoid stamp duty) to transfer both legal and equitable interests in these shares to the Royal College of Surgeons (RCS). It was not Vandervell's intention that the College should receive the shares absolutely, with all the implications that would have had for control of Vandervell Products Ltd. The intention, rather, was that it should receive large dividends on these shares, upon which, as a charity, it was not liable to pay tax. It actually received some £266,000 by these means. Vandervell retained an option to repurchase the shares themselves for a nominal amount (£5,000), however. He did not retain it in his own name, for that would have left him liable to pay surtax on the dividends. Instead, he set up a trustee company, Vandervell Trustees Ltd, to whom the option was granted.

At this stage, therefore, the legal interest in the shares had been transferred to the RCS. Vandervell Trustees Ltd had the legal interest in the option. If the equitable interest in either remained in Vandervell himself, however, he would be liable to surtax.

The shares and the option should be considered separately.

The shares

The Revenue initially claimed surtax from Mr Vandervell on the ground that he remained the equitable owner of the shares, although the legal interest had clearly been vested in the RCS, in the absence of a separate disposition in writing, of his equitable interest. This argument was rejected by the House of Lords, which held that s. 53(1)(c) had no application to the case where a beneficial owner, solely entitled, directs his bare trustees with regard to the legal and equitable estate. This is the most important part of the *Vandervell* litigation for formality purposes, and is in line with the policy discussed. As far as the shares themselves were concerned, therefore, both legal and equitable interests had been validly transferred despite lack of writing.

An interesting aside is that *Re Rose* was approved (see chapter 3): the transfer was effective as soon as Vandervell had performed his last act.

The option

Vandervell was liable to surtax nevertheless, because the House of Lords also held (Lords Reid and Donovan dissenting) that he had not succeeded in divesting himself of the equitable interest in the option, the legal interest of which was now in the trustee company, as this was held on resulting trust for him, along with liability to pay surtax on the dividends.

This did not raise a formalities point, however, but was the result simply of Vandervell's failure to state where the equitable interest was to go. Lord Wilberforce noted that the trusts upon which the option was supposed to be held were undefined and in the air, possibly to be defined later. The trustee company itself was clearly not a beneficiary, and an equitable interest cannot remain in the air, and so the only possibility was a resulting trust in favour of the settlor.

Vandervell No. 2

In order to avoid further surtax liability, Vandervell in 1961 instructed the trustee company to exercise the option and repurchase the shares, and this gave rise eventually to further litigation (*Re Vandervell's Trusts (No. 2)* [1974] Ch 269, CA) about whether Vandervell had divested himself of the option and the whereabouts of the equitable interest in the shares thereby purchased.

Clearly the legal interest in the shares was now vested in the trustee company, Vandervell Trustees Ltd, because it had pruchased the shares. They were also trustees under a separate trust for Vandervell's children. The £5,000 purchase money came from the children's settlement, and the trustee company regarded themselves as holding the shares on trust for the children under this settlement. In other words, they regarded the equitable interest in the shares as being in the children.

Liability to surtax now depended on the whereabouts of the equitable interest in the shares during that period (although in the event the Inland Revenue was excluded as a party to the action, and the taxation point was not in fact the main issue). It was argued that, as before, it remained with Vandervell. Again, let us consider separately the option and the shares.

The option
The Court of Appeal held that the option was destroyed when it was exercised by the trustee company in 1961, so Vandervell's equitable interest in it (resulting from the earlier litigation) was extinguished. This was not a disposition within s. 53.

The shares
The Court of Appeal held that the children had the equitable interest. The shares had been placed by the trustee company on the trusts of the children's settlements, and the Court of Appeal held the Vandervell had now succeeded in divesting himself of the entire interest in these shares, there being no longer a resulting trust in his favour. This was because the later trusts were precisely

defined, in favour of the children's settlements, so that it was no longer necessary for the equitable interest to remain in the settlor.

Lord Denning MR analysed the position as a termination of the resulting trust of the option in favour of Vandervell, and a fresh trust of the shares declared (presumably by the trustee company) in favour of the children. He thought that as to the first part, writing is not required to terminate a resulting trust, and that since the new trust was not of land no formalities were required for its creation.

So far as the formality aspects of the *Vandervell* decisions are concerned, at no stage did s. 53 operate to defeat a transaction in either case. Since none of the transactions could have been kept secret from the trustees this is in accord with the policy of the section.

In 1965 Vandervell, presumably by now justifiably fed up with his scheme, clearly relinquished by deed any interest, legal or equitable, he may still have had in the shares.

OUGHTRED v INLAND REVENUE COMMISSIONERS

The point which arose in a third important House of Lords case, *Oughtred* v *Inland Revenue Commissioners* [1960] AC 206, is logically quite separate from that which arose in the above cases. It is virtually a pure taxation case, though in general policy terms I suppose that if Oughtred had won, the possibility might have arisen of secret transfers of beneficial interests, at any rate for the short time between a contract for sale and the actual transfer.

Contracts for the sale of personalty (unlike land: see below) do not require writing, but equity recognises that the buyer has an interest as soon as the contract is made. A possible route round s. 53 (and therefore stamp duty) might therefore be to have an oral contract for the sale of (say) shares, followed later by a formal transfer. The argument is that the oral contract, not the written transfer, conveys the equitable title; the formal transfer merely conveys the bare legal title, which is worth hardly anything for the purposes of *ad valorem* stamp duty.

This was the essence of the scheme in *Oughtred* v *Inland Revenue Commissioners*. Mrs Oughtred owned 72,700 shares in William Jackson & Son Ltd absolutely; 200,000 shares in the same company were held on trust for Mrs Oughtred for life, thence for her son, Peter absolutely. The parties orally agreed to swap, so that Mrs Oughtred would obtain Peter's reversionary interest (she would then have 200,000 shares outright), and in exchange Peter would obtain Mrs Oughtred's 72,700 shares. Peter therefore stood to gain an immediate interest in a small number of shares, and to lose a reversionary interest in a large number of shares. The contract was later performed.

The Revenue claimed stamp duty on the transfer of the reversionary interest in the 200,000 shares, the actual transfer of which involved writing.

Oughtred's argument was that the equitable interest was transferred on the oral contract for sale, and that the later writing transferred only the bare legal title.

The argument was rejected by the House of Lords, Viscount Radcliffe and Lord Cohen dissenting. The essence of the majority view was that though equity, in appropriate circumstances, can grant specific performance of a contract of sale, and though in that case a constructive trust arises immediately in favour of the purchaser, the buyer does not have a full beneficial interest until the formal transfer. The situation was regarded as analogous to a sale of land, where the deed of conveyance is the effective instrument of transfer (and so liable to stamp duty). The minority view, on the other hand, was that the purchaser obtained a full beneficial interest immediately.

Essay Question

Examine the exact nature of the interest of a prospective purchaser of land, after the contract for sale has been concluded but before legal title has been conveyed.

This question clearly invites discussion of the majority and minority views in *Oughtred*, and little else. It is a short question, and was recently set as one part of the multi-part question.

SUGGESTED ADDITIONAL READING

- Green (1984) 47 MLR 385.

7 MATRIMONIAL PROPERTY AND BENEFICIAL INTERESTS OF COHABITEES

Most students seem to find this area of law quite interesting, and at any rate at a superficial level, it became much easier following the House of Lords' decision in *Lloyds Bank plc* v *Rosset* [1991] 1 AC 107. Do not be deceived, however. There are very real difficulties with Lord Bridge's speech in *Rosset*, and, arguably, the speech raises as many questions as it resolves. As usual, you should look for the difficulties, and the areas of doubt, since undoubtedly, that is where the marks (at the higher end of the scale) will be found.

PROBLEM QUESTION

Mr and Mrs Omega purchase a house, title to which is registered in Mr Omega's name alone. Mrs Omega provides one quarter of the purchase price. She also takes a job which contributes to the family income, replaces carpets and furniture, and brings up the children. They also treat all their property as shared within the marriage, although they never discuss this.

Unknown to Mrs Omega, Mr Omega mortgages the property (at some time after acquisition) in favour of the Alpha Bank, claiming to be solely entitled, in order to raise money for his business. The business folds and Mr Omega is unable to repay the mortgage. Alpha claims possession of the house, and Mrs Omega claims a half share, binding on the bank on the basis of the Land Registration Act 1925, s. 70(1)(g).

Would your answer be different if Mr and Mrs Omega had discussed the shares in which they were to hold the matrimonial home?

AN EASY ANSWER

This question looks deceptively easy, and, indeed, it is relatively easy to gain a lower second-class mark on a question of this type. All you really need to know is that, after many years where the leading cases were Court of Appeal decisions which were difficult to reconcile, the House of Lords eventually stepped in, with a remarkably clear statement by Lord Bridge speech in *Lloyds Bank plc v Rosset* [1991] 1 AC 107. The most important part of this speech is the following:

> The first and fundamental question which must always be resolved is whether, independently of any inference to be drawn from the conduct of the parties in the course of sharing the house as their home and managing their joint affairs, there has at any time prior to acquisition, or exceptionally at some later date, been any agreement, arrangement or understanding reached between them that the property is to be shared beneficially.
>
> The finding of an agreement or arrangement to share in this sense can only, I think, be based on evidence of express discussions between the partners, however imperfectly remembered and however imprecise their terms may have been. Once a finding to this effect is made it will only be necessary for the partner asserting a claim to a beneficial interest against the partner entitled to the legal estate to show that he or she has acted to his or her detriment or significantly altered his or her position in reliance on the agreement in order to give rise to a constructive trust or proprietary estoppel.
>
> In sharp contrast with this situation is the very different one where there is no evidence to support a finding of an agreement or arrangement to share, however reasonable it might have been for the parties to reach such an arrangement if they had applied their minds to the question, and where the court must rely entirely on the conduct of the parties both as the basis from which to infer a common intention to share the property beneficially and as the conduct relied on to give rise to a constructive trust. In this situation direct contributions to the purchase price by the partner who is not the legal owner, whether initially or by payment of mortgage instalments, will readily justify the inference necessary to the creation of a constructive trust. But, as I read the authorities, it is at least extremely doubtful whether anything less will do.

Applying the principles from this passage, it seems that, in general, where legal title to a house is conveyed into A's name, B will obtain an equitable title only where there have been express discussions between the parties, or where B has contributed to the purchase price. Here, there have been no discussions, and Mrs Omega has contributed one-quarter of the purchase price. The main part of the problem looks pretty straightforward, therefore. Mrs Omega gets a one-quarter share. It would make a difference if there had been discussions. Exactly what share she would get would depend on the discussions, but in the absence of contrary evidence, the courts would probably presume a half share.

That may seem to be a complete answer to the problem, and it is probably sufficient for a lower second-class answer, at any rate as long as you do not make silly mistakes. Last year (1995) I marked nearly 250 answers to a similar question, and made a note of the most common ways in which students lost marks. One of these was to refer to Bridge LJ in *Rosset*. Given that the area was, prior to 1990, crying out for a House of Lords' decision to clarify an area of law which was at that time far from clear, and that *Rosset* was that case, the reference to Bridge LJ suggested that the candidate had not even begun to understand the subject. This sort of thing is really throwing marks away, and the candidates probably never even realised their mistake. They probably came out of the exam thinking that they had produced a full answer, and maybe they had, but the reference to Bridge LJ told it all. They had not really understood, or indeed even thought about, the area at all. Students often underestimate how important it is to know in which court a case was decided.

A MORE THOUGHTFUL ANALYSIS: ROSSET SECOND CATEGORY

In fact, this question is much more difficult than it looks. Let us consider first the conclusion that, in the absence of express discussions between the parties, Mrs Omega's share is limited to the one-quarter share to which she is entitled, assessed on her contribution to the purchase price. This would be based on Lord Bridge's comment at the end of the passage set out above that 'it is at least extremely doubtful whether anything less will do'. However, he is not absolutely ruling out a lesser contribution, and other authorities (and, in particular, statements by Fox and May LJJ in *Burns v Burns* [1984] Ch 317) suggest that indirect financial contributions, referable to the acquisition of the property, will also suffice. The following passage is taken from Fox LJ's judgment in *Burns v Burns*, at p. 327:

> What is needed, I think, is evidence of a payment or payments by the plaintiff which it can be inferred was referable to the acquisition of the house.... If there is a substantial contribution by the woman to the family expenses, and the house was purchased on a mortgage, her contribution is, indirectly, referable to the acquisition of the house since, in one way or another, it enables the family to pay the mortgage instalments. Thus, a payment could be said to be referable to the acquisition of the house if, for example, the payer either (a) pays part of the purchase price or (b) contributes regularly to the mortgage instalments or (c) pays off part of the

mortgage or (d) makes a substantial financial contribution to the family expenses so as to enable the mortgage instalments to be paid.

This is obviously wider than Lord Bridge's view, and it may be that Mrs Omega can advance an argument based on this passage (we are not given sufficient information in the problem to know this). Lord Bridge does not, however, make clear whether his intention is to alter the law or merely to restate it, a point made by Patricia Ferguson (1993) 109 LQR 114, at p. 116:

[Lord Bridge's] requirement of 'direct contributions' where there is no express agreement runs contrary to previous authorities which held that indirect financial contributions which were 'referable to the acquisition of the house' — such as F's payment of all household expenses to free M's income for mortgage instalments — were sufficient. It is difficult to know … whether he intends to depart from this view of the law or not.

Throughout the article, M is assumed to be a male in a position similar to that of Mr Omega, whereas F is assumed to be a female in a position similar to that of Mrs Omega. If Lord Bridge's speech was intended to alter the previous law, then *Burns* v *Burns* is no longer relevant, whereas if it was intended merely to be a restatement, then clearly the issue needs to be examined more closely.

So, where do you go from here? One possibility, I would suggest, is to examine the principle upon which this second category is based. This is not clear from Lord Bridge's speech itself, but one could argue that the second category is based on resulting trust reasoning, whereas the first category is based on a constructive trust. *Tinsley* v *Milligan* [1994] 1 AC 340 (on which see further chapter 3) is probably a second-category *Rosset* case, and is clearly based on resulting trust reasoning; indeed, it would have been impossible to reach the same conclusion via a constructive trust, so the resulting trust analysis appears, at first sight, to be quite promising. You may, however, be surprised to learn how little analysis there has been in the literature of the ways in which the resulting trust arises, and how it works in the present context.

A definition of a resulting trust is where 'the beneficial interest "results" to the settlor or his estate' (see, e.g., AJ Oakley, *Parker & Mellows, The Modern Law of Trusts*, 6th ed, Sweet & Maxwell, 1994, at p. 189). It follows that in order for Mrs Omega to obtain an interest by way of resulting trust, she must settle property, or, in other words, she must start with legal and equitable title to some property, legal title to which she transfers to Mr Omega. One possibility would be where she starts off with legal and equitable title to the home itself, and transfers the bare legal title to Mr Omega, as in *Hodgson* v *Marks* [1971] 1 Ch 892. This is clearly not the present situation, but it is easy to see how a resulting trust can arise from Mr Omega's contributions to the purchase money. If Mrs Omega pays the purchase money (in which she has legal and equitable title) over to Mr Omega, then, in the absence of a presumption of advancement or consideration moving from him, she is presumed to retain equitable ownership in the money; *Dyer* v *Dyer* (1788) 2 Cox Eq Cas 92, *per* Eyre CB at p. 93. If the money is referable to the acquisition of property, then, on its acquisition by him, her interest in the money becomes converted into an interest in the property (on the principles stated by Sir George Jessel MR in *Re Hallett's Estate* (1880) 13 ChD 696 (an equitable tracing case), at p. 708). Alternatively, if both Mr and Mrs Omega pay the vendor, V, separately, then V becomes trustee of the money for both parties in the proportions in which they have paid it, until such time as the property is conveyed, when again the equitable interests are converted into interests in the property.

For these purposes the origin of the money advanced by Mrs Omega is irrelevant. If it is obtained by a loan, with her undertaking liability to repay the loan, the position is exactly the same, and, similarly, if she obtains the money through a mortgage on the property itself, accepting liability to repay the mortgage debt. This explains, for example, *Huntingford* v *Hobbs* [1993] 1 FCR 45, where Huntingford's undertaking to repay the mortgage debt was taken into account in calculating his share, although he had not actually paid off any of the capital.

It is difficult to see, however, how this type of analysis can work for the other types of contribution mentioned by Fox LJ in *Burns*, since only with the financial contributions can Mrs Omega be said to settle property which she owns. Therefore, a strict resulting trust analysis can probably operate only in respect of direct financial contributions, thereby supporting Lord Bridge's view, rather than that of Fox LJ.

On further investigation, however, it is clear that the *Rosset* second category cannot, in fact, be fully explained in terms of the resulting trust. There is authority that Mrs Omega can obtain an interest even if her contribution is in the form of a discount from the purchase price, rather than an actual cash payment. In *Springette* v *Defoe* [1992] 2 FCR 561, the Court of Appeal took into account, in assessing the size of her share, Springette's 41% discount, attributable to her council tenancy under a 'right to buy' scheme. Although the court purported to adopt a resulting trust analysis, it is difficult to see how *Springette* settled anything. In *Springette* v *Defoe*, her discount arose from a legal chose in action enforceable against the council, and you might investigate the possibilities of settling that, but even this could not explain *Marsh* v *Von Sternberg* [1986] 1 FLR 526, where the discount depended on increased bargaining power as a statutory tenant under the Rent Act 1974, and did not arise from a cause of action at all. It follows that resulting trust reasoning cannot explain the discount cases.

An alternative analysis is that of Staughton LJ in *Evans* v *Hayward* [1995] 2 FCR 313, at p. 319D:

> I do consider that the facts as to the existence of a discount and the source from which it is derived must be taken into account, and are capable of leading to the inference that the parties have made an agreement as to how the purchase price is provided.

In other words, the discount leads to the inference that the parties have made an agreement that they are to be treated as having provided the purchase price in proportions which take into account the discount. Once it is accepted that the true explanation of the discount cases is in terms of an inferred agreement, and does not depend on a resulting trust, then we can see that similar reasoning can also apply to the non-financial contributions mentioned in *Burns*. In principle, therefore, there is no particular reason to prefer Lord Bridge's views to those of Fox LJ.

You might care to consider what implications, if any, this discussion has on cases (such as *Pettit* v *Pettit* [1970] AC 777 and *Thomas* v *Fuller-Brown* [1988] 1 FLR 237), where one party argues the acquisition of an interest by improving the property of another. Can you infer an agreement, similar to that postulated by Staughton LJ in *Evans* v *Hayward*? If not, how, in your view, does the situation differ from that considered above? (*Hint*: you may conclude that different inferences are equally consistent with the fact of improvement, such as that the improver intended to make a gift of the improvements, or that he or she intended to be reimbursed for them, neither of which is necessarily consistent with an intention to acquire an interest in the property itself, whereas the alternative inferences look less likely in the discount case.)

ROSSET FIRST CATEGORY

Let us now consider the altnerative situation, where there has been express discussion between the parties. We know from Lord Bridge's speech that this makes a difference, but what is the nature of this difference? What precise share does Mrs Omega get? Does it depend on the discussions alone, or also on the nature and extent of her detrimental reliance?

Again, when one looks in more detail at Lord Bridge's speech the apparent certainties evaporate. It is not even clear whether the basis of the first category is constructive trust or proprietary estoppel, or whether Lord Bridge regarded them as the same or different. He did elaborate, however, as follows:

> Outstanding examples ... of cases giving rise to situations in the first category are *Eves* v *Eves* [1975] 1 WLR 1338 and *Grant* v *Edwards* [1986] Ch 638. In both these cases, where the parties who had cohabited were

unmarried, the female partner had been clearly led by the male partner to believe, when they set up home together, that the property would belong to them jointly. In *Eves* v *Eves* the male partner had told the female partner that the only reason why the property was to be acquired in his name alone was because she was under 21 and that, but for her age, he would have had the house put into their joint names. He admitted in evidence that this was simply an 'excuse'. Similarly, in *Grant* v *Edwards* the female partner was told by the male partner that the only reason for not acquiring the property in joint names was because she was involved in divorce proceedings and that, if the property were acquired jointly, this might operate to her prejudice in those proceedings. As Nourse LJ put it ([1986] Ch 638 at 649):

> 'Just as in *Eves* v *Eves*, these facts appear to me to raise a clear inference that there was an understanding between the plaintiff and the defendant, or a common intention, that the plaintiff was to have some sort of proprietary interest in the house otherwise no excuse for not putting her name onto the title would have been needed.'

The subsequent conduct of the female partner in each of these cases, which the court rightly held sufficient to give rise to a constructive trust or proprietary estoppel supporting her claim to an interest in the property, fell far short of such conduct as would by itself have supported the claim in the absence of an express representation by the male partner that she was to have such an interest. It is significant to note that the share to which the female partners in *Eves* v *Eves* and *Grant* v *Edwards* were held entitled were one-quarter and one-half respectively. In no sense could these shares have been regarded as proportionate to what the judge in the instant case described as a 'qualifying contribution' in terms of the indirect contributions to the acquisition or enhancement of the value of the houses made by the female partners.

Unfortunately, an investigation of the cases cited in this passage throws little more light on the issue, and both estoppel and constructive reasoning can be found, for example, in *Grant* v *Edwards*. It has further been argued that the agreement is entirely fictitious, because in each case the man clearly did not intend the woman to have any interest in the property. Thus, Simon Gardner writes ((1993) 109 LQR 263, at p. 265):

> But the fact that the men's statements were excuses (i.e., neither objectively valid nor even sincerely uttered) does not mean that the men were thereby acknowledging an agreement whereby the woman should have a share. If I give an excuse for rejecting an invitation to what I expect to be a dull party, it does not mean that I thereby agree to come: on the contrary, it means that

I do not agree to come, but for one reason or another find it hard to say so outright. The fallacious quality of the reasoning in *Eves* v *Eves* and *Grant* v *Edwards* is thus clear. It is hard to think that the judges concerned really believed in it.

Nicola Glover and I worked extensively on this area in the summer of 1995. This work has been published in [1995] 5 Web JCLI. The detailed analysis that is appropriate to an article in a refereed academic journal is not appropriate to this type of book; in any case, if you want to read the article it is freely available on the World Wide Web. What I hope I can do here is give you some idea of the academic thought-processes, and make some suggestions as to the types of issues you may care to think about. I can also summarise the conclusions of our article.

We were concerned first to consider if it made any difference whether a trust or estoppel analysis were adopted. Starting with the trust, in *Gissing* v *Gissing* [1971] AC 886, Lord Diplock gave explicit voice (at p. 904H) to what can be inferred from *Pettit* v *Pettit* [1970] AC 777, that the applicable principles are those of the general law of trusts. We should not be looking, therefore, for any special law which applies only to matrimonial property, but unfortunately, it appears that many of the writers in this area know surprisingly little about the general law of trusts, and, in particular, how trusts are created.

Remaining with *Gissing* v *Gissing*, however, Lord Diplock analysed this situation (at pp. 904H–905D) in terms of a declaration of trust by Mr Omega for Mrs Omega. The declaration would (if oral) be void for want of writing, which is required by s. 53(1)(b) of the Law of Property Act 1925, unless it was acted upon by her, so as to render it inequitable to allow him to deny the trust. It would then take effect as a constructive trust, to which, by virtue of s. 53(2), s. 53(1)(b) has no application. The explanation in *Lloyds Bank* v *Rosset* (at p. 129C) is similar: see also *Re Densham* [1975] 1 WLR 1519.

The important point about this analysis is that it assumes that all the incidents of an express trust are present. If the trust is in writing then detrimental reliance is not necessary, and, if not, then the only function of detrimental reliance is to invoke s. 53(2), and, hence, avoid the formality requirements. An obvious consequence of this is that Mrs Omega's interest ought to be capable of binding a third party (and here it needs to bind the bank). A second consequence is that the quantification of Mrs Omega's interest depends on the discussions alone, and not on the extent of her detrimental reliance, since the function of the detrimental reliance is simply to avoid the formality provisions of the Law of Property Act 1925. This can clearly be seen in cases such as *Hammond* v *Mitchell* [1991] 1 WLR 1127; Mitchell had not really done a great deal, and had contributed nothing at all to the house, but as a result of the discussions, was entitled (following *Grant* v *Edwards*) to a half share in the home.

We need next to dispose of Gardner's objection, that in *Grant* v *Edwards* and *Eves* v *Eves* the man did not intend the woman to have anything, so that the quantification of respectively a half and a one-quarter share in those cases was entirely fictitious. This is clearly correct if a subjective view is taken of intention, but when we looked at the cases (considered in chapter 3) on declaration of trusteeship, we found that intention is judged objectively. The courts appear to adopt the position of a reasonable observer. In *Richards* v *Delbridge* (1874) LR Eq 11, Sir George Jessel MR concentrated on the words used, as opposed to the actual intention, observing that 'however anxious the court may be to carry out a man's intention, it is not at liberty to construe words otherwise than according to their proper meaning'. This suggests that the actual intention is irrelevant. In *Re Kayford* [1975] 1 WLR 279, Megarry J (at p. 282A) also talked in terms of an intention being manifested, rather than merely held.

We therefore felt that Gardner's objection was misplaced. To take *Grant* v *Edwards* as the example, what Edwards was saying, in effect, was that although legal title must be vested in himself alone, this was for purely formal reasons (so as not to cause prejudice in the matrimonial proceedings pending between Linda Grant and her husband), and the reality was that the property (i.e., equitable title) was to belong to both of them. Once it is accepted that the test is objective, and does not depend on what Edwards actually thought, it is difficult to imagine a clearer declaration of trusteeship than that.

There are, however, other constraints on the constructive trust analysis, none of which affects the problem before us, but which could easily be relevant in a different fact situation. A trust operates as an immediate and irrevocable commitment, so that statements as to future intention will not suffice. The cases in chapter 3 show that before a trust can be inferred, Mr Omega must evince an intention to deal with the property in such a way as to deprive himself of his beneficial ownership, and to declare that he will hold it for that time forward on trust for Mrs Omega. Another limitation of some importance is that the property must be identified as existing property: *Re Ellenborough* [1903] 1 Ch 697. A trust analysis should not work, therefore, where the property has not been identified (e.g., where the statement concerns a house to be purchased at some future time). We had some difficulties in this regard with *Ungurian* v *Lesnoff* [1990] 1 Ch 206, which we felt was wrongly categorised as a constructive trust case. The statements relied on in that case ('We will have to look for and buy a house for us in London so that you will feel secure and happy, having lost your house in Poland'; and, 'You'll have to decide and find the house which you like. I want you to feel that you have something to rely on if anything happens to me'), cannot amount to a declaration of trust, both because there was no trust property at the time they were made, and because they were statements of future intention, not, therefore, amounting to a present irrevocable commitment.

By contrast, both types of statement were present in *Hammond* v *Mitchell* [1991] 1 WLR 1127. On its own, Hammond's promise (see p. 1131E of the judgment):

Don't worry about the future because when we are married it will be half yours anyway and I'll always look after you and [the boy]

was a statement of future intent which should not have led to the inference of a trust. However, Hammond also said (see p. 1131D):

I'll have to put the house in my name because I have tax problems due to the fact that my wife burnt all my account books and my caravan was burnt down with all the records of my car sales in it. The tax man would be interested, and if I could prove my money had gone back into a property I'd be safeguarded.

This is similar to the statements in *Eves* v *Eves* [1975] 1 WLR 1338 and *Grant* v *Edwards* [1986] Ch 638, considered above, where I argued that (despite Gardner's criticism) a trust analysis was entirely appropriate.

In the problem question there is no obvious reason why the discussions should not amount to a declaration of trust by Mr Omega, but where there are difficulties in the way of a constructive trust analysis, you may need also to consider an estoppel. Estoppels differ from constructive trusts in a number of significant respects. Whereas a trust is based on an irrevocable commitment, estoppel is based on the notion of A misleading B, and A is prevented from going back on his or her assurances only to the extent necessary to do justice to B. The commonly accepted formula for proprietary estoppel, adopted by Oliver J in *Taylors Fashions Ltd* v *Liverpool Victoria Trustees Co. Ltd* [1982] QB 133 at 151H–152A, requires only that 'it would be unconscionable for a party to be permitted to deny that which, knowingly or unknowingly, he has allowed or encouraged another to assume to his detriment', and in *Moorgate Mercantile Co. Ltd* v *Twitchings* [1975] QB 225, Lord Denning MR took the view (at p. 241) that encouragement can be by words or conduct. This is less stringent than the requirements for a declaration of trusteeship. A statement as to future intent will suffice, even where the property is not as yet identified (*Re Basham* [1986] 1 WLR 1498 at 1508–1509).

However, for estoppels, the quantification of B's interest may not depend on A's representation alone, but also on the extent of B's reliance. In *Crabb* v *Arun District Council* [1976] Ch 179, Scarman LJ (at p. 198G–H) took the view that quantification should be on the basis of 'the minimum equity to do justice to the plaintiff'. A's representation is undoubtedly relevant in that B cannot get more than was contemplated by the parties: *Baker* v *Baker* (1993) 25 HLR 408. However, while B's entitlement cannot be more than would be accorded on the basis of A's representation, it can certainly be less, as in *Dodsworth* v *Dodsworth* (1973) 228 EG 1115, and in principle, there seems no reason why, in satisfying the equity, it would be inappropriate to consider the extent of B's reliance.

In the problem, however, it is necessary for Mrs Omega's interest to bind the bank, and as Ferguson states (at p. 122), 'the consensus of opinion favours' the view that estoppels do not bind third parties, at any rate until the extent of the interest has been crystallised by a court. On this view an estoppel would not therefore suffice. There are, admittedly, strong arguments against this view advanced by Ferguson, and much of our article in the *Web Journal* was directed at countering these.

As I have said, for a full consideraton you will need to look at the detailed literature elsewhere. What I hope I have achieved in this chapter is to demonstrate that often deceptively easy legal problems are much more difficult than they appear at first sight. We have also used authorities from many different parts of the trusts course (e.g., constitution and tracing), although this is primarily a matrimonial property question. The message is that to do well at trusts, you need to have sufficient breadth of knowledge to be able to draw arguments from various areas, and also to have thought hard about the subject. I do not believe that you would come up with anything similar to the above discussion from an unthinking reading of notes and textbooks.

FURTHER THOUGHTS ABOUT EXAM QUESTIONS

As is obvious from the above discussion, Nicola Glover did a lot of work on this area in the summer of 1995, and I had also given the matter some thought earlier in the year. Not surprisingly, perhaps, I mentioned my then embryonic ideas in my course lectures. Many students in the exam then proceeded to quote me as authority for some of the propositions I have advanced here. However, at that time nothing had been published. It is a (common) mistake to quote as authority anything that has not been published — your lecture notes are authority for nothing at all.

Another mistake is simply to learn and reproduce the headings and outline information used in the lectures. Many of the candidates seemed simply to have learned up what I had said in the lectures without making much attempt to understand it. A properly considered exam question ought to make this obvious to the examiner.

At the risk of repeating, yet again, the central message of this book, therefore, I would say that you must, above all, think about what you are doing, and immerse yourself sufficiently in the subject to avoid obvious pitfalls. I started the chapter with the Bridge LJ howler (which virtually shouts at the examiner 'I know nothing about this area of law'). In examination answers I also saw references to Nourse J in *Grant* v *Edwards* and Slade J in *Thomas* v *Fuller-Brown*. I saw Court of Appeal cases being overruled by High Court decisions. The court in which a case was decided matters (especially with a landmark case like *Rosset*), and it is very obvious to an examiner if you get it wrong.

A number of students also mentioned Court of Appeal decisions in the early and mid-1970s, in particular *Cooke* v *Head* [1972] 1 WLR 518 and *Eves* v *Eves* [1975] 1 WLR 1338, where Lord Diplock in *Gissing* v *Gissing* was 'quoted out of context', particularly by Lord Denning MR. Few seemed to know what the context was, and why the quotes were 'out of context'. If you are going to say things like that, think about what they mean. Go and look at *Gissing* v *Gissing* and find out what the context was. Then, some students said, everything changed with *Burns* v *Burns* [1984] Ch 317, where the Court of Appeal took a different view. However, *Burns* v *Burns* was simply another decision of the Court of Appeal. So why should anybody prefer the reasoning there to that of Lord Denning MR in *Cooke* v *Head* or *Eves* v *Eves*? If you want to argue that, you need also to argue that *Burns* is easier to reconcile with House of Lords' decisions, such as *Gissing* v *Gissing*, *Winkworth* v *Edward Baron Development Co. Ltd* [1988] 1 WLR 1512 (where *Burns* was expressly upheld), and of course, *Rosset* itself. However, without the House of Lords' references, you simply have conflicting views expressed in the Court of Appeal.

Another common mistake was the assumption that the law of trusts no longer decides the issue where the parties are married, since statutory provisions, such as the Matrimonial Proceedings and Property Act 1970 and the Matrimonial Causes Act 1973, apply. This is clearly wrong, as the 1970 Act applies only to improvements, and the 1973 Act applies only where there is a judicial separation or divorce. Neither Act, therefore, applies to the problem considered here, which is therefore governed by the general principles of equity. The same was, of course, true in (among other cases) *Winkworth* v *Edward Baron Development Co. Ltd* and *Rosset* itself.

A final point is that where a question demands (for a good mark) a high level of analysis, you must leave yourself time to do the analysis. Do not bother to introduce the subject, or recount the history from *Pettit* v *Pettit* to the present. That was the job of the lecturer on the course (since you need to do it to teach the area properly), but it is not your job. Get straight to the heart of the problem; if your detailed analysis is good, it will be obvious enough to the examiner that you know the basic introductory material.

SUGGESTED ADDITIONAL READING

Far more detail than appears here can be found in Glover and Todd [1995] 5 Web JCLI. If you are not familiar with the *Web Journal*, it is accessible on the

World Wide Web using an appropriate browser (e.g., Mosaic or Netscape) at the following URL: http://www.ncl.ac.uk/˜nlawwww/ It is possible to download articles as RTF files, which can be read by most word-processing programs. The journal will also be published each year as a *Blackstone Yearbook*.

Recent references which we found particularly useful in writing our article were:

- Battersby, G. [1991] Conv 36.
- Baughen, S. (1994) 14 LS 147.
- Ferguson, P. (1993) 109 LQR 114.
- Gardner, S. (1993) 109 LQR 263.
- Hayton, D. [1990] Conv 370.

8 SECRET AND HALF-SECRET TRUSTS

The fact that there has been very little litigation on secret and half-secret trusts in recent years in no way diminishes the enthusiasm of examiners for this topic. Nor, I think, should it be assumed that secret trusts no longer have any practical relevance, although no doubt the reasons for using them have changed. It is less likely today that a testator will wish to keep hidden the existence of an extra-marital sexual partner, or an illegitimate child, and the Mortmain considerations (on which, see below) behind many of the early cases are clearly no longer applicable. Nevertheless, particularly with the increase in step-parenthood, informal secret trusts may well have a place even today. One spouse may be prepared to leave all his or her property to the other (current) spouse on the understanding that he or she will ensure that children of a previous marriage are adequately provided for, and may prefer to proceed in this way rather than risk upsetting the relationship, by making a new will. This could give rise to a secret trust, just as surely as the mistress and Mortmain cases of the nineteenth century.

Questions tend to fall into two types. The first is an essay which requires you to explain and account for the differences which exist between the rules governing fully and half-secret trusts: the second is a problem which demands that you remember exactly what those differences are and can apply them to a (usually uninspiring) set of facts. The two types of question involve different considerations, and it is as well to approach them separately.

UNDERLYING PRINCIPLES AND THE DIFFERENT RULES FOR SECRET AND HALF-SECRET TRUSTS

Almost any essay on this topic will seek to cover the basis of secret and half-secret trusts, and the different rules the courts have worked out for them although it is possible to slant the question towards various angles. Though the following discussion centres around an essay question, you will almost certainly not be able to put together a good, as opposed to merely passable, answer unless you have been prepared to go beyond the textbooks and lecture notes during study and revision.

In the first place the question is likely to be framed so as to encourage a comparison of differing opinions, and in any case you should be conscious of the range of views attributable to various academic writers. You should also have gained an impression of how these views fit together, where they clash, and on what terms it might be possible to reconcile some or any of them. If you lack this basic knowledge of the field, you might be advised to look for a different question to answer.

ESSAY QUESTION

Can any rational principles be offered to justify the different rules developed by the courts with regard to fully secret and half-secret trusts?

Because it is an essay and not a problem this sort of question often attracts very mediocre candidates. A common mistake is simply not to think about the question at all, or even to read it properly. Even a relatively poor candidate knows that all the textbooks say the distinction is illogical, so all that is necessary is to agree and to trot out all the standard cases on secret trusts mentioned in the textbooks, in the hope that somewhere in that lot will lie the reason why the distinction can be labelled illogical.

Such a candidate will get a poor second if there is nothing in the answer that is flagrantly wrong, or at best a third if there are substantial omissions or errors in the recital. The problem is simply that the question does not ask for a textbook treatise of the area, but is directed specifically towards discussion of principles. Obviously if you have thought about these during revision so much the better, because an examination is not an ideal situation in which to consider complex matters for the first time. But even if you have not given the matter much thought you should have close regard to the wording of the question (or do another question). The textbook treatise is frankly not an answer to the question at all, yet candidates who answer in that way are extremely common, and probably never even realise why they do not obtain a better result.

As with any other essay question you must determine its central point and its limits, so as to be able to judge how much information you can safely include without drifting into irrelevance. Also, though you ought to cover all arguments, you would be well advised to form a view yourself as to which view is correct. Before you start to write, decide where you are going, what authority you intend to use to get you there, and what arguments for the opposing view you will have to deal with on the way.

The question asks whether there is any rational principle which can account for the distinction, so the following discussion concentrates on reasons of principle upon which equity undertakes to enforce these trusts. Clearly, if there is no difference in principle between the grounds for enforcing fully and half-secret trusts, the assertion that the distinction is illogical is greatly strengthened. There are two principal theories on which enforcement of secret trusts can be justified, and both need to be examined.

In the following discussion, 'he' includes 'she' and 'himself' includes 'herself'.

WHAT ARE THE DIFFERENT RULES BETWEEN SECRET AND HALF-SECRET TRUSTS?

If you are asked to ascertain whether there are any rational principles which justify the different rules developed by the courts with regard to fully secret and half-secret trusts, quite a good starting point is an explanation of how the rules for the two in fact differ (assuming, of course, they do differ).

The main difference between the courts' treatment of fully secret and half-secret trusts concerns the time of communication of the terms of the trust of the secret trustee. For fully secret trusts it appears to be necessary for the existence of the secret trust to be communicated to the trustee before the death of the testator, and there is some authority that the terms also have to be communicated before the testator's *death* (below). Whether or not these communications precede or succeed the date of the *will* is irrelevant, however, to the enforcement of a fully secret trust.

For fully secret trusts, the authorities are *Wallgrave* v *Tebbs* (1855) 2 K & J 313, and *Re Boyes* (1884) 26 Ch D 531. In *Wallgrave* v *Tebbs* the testator had left property to close friends without informing them in his lifetime that he wished the land to be used for a religious charitable purpose. The court held that the friends were entitled to the property beneficially — a decision which, surprisingly enough, was most likely to give effect to the wishes of the testator, since if a secret trust had been found to exist it would have been void under the (now repealed) Statutes of Mortmain. As it was, the friends were free to carry out the testator's wishes. If, as the testator's relatives had argued, a secret trust had been created, they would have had to hold property on resulting trust *for those relatives*, the purpose of the trust being unlawful.

Hence the surprising situation that the very last people who might be expected to argue for a secret trust (the relatives) did so in that case, and in other cases to which the Statutes of Mortmain applied.

The case is authority for the proposition that for a fully secret trust to be enforced, the intended trustee must be told of the existence of the trust before the testator's death. In *Re Boyes*, however, the intended trustee was told of the existence of the trust before the testator's death, but was not told its terms, which were in favour of the testator's mistress. Kay J held that the intended trustee held the property on a resulting trust for the testator's estate.

If *Re Boyes* is correct, then not only the existence, but also the terms of a fully secret trust must be communicated to the trustee before the date of the testator. Kay J said (at p. 536):

> If the trust was not declared when the will was made [i.e., fully secret trust], it is essential in order to make it binding, that it should be communicated to the devisee or legatee in the testator's lifetime and that he should accept that particular trust.

For fully secret trusts, there is no authority that the date of the will is of any relevance. In the case of a half-secret trust, however, it appears that the terms of the trust have to be finalised before the date of the will. The leading authorities are *Re Keen* [1937] Ch 236 and *Re Bateman* [1970] 3 All ER 817. In *Re Keen*, a clause in the testator's will gave £10,000 on trust to two persons, who were directed to dispose of it 'as may be notified by me to them or either of them during my lifetime'. In fact, some months prior to the will, the testator had given one of the two trustees a sealed envelope containing a sheet of paper on which he had written the name and address of the proposed secret beneficiary (a lady to whom the testator was not married).

The Court of Appeal held that no valid half-secret trust had been created, and the £10,000 fell into residue. One reason was that, simply as a matter of construction, the clause in the testator's will referred to a *future* direction, whereas the direction had by then *already* been communicated to one of the two trustees. Therefore, the express terms of the will were inconsistent with the terms of the trust being contained in the sealed envelope. Had that been the only ground for the decision, the case would have created no difficulties, and the position for half-secret trusts would have been identical to that for fully secret trusts.

Lord Wright MR also said, however, that the testator having declared the existence of the trust in the will, should not be able to reserve to himself the power of making future dispositions without a duly attested codicil simply by notifying them during his lifetime. If that is correct, it follows that the terms of a half-secret trust must be finalised by the date of the will. In *Re Bateman's WT*, the trustees were directed by a clause in the will to dispose of the income from the testator's estate 'to such persons and in such proportions as shall be stated by me in a sealed letter in my own handwriting and addressed to my Trustees'. As in *Keen*, this refers to a *future* direction, but unlike *Keen*, the trustees in *Bateman* received their instructions by means of a sealed letter after the will, but before the death of the testator. Therefore, the express terms of the will were not inconsistent with the timing of the communication.

Nevertheless, the Court of Appeal held that the direction to trustees was invalid. The only possible explanation for the case, and indeed the one actually adopted by Pennycuick V-C, was that as a general principle, a half-secret trust is enforceable only where its terms are known at the date of the will.

There may be other differences between fully and half-secret trusts, but in this chapter we will concentrate on the main one, the timing of the communication of the terms of the trust in relation to the date of the will.

The differences having now been explained, we can return to the question to see whether they can be justified.

BASIS OF ENFORCEMENT OF SECRET AND HALF-SECRET TRUSTS

The authorities suggest that the basis of enforcement of fully and half-secret trusts is the same, that equity imposes upon the conscience of the secret trustee for the prevention of fraud. This is clear from the speech of Viscount Sumner in *Blackwell v Blackwell* [1929] AC 318 (at pp. 335-6):

> For the prevention of fraud equity fastens on the conscience of the legatee a trust, a trust, that is, which otherwise would be inoperative; in other words it makes him do what the will in itself has nothing to do with; it lets him take what the will gives him and then makes him apply it, as the Court of conscience directs, and it does so in order to give effect to wishes of the testator, which would not otherwise be effectual.

Blackwell v Blackwell is, of course, the leading authority on half-secret trusts, but it is clear that Viscount Sumner treats the two varieties as the same, and that these comments are intended to apply to both.

From the quote three propositions can be gleaned. First, the reason equity fastens on the conscience of the legatee is for the prevention of fraud. Secondly, the effect of the trust is to make the legatee 'do what the will in itself has nothing to do with'; in other words, the trust operates independently of the will. Thirdly, in order to prevent fraud, equity directs the legatee to give effect to wishes of the testator. This point is of some importance. The fraud whose commission is being prevented is not the taking of the property beneficially by the legatee, but, having taken it, not giving effect to the wishes of the testator.

Relevance of and Nature of Fraud

The need for fraud can be seen clearly in the House of Lords' decision in *McCormick* v *Grogan* (1869) LR 4 HL 82, where Lord Hatherley LC and Lord Westbury emphasised that the doctrine should be limited to cases where the intended trustee had committed a personal fraud upon the testator, by inducing the bequest on the clear representation that he would hold the property on behalf of the intended beneficiary. Lord Westbury in particular emphasised the need for a *'malus animus'* to be 'proved by the clearest and most indisputable evidence'.

But this immediately raises the question: if the object is merely to prevent the intended trustee from taking the property for himself, on what ground should equity disregard the requirement of the Wills Act 1837 by giving effect to the testator's oral instruction that the property should go to someone not named in the will? If the defeat of the intended trustee's fraudulent profit was all that was desired, it would be sufficient simply to compel him to hold the property on a resulting trust for the testator's estate. In fact, however, this is not all that is desired.

A historical reason why a resulting trust would not have provided a satisfactory solution is that, prior to the Executors Act of 1830, an executor was entitled to take as residuary legatee all property not specifically disposed of in the will. If, as might well happen, the intended trustee was also the executor, a resulting trust would merely have the effect of granting him indirectly what the court refused to allow him to take directly.

An early example is *Thynn* v *Thynn* (1684) 1 Vern 296. Here, the testator had made his wife his sole executrix, but his son, on a fraudulent pretext, persuaded her to step down in his favour. The court compelled him to hold the property on trust for the wife. If it had not enforced the trust, but allowed the property to result to the estate, the fraudulent son (as executor) would have taken beneficially, so this solution would clearly have been inappropriate.

By the time *McCormick* v *Grogan* was decided, the Executors' Act had altered the rule. Nowadays, the effect of a resulting trust in favour of the testator's estate will be to pass the property to the person named as residuary legatee, or, if there is none, to those close relatives of the testator who are entitled to take in the event of his total or partial intestacy. There can still be problems, as in *Re Rees* [1950] Ch 204, where the intended trustee (the solicitor who had drafted the will) was also the named residuary legatee, but such problems are less likely to arise today.

Nevertheless, the House of Lords in *McCormick* v *Grogan* would have been prepared to enforce the secret trust on its terms, though on the facts of the case no trust was held to have been created. Again, this may be explicable in the light of social considerations. A common reason for setting up a secret trust is the desire to benefit someone whose existence the testator would prefer to keep hidden from his family, such as a mistress or, as in *McCormick v Grogan* itself, an illegitimate child. A resulting trust would divert the property to the very last people whom the testator wished to benefit (his legitimate family). But for the court to give weight to this sort of consideration involves accepting that the testator's wishes are of sufficient importance to justify ignoring the clear terms of a statute in order to enforce the trust.

Hodge [1980] Conv 341 has a different explanation. He argues that the nature of the fraud lies not simply in keeping the property personally, but in the fact that it was the promise to carry out the testator's wishes *in their exact terms* which induced him to leave his property to the intended trustee. It is the intended trustee's failure to do this which makes the fraud, not the element of greed. He would be just as fraudulent with regard to the testator's confidence if he gave the property to a charity, as he would be if he kept it for himself. And the testator would be no less defrauded if the intended trustee were to (say) hand over the gift intended for the testator's mistress to his innocent and long-suffering wife. A deception practised out of high moral principle is still deceit. Therefore, nothing less than the enforcement of the testator's wishes will suffice to avert a fraud in this situation.

This explanation of the true meaning of fraud has the backing of authority. It is clear from the quote from *Blackwell v Blackwell* already considered, that fraud in this context does not necessarily require the trustee to keep the property beneficially, but merely for him, having taken the property, not to carry out the testator's wishes. A similar statement can be found in Lord Sterndale's judgment in *Re Gardner* [1920] 2 Ch 523 (at p. 529): 'The breach of trust or the fraud would arise when [the secret trustee] attempted to deal with the money contrary to the terms on which he took it.' It is not necessary for him to attempt to keep it beneficially, and indeed, in *Re Gardner* itself, he had no intention of so doing.

Lord Westbury's requirement in *McCormick v Grogan* was for a *'malus animus'* to be proved by clearest and most indisputable evidence. This seems to suggest that a deliberate intention to deceive him must be shown on the legatee's part (for example, where he had deliberately induced the testator to leave the property to him in the will, on the clear representation that he would hold it in trust for the secret beneficiary). It also appears that the standard of proof is as in common-law fraud; in other words, a very high standard indeed is required.

Lord Westbury's remarks were not essential to the decision in *McCormick v Grogan*, and indeed, seem not to have been adopted in later cases. For example, in the later House of Lords authority, *Blackwell v Blackwell* [1929] AC 518, Lord Buckmaster thought that all that was required to show a fraud was:

(a) the intention of the testator to subject the intended trustee to an obligation in favour of the intended beneficiary;

(b) communication of that intention to the intended trustee; and

(c) the acceptance of that obligation by the intended trustee, either expressly or by acquiescence.

In *Ottaway* v *Norman* [1972] Ch 698, Brightman J, relying on the criteria above, enforced a trust of land without any suggestion that the intended trustee had procured her prior life interest by deceit. At the time of the arrangement between herself and the testator, Ottaway, she clearly intended to carry out her promise to leave the land to Ottaway's son in her own will. Her failure in the event to do this might be rated as a breach of trust, and it is clearly a fraud in the sense that it defeats the intention of the testator, but no question of '*malus animus*' arose. Nor did Brightman J see any reason to depart from the ordinary civil standard of proof, i.e., balance of probabilities.

Is '*malus animus*', and the requisite higher standard of proof, therefore irrelevant? In *Re Snowden* [1979] Ch 528, Megarry V-C appears to suggest that it may have to be shown in some circumstances, but unfortunately these are not elaborated upon. This aspect of the case may in any event be limited to issues of proof: if the only way that a would-be beneficiary can assert the existence of a trust in his favour is to allege facts which necessarily impute fraud to the alleged trustee, then inevitably '*malus animus*' will need to be shown, and the standard of proof will be high. If the three elements listed earlier can be shown without proof of '*malus animus*', however, presumably he may still succeed on the balance of probabilities.

Secret and Half-secret Trusts Take Effect Independently of the Will

It is also clear from *Blackwell* v *Blackwell* [1929] AC 518 that secret and half-secret trusts operate independently of the will. It is possible that they operate as express trusts created *inter vivos* by the agreement reached between the testator and the intended trustee, the function or relevance of the will being to vest the property in the intended trustee at the agreed time for the assumption of his office. From the passage in Viscount Sumner's speech, however, to which allusion has already been made, it seems more likely that after the will has transferred legal title to the legatee, the court fastens on the conscience of the legatee by imposing on him a trust. This is probably best analysed as a constructive trust, imposed in order to prevent fraud.

A similar analysis was adopted by Lord Westbury in *McCormick* v *Grogan* (at p. 97).

The Court of Equity has, from an early period, decided that even an Act of Parliament shall not be used as an instrument of fraud; and if in the machinery of perpetrating a fraud an Act of Parliament intervenes, the Court of Equity, it is true, does not set aside the Act of Parliament but it fastens on the individual who gets a title under the Act, and imposes upon him a personal obligation, because he applies the Act as an instrument for accomplishing a fraud.

Whichever analysis is correct, whether secret and half-secret trusts are express *inter vivos* trusts or constructive trusts imposed once the legatee has received the property, the will does no more than constitute the trust, transferring the legal property to the secret trustee. It seems likely that the trust could also be constituted by intestacy, in the absence of any will, if the settlor refrains from making a will in the knowledge that the property will pass to the intended trustee by virtue of the Administration of Estates Act 1925, rather than using a more usual form of transfer for an *inter vivos* trust.

It is undoubtedly correct to say that the mechanism by which secret and half-secret trusts are enforced has nothing to do with the will. But to describe the mechanism is not the same thing as providing a reason for their enforcement. The reason that equity imposes on the conscience of the legatee is fraud, and the mere fact that the mechanism operates independently of the will in no way affects that requirement.

The operation of secret and half-secret trusts independently of this will does have other consequences, however. In *Re Young* [1951] Ch 344 a half-secret trust was enforced despite the fact that the beneficiary had witnessed the will, which under s. 15 of the Wills Act 1837 would normally have the effect of invalidating the gift to the witnessing beneficiary. Since he took outside the will, however, this rule did not apply. Dankwerts J commented:

> The whole theory of the formation of a secret trust is that the Wills Act has nothing to do with the matter . . ., since the persons do not take by virtue of the gift in the will, but by virtue of the secret trusts imposed upon the beneficiary, who does in fact take under the will.

In *Re Gardner (No. 2)* [1923] 2 Ch 230, a secret trust in favour of a beneficiary who had predeceased the testator was upheld. It is not possible to leave property to a dead person by will, and it is difficult to justify this decision even on the basis that the will has nothing to do with the matter. The usual analysis is that, at the very least, the will constitutes the trust by transferring legal title to the secret trustee. Romer J saw no reason why a declaration of trust by the secret trustee should not have occurred at the moment of communication of the trust to him (at p. 233):

> The rights of the parties appear to me to be exactly the same as though the husband [secret trustee], after the memorandum had been communicated

to him by the testatrix ..., had executed a declaration of trust binding himself to hold any property that should come to him upon his wife's [settlor's] partial intestacy upon trust as specified in the memorandum.

If Romer J's view is correct, then the consequences are not limited to an ability to make a secret or half-secret trust in favour of a beneficiary who predeceases the testator. If the trust comes into force from the moment of communication, then it must also follow that it is irrevocable from that moment, and the secret trustee would be unable later to change his mind. This would be an unfortunate consequence if the communication was made many years before the testator's death and circumstances had changed radically in the meantime. Suppose, for example, the secret beneficiary ran off with the secret trustee's wife. Could the secret trustee not inform the testator that he was no longer prepared to accept the property on the original terms? Or, if he were no longer able to get in touch with the testator, could he not refuse to take the property under the will? One would have thought that, in principle, he should be able to change his mind, but if Romer J is right, and the trust is created from the moment of communication, then it may well be that he cannot.

There is another difficulty with Romer J's analysis. The secret trustee must be declaring himself trustee of after-acquired property, since only on the testator's death is legal title vested in him. The conventional view is that trusts of future property are void (see further Chapter 3). The orthodox view is that *Gardner (No. 2)* is wrong.

CAN THE DISTINCTIONS BETWEEN SECRET AND HALF-SECRET TRUSTS BE JUSTIFIED?

There is no particular difficulty in justifying the decision in *Wallgrave v Tebbs*, since if the intended trustee knew nothing about the trust until after the testator's death, there could have been no fraud in the procuring of the bequest, and thus no reason for the court to compel the intended trustee to do anything in particular with what is now his own property. Another justification is that any other decision would have permitted the testator to derogate from his grant. A bequest ought not to be 'snatched back' after it has been made, any more than a birthday present could be later reclaimed.

Re Boyes is more difficult to justify, since there appears to have been a fraud on the testator, but it is clear from Kay J's judgment that his understanding of the basis of enforcement was substantially that outlined above:

> The essence of [the early cases on secret trusts] is that the devisee or legatee accepts a particular trust which thereupon becomes binding upon him, and which it would be a fraud in him not to carry into effect.

Further, the intended trustee was willing to carry out those terms. It seems that the case must be explained as one in which the scope of any possible fraud was limited to denying the existence of the trust. The intended trustee could hardly be said to have procured the bequest by a promise to adhere to its terms, since he did not know them. All he knew was that the testator wished him to take the property in the capacity of trustee and not beneficially, so by compelling him to hold as trustee the court had done all it needed to in order to make him comply with the terms on which the bequest had been granted. If the intended trustee had known where the terms of the trust could be found (e.g., in a letter to be opened after the testator's death) then it could be said that he accepted those terms and was bound by them. In this situation, he would hold the property on the terms of the secret trust (*Re Keen* [1937] Ch 236, 242).

There is nothing in the fraud basis of enforcement, however, which would require that an intended trustee must know the terms of the trust by the time the will is executed. There is no real difference between making a bequest on the strength of the intended trustee's promise, and leaving that bequest unrevoked on the strength of his later assurance. So there is no reason to refuse to enforce the trust where the intended trustee becomes aware of its terms only after the execution of the will. All that is necessary is that he should be aware of them, or where they are to be found, before the bequest takes effect, i.e., upon the testator's death.

It is also obvious that justifications for *Keen* and *Bateman* become even more difficult given that secret and half-secret trusts operate outside the will.

It is therefore difficult to justify *Keen* and *Bateman* simply on the basis of the principles of enforcement of secret and half-secret trusts. Are there any other justifications for these cases, therefore, or can they be justified by a policy which outweighs any of the above discussion?

Other Justifications for Keen and Bateman

It is sometimes argued that the fraud theory ought to draw a distinction between fully and half-secret trusts, on the ground that there is no possibility of an intended trustee of a half-secret trust claiming the property for himself, since the fact of the trust is plain from the will. All that is needed to avert fraud, therefore, is to compel him to hold on resulting trust for the testator's estate.

This may be an argument against enforcing half-secret trusts at all, but it is no argument for the rule regarding time of communication. To impose a resulting trust would be the same thing as refusing to enforce the trust, because a resulting trust is what would happen in any case where a testamentary bequest failed for whatever reason. But it is clear that the courts do enforce half-secret trusts, provided that the terms are communicated prior to or contemporaneously with the making of the will. It is also clear that they do this partly out of a desire to prevent fraud: see the speeches of the House in *Blackwell* v *Blackwell* [1929] AC 318.

In any case it is simply not adequate to say that a resulting trust would suffice to avert fraud; as suggested earlier, it would still amount to a fraud on the testator. Can we say that it is only a fraud on him if the intended trustee has assented to the scheme before the will was made, and so procured the bequest? Hardly — there is no difference between making the bequest and leaving it unrevoked on the strength of the trustee's later acquiescence. To argue that the rule regarding time of communication can serve to prevent fraud seems simply illogical.

A possible justification for the *Re Keen* distinction is that because the existence of a half-secret (but not fully secret) trust is openly declared in a formal testamentary bequest, any later addition or change to the statement that the property is to be held on trust must also be made in a properly attested will or codicil. Therefore, if the testator chooses to declare the terms of his trust later than the date of executing his will, he is committed to using the correct formalities. This argument only applies, of course, to half-secret trusts.

It has a superficial attraction, as it takes account of the fact that the problem of adequate proof is one which bedevils the whole area of secret trusts. If a testator has blandly asserted that property is to be held on trust, it is obviously vital to ensure that any other statements he may have made regarding the precise terms of that trust are indeed referable to that particular trust, and no other. B. Perrins [1985] Conv 248 explains the timidity of the courts in accepting evidence which post-dates the will.

In this, they appear to have been influenced by the probate doctrine of incorporation by reference. This, in brief, permits the incorporation into a will of any document which was in existence at the time the will was executed, and was referred to as such in the will itself. It is a useful doctrine in that it saves the bother of copying out lengthy trust documents in the will itself, merely for the purpose of adding a fresh sum to those trusts by way of bequest. The testator can instead simply refer to those documents and rely on a short declaration that the bequest is to be held on the terms set out in those documents. He cannot, however, incorporate a document which is not yet in existence at the time of making the will: to allow this would be to tempt fraudulent claims that this or that document was the one to which the testator meant to refer.

It is therefore easy to see why the courts, conscious of the wisdom of these limits to the doctrine of incorporation by reference, may have thought it prudent to import those limits into the enforcement of half-secret trusts. But as a principled justification for the communication rules, the explanation has defects.

It should be noted, for example, that it is not necessary to the enforcement of a half-secret trust that any document at all should exist to declare the terms of the trust. So long as he communicates the terms before signing his will, the testator is free to rely on a purely oral communication, which must be even more susceptible to later misrepresentation than a document. Further, since the courts are prepared to accept the existence of fully secret trusts on quite slender evidence, e.g., *Ottaway v Norman* [1972] Ch 698, it would be odd if they refuse to accept oral evidence to show the terms of a half-secret trust: the chance of a fraudulent claim is certainly no greater in the latter case.

In any case, to argue that the testator, having once committed himself to formality, remains bound by the need for further formality if he wishes to expound the terms of his trust later than the date of making his will, is merely to penalise him for partial compliance with the Wills Act 1837, while allowing the testator who ignores that Act entirely (by creating a fully secret trust) to have his wishes enforced. This seems to fall short of being a rational justification, therefore.

Another, related argument which was stated in *Blackwell v Blackwell*, and repeated in *Re Keen*, is that to permit a testator simply to state the existence of a trust and communicate its terms at his leisure would be to permit a will to be freely altered by unattested dispositions, thus defeating the policy of the Wills Act 1837.

The argument reflects a respect for the policy of the Wills Act, and it has been argued that the same policy ought to apply also to fully secret trusts (see T.G. Watkin [1981] Conv 335). This, it is argued, would allow the testator who has made up his mind where he wants his property to go, but wishes its destination to be secret, to fulfil his desires by making his communication prior to the will, while defeating the testator who is merely indecisive and wants the luxury of changing his will without the trouble and expense of making fresh testamentary provisions.

Whatever can be said for this view, as Watkin acknowledges, the practice of permitting indecisive behaviour via a fully secret trust is so firmly entrenched that a statute would be required to effect the change. In any case the argument, even if sound in principle, provides no reason for treating fully and half-secret trusts differently; indeed it is a strong argument for treating them in the same way.

Though the question does not ask for it, since I have concluded that there is no rational justification for the distinction, it is worth considering whether there is any possibility of reform.

The chances of any reform in this area are limited to statutory intervention to bring the two species of secret trust in line, and/or the possibility that the House of Lords may one day review *Re Keen* and decide that, after all, there is no sound basis for the distinction drawn in that case. It is arguable that the time of communication was not the true basis of the decision in *Re Keen*, since the alleged communication did not anyway match the description given in the will, but the rule derived from *Re Keen* has since been applied in *Re Bateman's WT* [1970] 1 WLR 1463. However, the question is still open to review by the House of Lords.

These, then, are some of the issues which a good answer to our hypothetical question ought to cover. It is not intended to be a model answer, however, and other views are possible. Model answers are in any case a bad thing. You should not attempt to parrot-learn a stock answer, but would be better advised to examine the above reasoning, and pick holes in it where you can.

PROBLEM QUESTIONS

A typical problem question on secret trusts will attempt to test you on several points. Almost inevitably, it will introduce the distinction between half and fully secret trusts discussed above. Other possible complications for which you should look out may include:

(a) The form of wording used to indicate a half-secret trust. Has the testator referred to the trust as something already known to the intended trustee, or has he made the *Re Keen* style error of using language which could be taken to indicate a future communication? If the examiner has chosen to use words which do not precisely match those in any decided case, you may have to use your own judgment here and be prepared to argue for your chosen interpretation.

(b) Possible contradictions between the words of the will and the directions given by the testator to the intended trustee. For example, the testator may have left property 'to X on trust', but informed X that only part of that property is to be held for the beneficiary and that X can keep the rest. You then have to consider whether X will be allowed to do so, and if not, what happens to the property — will it go to the beneficiary, or pass on resulting trust?

(c) More than one intended trustee. This raises issues concerning the rules for joint tenants and tenants in common (see B. Perrins (1972) 85 LQR 225) and perhaps whether they can be applied by analogy in the case of half-secret as well as fully secret trusts.

(d) The later addition of a codicil which has the effect of republishing the will. Can this affect a situation where the testator communicates with his intended trustee only after making the will which contains a half-secret trust?

(e) *Ottaway v Norman* complications. If the obligation imposed upon the intended trustee is to leave the property in his own will, what is the status of the trust in the lifetime of the intended trustee? Can property other than that received under the testator's will be bound by the trust?

(f)   The issue of whether a secret trust of land can be enforced without writing as required by s. 53(1)(b) of the Law of Property Act 1925, or possibly, whether a secret trust of an equitable interset can be created, and if so whether this requires writing by virtue of s. 53(1)(c).

(g)   The 'sealed envelope' situation. How far must the intended trustee be aware of its contents, and will it suffice if the envelope is not to be opened until the testator's death?

You would be very unlucky indeed to be faced with a problem which contained all of these elements together, but you should be ready to tackle all or any, if necessary. By way of example, let us consider such a problem. In order to cover all these aspects, the following problem is inevitably rather clumsy, but it may suffice for illustrative purposes.

Problem Question

In 1980, Tom made a will which contained the following dispositions:

(a)   My house, Blackacre, to Alice, absolutely.

(b)   My farms, Whiteacre and Brownacre, to Benjamin and Cecil jointly.

(c)   My country cottage, Greenacre, to Damion on trust to carry out my wishes.

(d)   All my personal property to Edgar on the trusts privately communicated to him by me.

(e)   All my residuary estate to Fenella.

Prior to making the will, Tom had told Damion that he wanted him to hold Greenacre on trust for George, Tom's illegitimate son. In 1982, Tom told Alice that he had left her Blackacre so that she would be assured of a home for life, but that he expected her to leave Blackacre, and any other property she might possess at her death, to George in her own will. He then told Benjamin, but not Cecil, that he wanted them to hold Whiteacre on trust for George, but that they could keep Brownacre for themselves. Finally, he wrote a letter to Edgar, telling him that he wished him to hold certain items of the personal property on trusts which he would find contained in a sealed envelope, which should not be opened until after Tom's death. The envelope contained the direction that Edgar should hold 10,000 shares on trust for George, but that he could keep the rest of the personalty for himself.

In 1985, Tom won £10,000 on the football pools, and executed a codicil, which left the £10,000 'to Edgar, on the trusts known to him'. Damion died in 1986, a fortnight before Tom also died.

Advise all the parties.

This is simpler than it looks to work through, so long as you do not confuse the parties with one another. A rough plan, showing who gets what, and on what terms, is strongly recommended. It should also note the issues raised, after which it is simply a matter of working your way through the apparent jungle of legal issues in your list.

Depending on how much time is available, some students like to open a problem with a short résumé of the area of law. In the context of a monster problem like this, this practice is unlikely to be helpful, since you would need to cover practically every aspect of secret trusts in your 'short' résumé. Let us jump straight in, then, and start with Alice.

Alice exists simply to fulfil the role of Miss Hodges, the housekeeper in *Ottaway v Norman* [1972] Ch 698. Miss Hodges was employed by Mr Ottaway who left her his bungalow in his will, on terms that she would leave it by her own will to Mr Ottaway's son. According to the evidence given by the son and his wife, she also undertook to leave them the furniture and other contents, including her money.

It was established in *Re Gardner (No. 1)* [1920] 2 Ch 523 that an agreement to make provision for beneficiaries after one's death could be enforced. In that case, a wife had left her estate to her husband who had agreed to divide the property among beneficiaries on his death, but he died before making his will. The Court of Appeal found that he held the property for himself for life, and for the beneficiaries after his death.

Brightman J, in *Ottaway v Norman*, accepted that there had been an arrangement between old Mr Ottaway and Miss Hodges that she should leave the bungalow to the son, and was prepared to enforce that agreement by imposing what he called a constructive trust upon the bungalow in the hands of Miss Hodges's executor (she having later changed her mind and left her property to a cousin). He also accepted that the trust comprised such furnishings and fixtures as Miss Hodges had received under Mr Ottaway's will, but not that it included all Miss Hodges's other property and cash from whatever source.

In respect of the last, it seems that he was not convinced that so far-reaching an obligation had in fact been envisaged in the agreement, but if, as in our problem, the intended trustee has clearly accepted such an obligation, it may well be, on analogy with mutual wills (on which, see chapter 6), that this obligation also could be enforced against her estate.

This raises the issue of the status of the trust during Alice's lifetime. In *Ottaway v Norman*, Brightman J employed the concept of a 'floating trust', derived from the Australian case of *Birmingham v Renfrew* (1937) 57 CLR 666, which would remain in suspense during the life of the trustee and crystallise on her death, attaching to whatever property was comprised within her estate. This, as the learned judge noted, would seem to preclude Alice from making even a small pecuniary legacy in favour of her relatives or friends.

Compare the views of Nourse J in *Re Cleaver* [1981] 1 WLR 939 in the context of mutual wills, discussed in chapter 6.

George can enforce the secret trust, therefore, at least with regard to Blackacre, and perhaps also with regard to Alice's other property, as it seems she accepted this obligation. The fact that the trust is not contained in writing ought, I would suggest, to be no bar to its enforcement, despite the Law of Property Act 1925, s. 53(1)(b). In *Ottaway* v *Norman* itself the section was avoided as the executor was held to be a constructive trustee of the bungalow. Whether or not this analysis was correct, in principle a fully secret trust of land should be enforceable despite the absence of writing, either on the assumption that such trusts are to be regarded as constructive since they are imposed on the ground of conscience, or more probably because equity will not allow a statute intended to prevent fraud to be used as a cloak for fraud.

The devise of the farms to Benjamin and Cecil raises the issue of whether communication to one of several trustees can bind them all. Where a gift is made (as here) to trustees as joint tenants, the orthodox view is that if communication is made before the execution of the will, all will be bound, whereas if communication is made after the execution of the will but before the death of the testator, only those who have accepted the trust are bound by it, on the basis that the gift to an intended trustee who does not consent is not tainted with any fraud in procuring the execution of the will (see Farwell J in *Re Stead* [1900] 1 Ch 237 at p. 241).

Though it does not arise in the problem, note for the sake of completeness that where the gift is to the intended trustees as tenants in common, only those who are aware of the trust are bound, whether they obtain this knowledge before or after the will is executed.

This orthodox distinction lacks credibility, and B. Perrins (1972) 88 LQR 225 has argued that the true rule rests on the principle of *Huguenin* v *Baseley* (1807) 14 Ves Jr 273, that no man may profit from the fraud of another. On this argument, Cecil would be bound if Tom was induced to leave the farms to him on the strength of Benjamin's promise, and the question of when communication occurred would be a matter of evidence only. The argument has much to commend it, but is inconsistent with *Re Stead*.

On the facts of our problem, Cecil would not on the basis of *Re Stead* be bound by the trust, since it was not communicated to him until after the making of the will (or indeed at all).

Benjamin can of course claim that his share of Brownacre at least is free from the trust in favour of George, because clearly Tom intended only to impress Whiteacre with the trust. The extrinsic evidence difficulties, discussed below in relation to half-secret trusts, almost certainly do not apply to fully secret trusts, so Benjamin should be permitted to adduce evidence to show that Tom indeed intended him to take his interest in Brownacre beneficially.

Greenacre may be subject to a half-secret trust in George's favour. Tom has communicated his wishes, which Damion must be taken to have accepted, prior to the execution of the will, but there is still an issue as to whether a half-secret trust of land requires to be evidenced in writing under s. 53(1)(b) of the Law of Property Act 1925. In *Re Baillie* (1886) 2 TLR 660 it was said that a half-secret trust of land will not be enforced unless evidenced in writing, but the case is of doubtful authority, pre-dating as it does *Blackwell v Blackwell* [1929] AC 318 (when *Re Baillie* was decided, the enforceability at all of half-secret trusts was not beyond doubt). I would suggest that writing ought not to be required, on the same basis as for fully secret trusts (see above).

Damion has died before Tom, which makes it necessary to consider whether a secret trust can be enforced in the absence of the intended trustee. For a fully secret trust, there is some authority that it must fail, since the gift upon which it is engrafted will lapse with the death of the intended trustee (see Cozens-Hardy LJ in *Re Maddock* [1902] 2 Ch 220 at p. 251). Half-secret trusts may, however, be saved, for the trust is plain on the face of the will, and the maxim that 'Equity will not allow a trust to fail for want of a trustee' ought to impose a trust upon Greenacre in the hands of Tom's executor. He will therefore be taken to hold Greenacre for George, and not for Fenella as residuary legatee.

Edgar's situation raises several problems. Half-secret trusts must, of course, be communicated prior to, or contemporaneously with, the execution of the will, but it is only in 1982 that Tom informs Edgar that he is to hold all Tom's personal property on trust. This raises the question of the effect of the codicil. A codicil has the effect of republishing a will, i.e., it is as though the will itself had been made at the date of the later codicil. Can we therefore say that, since Edgar was aware that he was to be a trustee by the date of execution of the codicil, he is therefore bound?

In *Blackwell v Blackwell* itself, the gift which was subject to the half-secret trust was contained in a codicil, but in that case the gift was created for the first time by the codicil, and the trustees had been duly informed in advance. Here, the half-secret trust is originally created earlier, in the will, and the intended trustee has not been informed in advance. There is no direct authority whether the later reference to that trust in the codicil, at a time when Edgar has been informed of the trust, will suffice first to create the trust contained in the will, and secondly to add to this trust the extra £10,000.

On the method of communication, via a sealed envelope, *Re Keen* [1937] Ch 236 is authority that it is permissible, provided, as here, the trustee knows that it contains the terms of a trust and has agreed to carry out those terms, whatever they may turn out to be.

On the main issue, in favour of allowing the trust, it can be argued that the policy of the *Re Keen* rule is merely to ensure that the trust is communicated prior to some properly executed testamentary disposition which indicates its terms, and that, this being the case here, the mention of the trust in the codicil should be good enough.

Against this, however, is a possible argument based on *Re Cooper* [1939] Ch 811. In that case, a testator had left £5,000 to trustees on half-secret trust in his will, having duly informed them in advance and obtained their agreement, and later added a further £10,000 to this trust in a codicil. The Court of Appeal held that only the first amount mentioned in the will could be subject to the half-secret trust, and that the amount added by the codicil fell into residue. This might be taken to mean that a testator is obliged to inform his trustees of each and every alteration or addition, and secure their agreement prior to that alteration or addition. If this were so, it could be argued that no subsequent agreement could retroactively validate the trust in the will, despite the republication doctrine.

An alternative, and in my view better, interpretation of *Re Cooper*, is that trustees are bound by what they agree to, and that this is a question of fact to be determined on the evidence. In *Re Cooper*, the trustees had agreed to hold £5,000, and that was the limit of their obligation, since they never knew of the further obligation imposed in the codicil. As Greene MR said (at p. 818):

> it was not with regard to any sum other than the £5,000 that the consciences of the trustees (to use a technical phrase) were burdened.

He seemed to envisage, however, that if the agreement had been that the trustees would hold £5,000 or whatever sum the testator finally chose to bequeath, it would have been enforceable on those terms. This also accords with the view taken by the courts that a sealed envelope may be sufficient communication, despite the fact that the terms are, *ex hypothesi*, unknown to the trustee, who assents to carry them out whatever they might turn out to be. It is suggested therefore that this case offers no obstacle to a decision that Tom's codicil is effective to create the half-secret trust in favour of George.

Even if the half-secret trust is validated by the codicil, the words in the will, 'to Edgar on the trusts privately communicated to him by me', are arguably ambiguous as to whether a past or future communication is indicated (the other ground of the decision in *Re Keen*). Presumably they would have to be construed as past if the codicil is regarded as republishing the will.

One further complication is that, on the facts of our problem, it appears that the money bequeathed by the codicil is, in fact, intended for Edgar beneficially, since the letter, when opened, directed him to hold only the shares in trust for George and to keep the rest of the personal property for himself. In principle, there seems no reason why this should be unacceptable.

Assuming that the half-secret trust might thus be held valid, there remains the issue of whether Edgar may indeed retain for himself the personalty other than the shares intended for George. The courts have shown themselves reluctant to admit any evidence to contradict the terms of a will. In *Re Rees* [1950] Ch 204, the testator had left his whole estate on half-secret trust and privately informed his trustees that they were to make certain payments and retain the surplus for themselves. Since one of the trustees was the solicitor who had drafted the will, the court was, perhaps, especially disposed towards caution in this case, holding that on the proper construction of the will, the half-secret trust was imposed upon the entire estate. The trustees would not therefore be allowed to introduce extrinsic evidence to contradict this by showing that they were intended to take beneficially subject only to making the payments. The issue seems to turn on the construction of the will. If it can be said that the will creates a conditional gift, then the trustees may take, subject to fulfilling the condition. If, however, it imposes a trust, the trustees will not be allowed to bring evidence to contradict the will.

Re Rees was in any case doubted in *Re Tyler* [1967] 1 WLR 1269. Our problem provides strong evidence, in the shape of the letter, of Tom's true intentions concerning the terms of his trust, and there is no reason in principle why the court should not enforce these terms, permitting Edgar to take the rest of the personalty beneficially. It can hardly be said that this would involve adducing evidence to contradict the will: rather, the evidence is directly *upon* its terms.

Had the facts of our problem been closer to those in *Re Rees*, however, probably no evidence in contradiction to the will could have been brought. In that case, Edgar would hold the shares for George, and the rest of the personalty for Fenella as residuary legatee.

It can be seen, then, that none of the points in the problem is especially difficult, so long as you work through it in a logical manner.

SUGGESTED ADDITIONAL READING

- Hodge [1980] Conv 341;
- Perrins [1985] Conv 248.

9 CHARITABLE TRUSTS

Questions on charities also often arise in problem form but it would be rare for a problem question to be limited to charities issues alone. Almost invariably knowledge of private purpose trusts and/or unincorporated associations, considered already in chapter 5, would also be required. For example, in the problem considered in the section on self-help organisations, the only issue is distribution of surplus funds. If the purposes are charitable (for the relief of poverty) then when continued pursuit of the purposes became impossible a *cy près* scheme ought to be effected. None of the money ought to return to the original contributors. On the other hand, if this is a non-charitable purpose trust, or the funds are held by a non-charitable unincorporated association, then there can be no *cy près* scheme, but distribution will be effected among the contributors. The basis of distribution will be on the principles examined at the end of chapter 5.

The point of this example is to show you that it is not always possible to treat charities in isolation, and if you intend to concentrate on charities for the exam, make sure you also know about non-charitable purpose trusts and unincorporated associations. Indeed, the cases themselves often raise issues from both areas. *Re Shaw* [1957] 1 WLR 729, (the 40-letter alphabet case) was argued (unsuccessfully) as an educational charity, or alternatively (equally unsuccessfully) as a non-charitable purpose trust. *Re Hobourn Aero Components Ltd's Air Raid Disaster Fund* [1964] Ch 194, a case considered later in this chapter under self-help organisations, was entirely concerned with the distribution of surplus funds. If, as the Charity Commissioners unsuccessfully argued, the fund's purposes were charitable, a *cy près* scheme would have been appropriate. If, as was held in the Court of Appeal, the fund was not charitable, it should have been distributed among the contributors. In both those cases, issues from this chapter and issues from chapter 5 were mixed, and the last of the above problems appears to be based closely upon the *Hobourn Aero* case.

Space considerations do not permit a full review of the heads of charities, and in any case some of the issues in the above problem, and that alluded to in chapter 1, have already been considered in chapter 5. Instead, an essay question is considered, on the issue of public benefit, which is really central to the law of charities.

THE REQUIREMENT OF PUBLIC BENEFIT

Essay Question

ANSWER ALL PARTS

    (i)   What is meant by the *Oppenheim* personal nexus test? To which heads of charity, if any, does it apply?
AND
    (ii)   In an educational charity, to what extent, if at all, can a settlor show a preference for a class which, were members of that class to be the only recipients of the charity, would fall foul of the *Oppenheim* personal nexus test?
AND
    (iii)   What test (or tests) of public benefit apply under the 4th head of charity (as categorised by Lord Macnaghten in *Commissioners for Special Purposes of the Income Tax* v *Pemsel* [1891] AC 531)?

Charitable trusts are of a public nature, in that they are publicly enforced and controlled, and enjoy certain tax concessions. It is not therefore surprising that, in order to be charitable a purpose must, in addition to falling within the *Pemsel* heads, involve a public benefit.

The *Pemsel* heads, from Lord Macnaghten's speech in *Commissioners for Special Purposes of the Income Tax* v *Pemsel* [1891] AC 531, are relief of poverty, advancement of religion, advancement of education, and other purposes beneficial to the community. The Recreational Charities Act 1958 has added an extra category, with a requirement of social welfare, which is probably similar to the public benefit requirement for the other heads.

There are therefore two requirements for a purpose to be charitable. It must confer a benefit (defined by the *Pemsel* heads) upon those who are directly the objects of the charity, and it must also confer an additional benefit upon the public at large.

For example, if a charitable purpose such as education is to be advanced, it must not only confer a benefit on those in direct receipt of the education, but must also be advanced in some way that benefits the public, or at least a substantial section thereof, rather than providing benefits for some artificially limited class of people.

However, this requirement is not applied with the same rigour to each of the four heads of charity, and in the case of the relief of poverty, its role is minimal. For this reason, the public benefit requirement will be dealt with separately under each head.

It is convenient to begin with trusts for the advancement of education, because the leading House of Lords' authority concerned an attempt to set up an educational charity.

Advancement of Education

Whereas in the case of relief of poverty, even benefiting a small number of people may be regarded as conferring a public benefit, with educational charities the problem of public benefit is thrown into a clearer relief. It is perhaps not surprising, then, that the leading House of Lords' authority should concern this head of charity.

Obviously education constitutes a benefit to those in immediate receipt of it, but it is not self-evident that educating a few people constitutes a benefit to the general public. Indeed, given that many of the cases under this head are in reality disputes over tax relief, it would be strange if the education of a privileged few were to be regarded as charitable. That is why under this head in particular it is necessary that there is some additional benefit to the general public, or some appreciable sector thereof.

That is not to say that a particular form of education has to be capable of being enjoyed by everyone, so long as access to it is reasonably open. Thus public schools may be charitable as long as they are not operated as profit-making ventures, although their fees may place them beyond the means of the majority. Even scholarships or endowed chairs, which can be enjoyed only by one person at a time, present no difficulty. The problems arise where it is sought to limit the range of potential beneficiaries within a class which cannot be said to constitute a section of the public.

There are in effect two separate requirements. First, the class must be able genuinely to be described as a section of the community, rather than simply a body of private individuals. Persons following a common profession or calling, people of common nationality, religion or sex, or the inhabitants of a town or county can be described as a section of the community. Special provisions for people suffering disability are also permissible, since they are a section of the public in a meaningful sense. But in *Davies v Perpetual Trustee Co. Ltd* [1959] AC 459, the Privy Council held non-charitable a trust which was confined to Presbyterian youths who were descended from settlors in New South Wales who had originated from the North of Ireland. Although quite large in number, this category of potential beneficiaries was held not to be a section of the public.

Secondly, under this head, and probably under all the heads except relief of poverty, it will also be fatal if the class of potential beneficiaries (however large) is defined in terms of relation to particular individuals or a company. This approach originated in Re Compton [1945] Ch 123, where charitable status was denied to a trust to educate the children of three named families. It is understandable that the courts are reluctant to allow an essentially private arrangement to enjoy charitable privileges, especially tax advantages, but it seems that the principle extends to cases where the class of potential beneficiaries is defined in terms of a relationship with an employer, even where the employer is a substantial concern.

The most authoritative statements are those of Lord Simonds in Oppenheim v Tobacco Securities Trust Co. Ltd [1951] AC 297, where Re Compton was approved in the House of Lords. He said that first, the number of possible beneficiaries must not be negligible, and secondly, that the class must not be defined so as to depend on any relationship to a particular individual or employer.

In the trust with which the House of Lords was concerned, the number of potential beneficiaries (at least in theory) was certainly not negligible. The income of the trust fund was directed to be applied 'in providing for ... the education of children of employees or former employees of the British-American Tobacco Co. Ltd ... or any of its subsidiary or allied companies in such manner ... as the acting trustees shall in their absolute discretion ... think fit'. The number of present employees alone exceeded 110,000, so it was only the personal nexus rule which was fatal (because they were all connected with the same company).

The test is arguably inappropriate in large companies. Though perhaps the special tax concessions of charitable status should not be given to any arrangement for a private class, the personal link between employees is not as obvious as that between members of a family, among whom consider-ations of mutual interest might be considered to negate the altruistic status of the trust.

Of course, if you take a hard line on private arrangements the Oppenheim decision logically follows. But perhaps the real, if unstated, justification for the result was the extent of the trustees' discretion in Oppenheim. The benefit to 110,000 or more people may in fact have been entirely theoretical — for example, if the trustees had used the funds to pay 15% of fees to those employees who sent their sons to boarding school, only the relatively small number who could afford the other 85% would actually have benefited. Indeed, it is perhaps a pity (unless you are a hard-liner) that the test in

Oppenheim does not address the real problem, which is the extent of the trustees' discretion to reduce the size of the class, rather than the theoretical personal nexus.

Interesting questions can arise where most but not all the fund is directed towards people connected with a particular employer. In *Re Koettgen's WT* [1954] Ch 252, an educational trust succeeded despite a direction that the trustees should give preference to the families of employees, up to a maximum of 75% of income, but a preference for the grantor's family rendered a gift non-charitable in *Caffoor v Commissioner of Income Tax, Colombo* [1961] AC 584. The trust also failed in *Inland Revenue Commissioners v Educational Grants Association Ltd* [1967] Ch 123, affirmed [1967] Ch 993, where between 76% and 85% of the income (varying from year to year) was paid for the education of persons connected with the Metal Box Co. Ltd. Pennycuick J found 'considerable difficulty in the *Koettgen* decision', and thought that a preference for a private class might always be fatal (though he did not need actually to decide that). The problem with laying down a clear rule of this nature would be that extreme cases could be envisaged (e.g., a preference up to 5% of income) where its application would further no obvious policy (unless again, of course, an objection is taken in principle to charitable status for an arrangement with *any* purely private content).

This problem is similar to that in *Oppenheim v Tobacco Securities Trust Co. Ltd* itself, i.e., that the rule is arguably too rigid. The real problem in *Oppenheim*, as has been seen, was the extent of the trustees' discretion to limit the number of people who could in practice have benefited, rather than the nexus with the company (unless again, objection is taken to *any* private arrangement). It would have been difficult to formulate a clear rule on trustees' discretion, however, where the problem is essentially one of where to draw the line, just as it is difficult to draw the line in the *Re Koettgen's WT* situation. In both cases, therefore, a rigid rule may well be the only answer.

Relief of Poverty

It is unquestioned law that to relieve poverty is to confer a benefit upon the public at large, if only by mitigating the burden of support for the poor which would otherwise fall upon the community. There is no need for the *Oppenheim v Tobacco Securities Trust Co. Ltd* test to apply, and it does not apply in fact.

The *Oppenheim* case exempted the 19th-century 'poor relations' cases as anomalous, and left open the position regarding them. Since then the House of Lords has considered them directly in *Dingle v Turner* [1972] AC 601, and expressly upheld them. In that case a trust for 'poor employees of E. Dingle & Co.' was held charitable, though it would have failed under the personal nexus test.

It is clear, therefore, that the personal nexus test does not apply to this head of charity.

It is, however, necessary that the trust should be intended to benefit a class of persons, and not simply to make a gift to an individual, or group of individuals, who happen to be poor. In *Re Scarisbrick* [1951] Ch 622 Jenkins LJ (at p. 655) stated the rule thus:

> I think the true question in each case has really been whether the gift was for the relief of poverty amongst a class of persons, or ... a particular description of poor, or was merely a gift to individuals, albeit with relief of poverty amongst those individuals as the motive of the gift, or with a selective preference for the poor or poorest amongst those individuals.

This statement received the approval of Lord Cross of Chelsea in *Dingle* v *Turner*. In *Re Scarisbrick* itself the class of potential recipients was so wide as to be incapable of exhaustive ascertainment ('such relations of my said son and daughters as shall be in needy circumstances'), so the trust was charitable.

Advancement of Religion

There are dicta in *Oppenheim* v *Tobacco Securities Trust Co. Ltd* [1951] AC 297 that the public benefit tests advanced in that case apply to all heads of charity except the relief of poverty. If these dicta are correct, the personal nexus rule applies to religious charities, therefore. This seems surprising because:

(a)   The rationale of the personal nexus rule, which is to deny tax and rates advantages to private educational schemes for élite family groups, does not apply as easily in the field of religion.

(b)   If a religious family group mixes actively in the community, arguably the benefit is to the community as a whole, rather than just to the family members. Therefore the *Oppenheim* test is satisfied unless the group shuts itself off from the rest of the community, as occurred in *Gilmour* v *Coats* [1949] AC 426 (see below).

In practice, therefore, there seems to be a substantial overlap between the personal nexus rule and the requirement that religion be *advanced*. Apart from requiring some positive action, it seems that there must by virtue of this requirement be an element of public contact. Private salvation, however commendable, is not charitable. Thus in *Yeap Cheah Neo* v *Ong Chen Neo* (1875) LR 6 PC 381 a provision for the performance of ancestor worship was held non-charitable (by the Privy Council), and a possible reason was that it could benefit only the family group.

The leading case is *Gilmour v Coats* [1949] AC 426, where the House of Lords had to consider a gift of £500 towards a Carmelite priory. The priory housed about 20 cloistered nuns who devoted themselves to intercessory prayer, and had no contact at all with the outside world. This was held non-charitable on the grounds that there was no contact with the outside world. Arguments based on Catholic doctrine, to the effect that everyone benefited from the intercessory prayers, were rejected as being not susceptible to legal proof. Nor could any benefit be found merely in the example of the piety of the women, as it was too vague and intangible. The House of Lords also rejected the argument that, entry being open to all women, the priory should be treated on analogy with an educational institution offering scholarship entry, holding that an educational establishment which required its members to withdraw from the world and leave no record of their studies would not be charitable either.

On the other hand, in *Re Caus* [1934] Ch 162, Catholic masses for the dead were held charitable. This case was doubted in *Gilmour v Coats*, but in principle the case seems correct, and *Caus* was applied by Browne-Wilkinson V-C in *Re Hetherington* [1989] 2 All ER 129. The point is that Catholic masses are open to the public at large even where a private function, such as a funiary rite, is incorporated into the celebration, so in principle *Caus* is distinguishable from *Gilmour v Coats*.

In *Re Hetherington*, Browne-Wilkinson V-C was called upon to consider a gift for the saying of masses, which did not exclude the possibility that the masses would be said in private. In practice, however, all or most of the masses would be open to public. Reviewing the cases, he said (at pp. 134-5):

1. A trust for the ... the advancement of religion is *prima facie* charitable, and assumed to be for the public benefit ... This assumption of public benefit can be rebutted by showing that in fact the particular trust in question cannot operate so as to confer a legally recognised benefit on the public, as in *Gilmour v Coats*.

2. The celebration of a religious rite in public does confer such a benefit because of the edifying and improving effect of such celebration on the members of the public who attend ...

3. The celebration of a religious rite in private does not contain the necessary element of public benefit since any benefit by prayer or example is incapable of proof in the legal sense, and any element of education is limited to a private, not public, class of those present at the celebration: see *Gilmour v Coats* itself ...

4. Where there is a gift for a religious purpose which could be carried out in a way which is beneficial to the public (i.e., by public masses) but could also be carried out in a way which would not have sufficient public benefit (i.e., by private masses) the gift is to be construed as a gift to be

carried out only by the methods that are charitable, all non-charitable purposes being excluded ...

Applying these principles to the case before him, he concluded that:

> a gift for the saying of masses is *prima facie* charitable, being for a religious purpose. In practice, those masses will be celebrated in public, which provides a sufficient element of public benefit ... The gift is to be construed as a gift for the saying of public masses only ..., private masses not being permissible since it would not be a charitable application of the fund for a religious purpose.

In other words, he construed the gift in such a way as to exclude purposes which were non-charitable.

It follows that the mere attendance by the public at a prayer service is sufficient to distinguish *Gilmour* v *Coats*. Suppose, on the other hand, the religious organisation conducts all its affairs in private, but unlike *Gilmour* v *Coats* its members have not cut themselves off entirely from the outside world, but mix with it. This also seems sufficient to distinguish *Gilmour* v *Coats*. In *Neville Estates* v *Madden*, Cross J held charitable a trust for the members of Catford Synagogue. He thought that the rejection of example as a benefit in *Gilmour* v *Coats* would not apply to a restricted religious group if its members lived in the world and mixed with their fellow citizens, because they could thereby extend their example of religious living to the public at large.

It would seem to follow, therefore, that the requirement of public contact is not especially onerous. On Cross J's view, religion can be advanced by example, so long as one mixes in the world in a *physical* sense. *Neville Estates* is authority that no more is required.

Other Purposes Beneficial to the Community

Under this head, where the benefit is limited to a restricted class, such a class must be a section of the public. Certainly the personal nexus test applies, and it may even be that the courts adopt a more stringent approach to public benefit under this head than under the other three heads.

For example, in *Williams's Trustees* v *Inland Revenue Commissioners* [1947] AC 447, doubt was expressed by Lord Simonds as to whether Welsh people in London could be a section of the public. In *Inland Revenue Commissioners* v *Baddeley* [1955] AC 572 it was said that the persons to be benefited must either be the whole community or the inhabitants of a particular area. If some further restriction is imposed, thus creating in effect a class within a class, the test of public benefit will not be satisfied. In *IRC* v *Baddeley*, the limitation was to Methodists living in West Ham and Leyton, and the trust was held not to be charitable.

Neither of these cases of course falls foul of the personal nexus test, and it may be that *Williams's Trustees* v *IRC* at any rate is more stringent than the test in *Davies* v *Perpetual Trustee Co. Ltd* [1959] AC 439, which applies to educational charities (see above). Viscount Simonds in *IRC* v *Baddeley* thought it possible 'that a different degree of public benefit is requisite according to the class in which the charity is said to fall', and that public benefit considerations 'have even greater weight [than in the case of educational trusts] in the case of trusts which by their nominal classification depend for their validity upon general public utility' (though Lord Reid thought otherwise in his dissenting speech).

It is possible that what constitutes a section of the public depends on the purposes of the particular trust, and the courts are more likely to strike down arbitrary restrictions which are irrelevant to those purposes, but which simply serve to exclude other sections of the public. As Lord Simonds observed in *IRC* v *Baddeley* (at p. 592): 'Who has ever heard of a bridge to be crossed only by impecunious Methodists?' He went on to say that what is true of a bridge for Methodists is equally true of any other public purpose falling within the fourth head, and of the adherents of any other creed. The point is surely that if a purpose is so clearly beneficial as to be charitable under the fourth head, the arbitrary exclusion of *any* section of the public renders the disposition in effect a private gift.

There is some authority that the test of public benefit can vary within the fourth head itself. In *Re Dunlop (dec'd)* (1984) Northern Irish Judgments Bulletin (noted by Norma Dawson [1987] Conv 114), Carswell J upheld as charitable a bequest 'To hold the remainder of my residuary estate for the Presbyterian Trust . . . to found or help to found a home for Old Presbyterian persons,' and a *cy près* scheme was ordered. There was earlier Northern Irish authority that the Presbyterians of Londonderry were not a sufficient section of the public under the fourth head, and it was accepted that there was no difference between Irish and English definitions of charity. Carswell J took the view, however, that public benefit depended upon the nature of 'the advantage which the donor intends to provide for the benefit of all of the public'. A 'bridge to be used only by Methodists should clearly fail to qualify, whereas a gift for the education of the children of members of that church might be a valid charity'. But he was also prepared to distinguish between purposes within the fourth head itself.

It should be noted that neither *IRC* v *Baddeley* nor *Williams's Trustees* v *IRC* actually turned on the issue of public benefit. In the former case the purposes were not exclusively religious, but included social purposes and the provision of playing fields, and in the latter case purposes were exclusively social and recreational. They would therefore have failed because of the inclusion of a social content, whatever view had been taken on the public benefit issue.

Recreational Charities Act 1958

This Act was in response to a number of decisions about 30 years ago, including those mentioned in the previous paragraph, where doubt was cast on the charitable status under the fourth head of a number of social trusts which had always been assumed to be charitable.

Section 1 states that it shall be and be deemed always to have been charitable to provide, or assist in the provision of, facilities for recreation or other leisure-time occupation, if the facilities are provided in the interests of social welfare. A proviso adds that nothing in the section shall be taken to derogate from the principle that a trust or institution to be charitable must be for the public benefit. Under s. 1(2), the requirement that the facilities are provided in the interests of social welfare is not to be satisfied unless the facilities are provided with the object of improving the conditions of life for the persons for whom the facilities are primarily intended, and either:

(a) those persons have need of such facilities as aforesaid by reason of their youth, age, infirmity or disablement, poverty or social and economic circumstances; or

(b) the facilities are to be available to the members or female members of the public at large.

Subject to the requirement of social welfare, there is specific reference to the provision of facilities at village halls, community centres and women's institutes, and to the provision and maintenance of grounds and buildings to be used for the purposes of recreation or leisure-time occupation, extending to the provision of facilities for these purposes by the organising of any activity.

There is also express provision (in s. 2) for miners' welfare trusts.

Where the Act applies, the spirit of the preamble to the Statute of Charitable Uses 1601 seems no longer to be relevant, and it must therefore be taken that the statute has added a fresh head of charity.

Section 1(2)(b) above allows for the provision of facilities for recreation or other leisure-time occupation where the facilities are made available to the public at large, but under s. 1(1) they have also to be provided in the interests of social welfare. In *IRC* v *McMullen*, Walton J at first instance ([1978] 1 WLR 664, [1978] 1 All ER 230) held that the requirement of social welfare in s. 1(1) implied that for a charity to succeed under the Act, the recipients must be limited to those who are in some way 'deprived persons'. The Court of Appeal ([1979] 1 WLR 130, [1979] 1 All ER 588) split on the issue, the majority

(Stamp and Orr LJJ) holding that the class to be benefited must be disadvantaged in such a way as to have a special need for the facilities. There was no such limitation in *McMullen* itself, where the gift was to the Football Association Youth Trust. Bridge LJ dissented, preferring a wider view that social welfare may be promoted by benefits which extend to the better off as well as the socially deprived, observing that he could

> see no reason to conclude that only the deprived can have their conditions of life improved. Hyde Park improves the conditions of life for residents in Mayfair and Belgravia as much as for those in Pimlico or the Portobello Road, and the village hall may improve the conditions of life for the squire and his family as well as for cottagers.

The House of Lords ([1981] AC 1) left the issue open, allowing the appeal on the grounds that the trust was charitable as an educational charity. Indeed, their Lordships expressly refused to decide which of the approaches adopted in the Court of Appeal was correct, but the issue has now been resolved in *Guild* v *IRC* [1992] 2 All ER 10, where the House of Lords came down in favour of Bridge LJ's view. It is therefore not fatal that benefits are not limited to deprived persons.

Presumably, social welfare indicates some element of provision for others, so that a group acting purely to benefit themselves would fail to qualify. In any event, such an enterprise would lack the necessary element of public benefit preserved by the Act.

Self-help Organisations

The issue of public benefit, and in particular the less stringent requirements for poverty charities, also affects the status of self-help organisations and disaster appeals. Consider the following problem question which appeared on a recent university examination paper:

> In 1992 a street in Cardiff is destroyed by a gas explosion. An association is set up where members are invited to contribute £100 per month to provide temporary accommodation in Portakabins while their homes are being rebuilt. A and B are both among the 200 contributors to the fund. By 1993, however, B wishes to move to London, where he has obtained employment, so he ceases to contribute, and moves out of the Portakabin. By 1994 all the houses have been rebuilt, and the fund is wound up. At this time A is still a contributor. There is a substantial surplus.
>
> The Charity Commissioners would like to apply the moneys collected *cy près*, claiming that the association is a poverty charity. A argues that the surplus should be distributed equally among the contributors at the time

the fund was wound up. B argues that the surplus should be distributed among all contributors, past and present, in proportion to the total amount of their contributions.

Discuss.

As was observed at the beginning of the chapter, if this association is not charitable, then this question raises the issues discussed at the end of chapter 5. We are also told, however, that the Charity Commissioners would like to apply the moneys collected *cy près*, claiming that the association is a poverty charity. The problem is that it is a self-help organisation.

Self-help organisations are probably not charitable, because they lack the necessary element of altruism. If they are not poverty charities they clearly also fail on the *Oppenheim v Tobacco Securities Trust Co. Ltd* personal nexus test, so the public benefit test is here tied in with the element of altruism. Hall V-C in *Re Clark* (1875) 1 Ch D 497 envisaged that they may succeed as poverty charities, where of course public benefit tests are less stringent, but this also must now be regarded as doubtful, as a second principle has developed independently of the public benefit test that the benefits of charity must be provided by bounty and not bargain. Where, as is the case with many friendly societies, the beneficiaries have, in effect, bought their entitlement in a contractual arrangement, it is again considered that the element of altruism essential to charity is lacking.

In *Re Hobourn Aero Components Ltd's Air Raid Disaster Fund* [1946] Ch 194 (see also chapter 5), a fund established by employees to relieve members suffering in consequence of air raids on Coventry was held by the Court of Appeal to be non-charitable on the grounds that the employees among whom benefit was confined could not be a section of the public. It was not argued as a poverty charity, and the issue was left open whether it could have been charitable had it been so limited. Nevertheless, there are passages in Lord Greene MR's judgment which suggest that it could not have been charitable even as a poverty charity, because the members' entitlement to benefit turned upon the fact of their having subscribed to the fund. This was, in his view, a private trust. If this is correct, then no self-help organisation will be charitable.

It should perhaps be observed that the contributors did not want the fund in *Hobourn Aero* to be charitable, since if it had been the Charity Commissioners would have applied their contributions *cy près* (as in the problem) when the fund was wound up.

Disaster Appeals

These will be valid if for the relief of poverty, otherwise, like self-help organisations, will usually fail on the grounds of public benefit. Here again then, it is the public benefit test which is in effect defining what is charitable.

The organisers of such funds are left with two alternatives. They can apply a means test criterion to the receipt of benefit, in order to fall within the poverty head, but they may regard this as invidious. The other possibility, often favoured by fund organisers (e.g., Penlee lifeboat disaster fund in 1982), is to avoid the means test and draft the appeal in such a way as to avoid charitable status altogether. In that event, of course, the tax concessions will also be foregone. Perhaps more importantly, the *cy près* doctrine will not apply, and there may be difficulties over distribution of any surplus left over after the purposes have been achieved. It may even be that the Crown will take some or all of the surplus as *bona vacantia*, not perhaps the most fitting consequence of the altruism of the donors.

Problem Question

In October 1995 Britain's relations with the newly formed state of Aquarius deteriorate to a very low level. Aquarius is not in a position to do much about this, but it does have a spy satellite whose (geosynchronous) orbit takes it over Devon and Cornwall early every afternoon. Since, however, the orbit is from South East to North West, no other part of the United Kingdom is affected. It is rumoured that the satellite is capable of observing people on the ground at high resolution, and as a result the tourism industry is seriously adversely affected.

In his will Alpha, who died in December 1995 after leaving £10,000 to each of seven well-known charities, left a further £10,000 to 'The Spy Satellite Relief Fund, for relieving persons adversely affected by the spy satellite'. The Relief Fund is maintained by an unincorporated association (which has not applied for registration as a charity) whose purpose is, for up to five years, to compensate the hoteliers adversely affected by the satellite, and to further the interests of tourism in Devon and Cornwall by providing indoor facilities (which are believed to be invisible to the satellite). The fund's total receipts are £10 million. After only 10% is spent, the satellite is hit by a meteorite and destroyed.

Alpha's executors claim to recover 90% of the £10,000 they had paid to the association under cover of a letter setting out the exact wording of the bequest. The Charity Commissioners wish to apply the surplus, *cy près*.

Discuss.

We have observed that disaster appeal funds are usually non-charitable on the grounds of public benefit, unless they are for the relief of poverty. Exceptionally, however, there may be a sufficient public benefit, even to satisfy the requirements of the fourth head, as in *Re North Devon and West Somerset Relief Fund Trusts* [1953] 1 WLR 1260, where an appeal fund set up after the Lynmouth flood disaster of 1952 was held charitable as being for the benefit of the community at large. The public benefit test was satisfied, although the purposes were not confined to the relief of poverty, because the trust benefited an entire area. The purposes here are arguably comparable, in which case the Spy Satellite Relief Fund ought also to be charitable.

If the fund is not charitable, then, even if *Re West Sussex Constabulary's Widows, Children and Benevolent (1930) Fund* [1971] Ch 1 casts doubt on *Re Gillingham Bus Disaster Fund* [1958] Ch 300 as far as unidentifiable donations are concerned, since Alpha is identifiable, his executor ought to be able to claim on the basis of a resulting trust, as in *West Sussex* itself. This would require the donation to have been made on trust, rather than the more usual interpretation of an out-and-out gift to the existing members of the association, subject to their contractual rights and duties *inter se* (on which see the discussion of *Neville Estates v Madden* in chapter 5). However, since the fund's purposes are limited to five years' duration, the perpetuity problems discussed there, and further below, would not apply. An out-and-out gift to the members of the association would also require an unnatural construction of Alpha's intention, since he clearly never intended to confer any benefit on the members themselves.

If the purposes of the fund are charitable, then it could be argued that the same result obtains, since there is no more reason to suppose that Alpha has made an out-and-out gift to charity, than that, in the previous paragraph, he made an out-and-out gift to the members of the association; but the authorities are against this conclusion. In *Re Welsh Hospital (Netley) Fund* [1921] 1 Ch 655, Lawrence J held that anonymous contributors to a charitable fund must be taken to have parted with their money out-and-out, and that individual subscribers 'must be taken to have known that they were contributing to a general fund which was being raised in [that] manner ...'. The entire fund was therefore applied *cy près*, and a similar view was taken by Wynn-Parry J in *Re North Devon and West Somerset Relief Fund Trusts*. It might be objected that these decisions depend on some of the fund having been raised by anonymous contributions, whereas we have no information to that effect here. It might also be objected that the cases do not survive *Gillingham* and *West Sussex*, especially as, in the latter case, a distinction was expressly drawn between identified and anonymous contributions. However, in *Re Ulverston and District New Hospital Building Trusts* [1956] Ch 622, Jenkins LJ explained the earlier charity cases as straightforward cases of subsequent failure, since some of the money had already been spent, and that is obviously also the case here. If Jenkins LJ's views are correct, then regardless of whether there were also anonymous contributions to the fund, and whatever the effect of *Gillingham* and *West Sussex*, the entire fund would be applied *cy près*. It is to be noted that neither *Gillingham* nor *West Sussex* were charity cases, so that in neither case did the possibility of a *cy près* scheme arise; in *Gillingham* this was regarded by Harman J as a material factor, and a reason for distinguishing *Re Welsh Hospital (Netley) Fund*.

CY PRÈS

Problem Question

Mr Smith changes his name to the Rev. Why Taz Daz, and attracts a substantial religious following. A fund is organised to hire Wembley Stadium for a rally, to celebrate the Rev. Why Taz Daz's immortality, and to learn from his infinite wisdom. All contributions are obtained from anonymous street-collection boxes. Before any money has been paid out towards the hire, the Rev. Why Taz Daz is run over by a bus and killed.

The Charity Commissioners would like to apply the fund *cy près*. The Crown claims it as *bona vacantia*. The trustees of the fund would like to repay the money raised to the original donors.

Discuss.

The first question is whether this is a charitable purpose for the advancement of religion. The fact that this is not either Christian or any other accepted religion is not necessarily fatal, since as Cross J remarked in *Neville Estates* v *Madden* [1962] Ch 832, in which a trust for the members of the Catford Synagogue was held charitable: 'As between different religions the law stands neutral, but it assumes that any religion is at least likely to be better than none'. In *Bowman* v *Secular Society Ltd* [1917] AC 406, Lord Parker of Waddington thought that a trust for the purpose of any kind of monotheistic theism would be a good charitable trust.

In *Re South Place Ethical Society* [1980] 3 All ER 918, Dillon J said:

Religion, as I see it, is concerned with man's relations with God, and ethics are concerned with man's relations with man. The two are not the same, and are not made the same by sincere inquiry into the question, what is God?

Here, we have a man setting himself up as a god, and there is no direct authority covering this situation. However, there is a supernatural element, and this is not simply a matter of reason or ethics, so there is no obvious reason to hold the purposes non-charitable on these grounds.

It may also be argued, on the authority of *United Grand Lodge of Ancient Free & Accepted Masons of England and Wales* v *Holborn BC* [1957] 1 WLR 1080, that religion is not being advanced, but the function of the rally includes learning from Why Taz Daz's infinite wisdom, so, again, this is not necessarily a ground for holding these purposes non-charitable.

If the purposes are non-charitable, then (on the assumption that the purposes have failed) the question depends on whether you prefer the views expressed by Harman J in *Re Gillingham Bus Disaster Fund* [1958] Ch 300, or those expressed by Goff J in *Re West Sussex Constabulary's Widows, Children and Benevolent (1930) Fund* [1971] Ch 1. In the former case, there was a resulting trust for the donors, but in the latter case, Goff J took the view that by contributing anonymously the donors must be taken to have parted with their money out-and-out. Hence, they retained no interest in it, and on the failure of the purpose the money went to the Crown as *bona vacantia*.

If this is a charitable trust then there appears to be an initial failure of purpose, since (as in *Re Ulverston and District New Hospital Building Trusts* [1956] Ch 622) none of the money has been spent, although it may be possible to argue that the original purposes can still be carried out. An interesting question is whether the question of failure is decided by the pre-1960 law, or by s. 13 of the Charities Act 1993 (re-enacting the same s. 13 of the 1960 Act), subss. (1) and (2) of which provide:

(1)   Subject to subsection (2) below, the circumstances in which the original purposes of a charitable gift can be altered to allow the property given or part of it to be applied *cy près* shall be as follows —

(a)   where the original purposes, in whole or in part —

(i)   have been as far as may be fulfilled; or
(ii)   cannot be carried out, or not according to the directions given and to the spirit of the gift; or

(b)   where the original purposes provide a use for part only of the property available by virtue of the gift; or

(c)   where the property available by virtue of the gift and other property applicable for similar purposes can be more effectively used in conjunction, and to that end can suitably, regard being had to the spirit of the gift, be made applicable to common purposes; or

(d)   where the original purposes were laid down by reference to an area which then was but has since ceased to be a unit for some other purpose, or by reference to a class of persons or to an area which has for any reason since ceased to be suitable, regard being had to the spirit of the gift, or to be practical in administering the gift; or

(e)   where the original purposes, in whole or in part, have, since they were laid down, —

(i)   been adequately provided for by other means; or
(ii)   ceased, as being useless or harmful to the community or for other reasons, to be in law charitable; or
(iii)   ceased in any other way to provide a suitable and effective method of using the property available by virtue of the gift, regard being had to the spirit of the gift.

(2)   Subsection (1) above shall not affect the conditions which must be satisfied in order that property given for charitable purposes may be applied *cy près* except in so far as those conditions require a failure of the original purposes.

Subheads (a) to (e) of subs. (1) will generally be wider than the pre-1960 definition of failure, and apparently supersede it; in *Oldham Borough Council v Attorney-General* [1993] 2 All ER 432, Dillon LJ took the view that the s. 13 heads were exhaustive:

Broadly, the effect of that section is that an alteration of the 'original purposes' of a charitable gift can only be authorised by a scheme for the *cy près* application of the trust property and such a scheme can only be made in the circumstances set out in subheads (a) to (e) of subsection (1) of section 13.

Section 13 defines failure and arguably applies to define initial as well as subsequent failure. However, the section begins by talking of 'the original purposes of a charitable gift', which supposes that a charitable gift has taken place. This will not be true in many cases of initial failure and, arguably, has not done so here. In that case the question of whether there has been a failure will be determined on the basis of the pre-1960 law.

If there has been a failure, then, because the donors are anonymous, it might be thought that this is a classic situation to which s. 14 of the Charities Act 1993 applies, to apply the fund *cy près*. However, a close reading of the section reveals that this may not be the case. Consider the following essay question.

Essay Question

What, if anything, is the effect of Charities Act 1993, s. 14 (re-enacting Charities Act 1960)? Do you agree with David Wilson [1983] Conv 40 at 49 that it is 'a dead letter of English law'?

Subsections (1) and (3) of s. 14 provide:

(1)   Property given for specific charitable purposes which fail shall be applicable *cy près* as if given for charitable purposes generally, where it belongs —

(a)   to a donor who after —

(i)   the prescribed advertisements and inquiries have been published and made, and

(ii)   the prescribed period beginning with the publication of those advertisements has expired,

cannot be identified or cannot be found; or

(b)   to a donor who has executed a disclaimer in the precribed form of his right to have the property returned.

...

(3)   For the purposes of this section property shall be conclusively presumed (without any advertisement or inquiry) to belong to donors who cannot be identified, in so far as it consists —

(a)   of the proceeds of cash collections made by means of collecting boxes or by other means not adapted for distinguishing one gift from another; or
(b)   of the proceeds of any lottery, competition, entertainment, sale or similar money-raising activity, after allowing for property given to provide prizes or articles for sale or otherwise to enable the activity to be undertaken.

This appears, at first sight, to apply clearly to the present problem, since property appears to have been given for specific purposes which fail, whereas if it had been given for charitable purposes generally (as provided by s. 14(1)), then a *cy près* scheme would have been ordered. However, s. 14(1) applies only where the property belongs to a donor. However, if Goff J was correct in *Re West Sussex Constabulary's Widows, Children and Benevolent (1930) Fund* [1971] Ch 1, doubting Harman J in *Re Gillingham Bus Disaster Fund* [1958] Ch 300, anonymous contributors do not intend to retain any interest in the property, and hence, s. 14 is never triggered. It might be thought that the presumption in s. 14(3) cures the problem, but arguably, the presumption goes only to the question of identification, rather than whether the property also 'belongs to donors'. Indeed, it is natural to read s. 14(3) as applying to identification only. In that case, the property will, as in *West Sussex*, still go to the Crown as *bona vacantia*, and s. 14 will make no difference: see further the article by David Wilson referred to in the question.

If, on the other hand, any of the fund had actually been applied towards the charitable purpose, then, on Jenkins LJ's views (above) in *Re Ulverston and District New Hospital Building Trusts* [1956] Ch 622, the failure would be a subsequent failure, and a *cy près* scheme would be ordered. In that case, there would be no need for s. 14.

POLITICAL OBJECTS

Problem Question

The North Cardiff Anti-Vivisection Society has purposes similar to the Natonal Anti-Vivisection Society. Beta has been a member for five years and Gamma for 10. In 1985, Alpha gratuitously transferred shares he held in ICI plc to the officers of the North Cardiff Anti-Vivisection Society, for the purposes of the society and for a 21-year period, so that it could use the dividends to benefit the society. In 1996, vivisection is abolished in the United Kingdom.

ANSWER ALL PARTS

(i)   Consider the extent to which, if at all, Alpha, Beta and Gamma have interests in the North Cardiff Anti-Vivisection Society's surplus funds.
(ii)   Would your answer be different if Alpha's gift had been for an 80-year period?
(iii)   Would your answer be different if Alpha's gift had been for an unlimited period?

It is fairly clear that the objects of the North Cardiff Anti-Vivisection Society are not charitable, following the decision of the House of Lords in *National Anti-Vivisection Society* v *Inland Revenue Commissioners* [1948] AC 31. The National Anti-Vivisection Society was not a charity within the fourth head, because its purposes were not beneficial for the community (the special commissioners for income tax having found that any assumed public benefit in the advancement of morals was outweighed by a detriment to medical science and research); also, its objects (*necessarily* requiring an alteration in the law) were political. Since the North Cardiff Anti-Vivisection Society has purposes similar to the National Anti-Vivisection Society, it may be assumed that it is also a non-charitable unincorporated association.

That being so, the distribution of its funds raises similar issues to those considered at the end of chapter 5. If *Neville Estates* applies, then, of course, the members of the association at the time of dissolution are entitled to the whole of the fund, but here we are specifically invited to consider an alternative trust solution, since, if the gift is limited to 21 years, the perpetuity problems considered at the end of chapter 5 do not arise. There is no reason, therefore, why Alpha should not have set up a *Denley*-type trust, in which case as an identifiable donor he ought to be entitled to a resulting trust of the shares.

Under s. 1 of the Perpetuities and Accumulations Act 1964, it is possible to stipulate an 80-year perpetuity period, as in part (ii) of this question, but only for dispositions, which include (under s. 15(2)) conferring of equitable interests in property, but exclude (under s. 15(4)) purpose trusts. The 80-year period can only be specified, therefore, if the *Denley*-type trust confers full beneficial interests on the members for the time being, but, arguably, not if the interests thereby conferred are less than full beneficial interests: see further the discussion of *Denley* in chapter 5.

If the gift had been for an unlimited period, as in part (iii) of the question, then it could normally take effect only on the contractual basis discussed in chapter 5, although it might be argued that the wait-and-see provisions of s. 3 of the 1964 Act can still enable it to take effect as a *Denley*-type trust. I would suggest, however, that where the courts can construe a gift either on the contractual basis which is known to work, or on the basis of a trust where the effect of the disposition will only be finally determined at some unknown future date, they will prefer the former construction to the latter. In the absence of clear words of trust, therefore, I would suggest that Alpha's gift in part (iii) takes effect as an out-and-out disposition of the shares to the existing members of the association, subject to their contractual rights and duties *inter se*, as in *Neville Estates* v *Madden*.

SUGGESTED ADDITIONAL READING

For general background, see:

• *Charities: A Framework for the Future* (HMSO, May 1989).

On s. 14 of the Charities Act, see:

• David Wilson [1983] Conv 40.

10 VARIATION OF TRUSTS

This is a relatively self-contained area which frequently crops up in examinations. It is possible to effect a variation without using the Variation of Trusts Act 1958, but the inherent jurisdiction and other statutory powers are fairly limited. In any case, the most interesting areas conceptually concern the 1958 Act, so we shall concentrate on that in this chapter.

VARIATION OF TRUSTS ACT 1958

The main conceptual areas likely to be covered in an exam are on whose behalf the court may approve a variation, and the question of what constitutes a benefit, especially where there is an element of risk. First, however, we shall consider what was the aim of the 1958 Act, and why it was thought to be desirable.

Policy behind the 1958 Act

The main reason for wishing to vary trusts today is usually to reduce liability to taxation. Equity does not generally, however, in the absence of an express power to vary the trust, allow the trustees to recast its terms. Until recent statutory reforms, therefore, and in particular the 1958 Act, powers to vary have been extremely limited, especially where tax planning is the motive.

There are nevertheless some possibilities apart from the 1958 Act. In the absence of an express power, it may be possible to invoke the rule in *Saunders v Vautier* (1841) 10 LJ Ch 354. Collectively, the beneficiaries, so long as they are all adult, *sui juris* and between them entitled to the entirety of the trust property, can bring the trust to an end and resettle the property on any terms they wish. They can also collectively consent to any act by the trustees which has the effect of varying the terms of the trust.

It is very important, however, to appreciate that the *Saunders* v *Vautier* doctrine depends on the beneficiaries all being collectively entitled, and able to consent. If some of the beneficiaries are infants, or if the settlement creates any interests in favour of persons who are not yet born or ascertained, variation of the trust upon this basis will not be possible. This is a serious limitation when dealing with family settlements of the usual type, which almost invariably give interests to such persons (termed non *sui juris* persons).

Even where not all the beneficiaries are adult and *sui juris* the courts will occasionally permit a variation of trust under their inherent jurisdiction. These circumstances are very limited, but it has long been recognised that the court may, in the case of necessity, permit the trustees to take measures not authorised by the trust instrument.

In *Chapman* v *Chapman* [1954] AC 429, the House of Lords indicated that this inherent jurisdiction is narrow, encompassing for the most part only emergency and salvage. It is confined to cases where some act of salvage is urgently required, such as the mortgage of an infant's property in order to raise money for vital repairs. It does not cover other contingencies not foreseen and provided for by the settlor, of which the most pertinent example would be changes in the basis of tax liability.

The court can also approve a compromise of some dispute regarding the beneficial entitlements on behalf of infant or future beneficiaries. Arguably, this is not a case of genuine variation of the trust, since the House of Lords in *Chapman* v *Chapman* held that the jurisdiction was confined to instances where a genuine element of dispute exists, i.e., where the terms of trust are genuinely unclear.

There are also statutory powers to vary trusts, apart from the 1958 Act, but these are limited to specified situations. The 1958 Act was important because it was the first provision of general application allowing variation of trusts for tax-avoidance purposes, even where not all the beneficiaries were adult and *sui juris*. The Act follows on the recommendations of the Law Reform Committee, Sixth Report (Court's Power to Sanction Variations of Trusts) (Cmnd 310). Whatever political views one holds about tax-avoidance schemes, it can at least be argued that infants and the unborn, for example, should not be deprived *for that reason* of the advantages which their adult counterparts could obtain on *Saunders* v *Vauier* principles; nor should their incapacity prevent the opportunity of gain to the trust as a whole.

The main application of the Variation of Trusts Act 1958 has been to vary the beneficial interests for tax-saving purposes, and this has been assumed to be its natural sphere of operation.

The Operation of the Act (in General Terms)

You ought to be aware of the general operation of the Variation of Trusts Act 1958, because essay questions will often address themselves to it.

Under s. 1(1) of the Act, the court has discretion to approve, on behalf of the following categories of person, any arrangement varying or revoking all or any of the trusts, or enlarging the trustees' powers of management and administration over the property subject to the trusts:

(a) any person having, directly or indirectly, an interest, whether vested or contingent, under the trusts who by reason of infancy or other incapacity is incapable of assenting [i.e., infants or people mentally incapacitated], or

(b) any person (whether ascertained or not) who may become entitled, directly or indirectly, to an interest under the trusts as being at a future date or on the happening of a future event a person of any specified description or a member of any specified class of persons, so however that this paragraph shall not include any person who would be of that description, or a member of that class, as the case may be, if the said date had fallen or the said event had happened at the date of the application to the court [in effect, the paragraph includes people who have a mere expectation of benefiting under the trusts, but those with interests, whether vested or contingent, should consent on their own behalf], or

(c) any person unborn, or

(d) any person in respect of any discretionary interest of his under protective trusts where the interest of the principal beneficiary has not failed or determined.

Proposals to vary the beneficial interests under a trust may thus be approved, provided (except in the case of para. (d) persons) that the court is satisfied that such variation will be for the benefit of those persons on behalf of whom approval is given.

In deciding whether to approve a proposed settlement, the court will consider the arrangement as a whole, since it is the arrangement which has to be approved, and not just those aspects of it which happen to affect a person on whose behalf the court is being asked to consent.

The application should be made by a beneficiary, preferably by the person currently receiving the income, but the settlor may also apply, and as a last resort the trustees may apply if no one else will apply and the variation is in the interests of the beneficiaries. Otherwise, it is undesirable for trustees to apply, as their position as applicant may conflict with their impartial duty to guard the interests of the beneficiaries. The settlor, if living, and all the beneficiaries, including minors, should be made parties, special attention being paid to ensure proper representation for minors and the unborn.

According to Megarry J in *Re Ball's Settlement* [1968] 1 WLR 899, the courts will not approve a proposal for a total resettlement which alters completely the substratum of the trust. This is a question of substance not form, and if Megarry J is correct the courts' jurisdiction does not therefore extend to the approval of such proposals at all.

Persons on whose Behalf the Court may Give its Approval

The way in which the Variation of Trusts Act 1958 works is to allow the court to give consent on behalf of non *sui juris* beneficiaries, but the principles underlying the rule in *Saunders* v *Vautier* were preserved by the Act, inasmuch as the court will not provide a consent which ought properly to be sought from an ascertainable adult, *sui juris* beneficiary. Hence the limits placed on s. 1(1)(b).

The difficulty with para. (b), which limits the discretion of the courts, arises with interests which are very remote, such as interests in default of appointment, or in the event of a failure of the trust. There is no problem over, for example, potential future spouses, since they clearly have a mere expectation of succeeding. They clearly come within para. (b), and the court can consent on their behalf. But if somebody is named in the instrument as having a contingent interest, however unlikely that contingency is to arise, the court cannot consent on their behalf. They must consent themselves to any variation.

This can seriously limit the scope of the 1958 Act, and *a fortiori* the discretion of the courts. For example, in *Re Suffert's Settlement* [1976] Ch 1, the court could not consent on behalf of a cousin who benefited only if Miss Suffert died without issue, and even then subject to a general testamentary power of appointment. Other examples are *Re Moncrieff's ST* [1962] 1 WLR 134, and *Knocker* v *Youle* [1986] 1 WLR 934. In the latter case the court could not consent on behalf of sisters who would benefit only in the event of failure or determination of the trust, and Warner J felt constrained to adopt a fairly literal interpretation of the Act.

What is Benefit?

It is not possible to state categorically what the court will regard as benefit, except that it will adopt the test of what a reasonable *sui juris* adult beneficiary would have done in the circumstances.

Financial benefit is clearly included, and most tax-saving schemes will satisfy the requirement, since such saving preserves the total quantum of property available for distribution among the beneficiaries.

In assessing financial benefit, the court may have to balance short-term against long-term factors, and to take account of the character of the persons on whose behalf approval is sought. In *Re Towler's ST* [1964] Ch 158, Wilberforce J was prepared to postpone the vesting of capital to which a beneficiary was soon to become entitled, upon evidence that she was likely to deal with it imprudently. In *Re Steed's WT* [1960] Ch 407, the proposed scheme was for the elimination of the protective element in a trust relating to land. The principal beneficiary, who was a life tenant (but not *sui juris* because of the protective element), wanted a variation such that the trustees held the property on trust for herself absolutely. Clearly this was in theory to her financial advantage, but evidence suggested that advantage would in fact be taken of the life tenant's good nature by the very persons against whose importuning the settlor had meant to protect her, and the Court of Appeal refused its consent.

It may be wondered why the court needed to be satisfied of a benefit in this case, since as noted above, there is no express statutory requirement of benefit for para. (d) persons. It is here that it should be remembered, however, that once it is clear that the court has jurisdiction, it has an unfettered discretion to exercise its powers under the Act *'if it thinks fit'*. In *Re Steed* the Court of Appeal (commenting that the Variation of Trusts Act 1958 conferred upon the courts a 'very wide, and indeed, revolutionary discretion') refused its consent even in a para. (d) case, where it thought no benefit was shown. In effect, whereas the court obviously cannot approve a variation except where the Act so provides, it has an apparently unlimited discretion to *refuse* its approval where it is given jurisdiction under the Act.

Though it will be rare for the court to look beyond the financial advantages contained in the proposed arrangement, the unfettered discretion given by the Act to the courts can lead them to refuse a variation where there is a clear financial benefit. In *Re Weston's Settlements* [1969] 1 Ch 223, the Court of Appeal refused to approve a scheme which would have removed the trusts to a tax haven (Jersey), where the family had moved three months previously, on the ground that the moral and social benefits of an English upbringing were not outweighed by the tax savings to be enjoyed by the infant beneficiaries. Harman LJ said that 'this is an essay in tax avoidance naked and unashamed', and Lord Denning MR noted (at p. 223) that:

> There are many things in life more worthwhile than money. One of these things is to be brought up in this our England, which is still 'the envy of less happier lands'. I do not believe it is for the benefit of children to be uprooted from England and transported to another country simply to avoid tax ... Many a child has been ruined by being given too much. The avoidance of tax may be lawful but it is not yet a virtue.

Re Weston is perhaps atypical, and the court will not always refuse approval to the removal of a trust from the jurisdiction. It will depend on the circumstances. In *Re Windeatt's WT* [1969] 1 WLR 692, a similar scheme was approved by Pennycuick J, but there the family had already been in Jersey for 19 years and the children had been born there: there was no question of uprooting them. Similarly, in *Re Seale's Marriage Settlement* [1961] Ch 574, Buckley J approved a scheme removing the trusts to Canada, to which country again the family had moved many years previously, with no thought of tax avoidance, and had brought up the children as Canadians.

In reality, the use of the 1958 Act to export trusts is quite common, but *Re Weston* shows that all circumstances will be taken into account, and that the existence of a clear financial benefit will not necessarily be conclusive.

Another possibility, included for the sake of completeness, is that some beneficiaries will benefit at the expense of others. An example is *Re Remnant's ST* [1970] Ch 560, where Pennycuick J approved the deletion of a forfeiture clause in respect of children who became Roman Catholics. Some of the children were Protestant and others Roman Catholic, but the court deleted the clause on policy grounds, as being liable to cause serious dissension within the family, although this was clearly to the disadvantage of the Protestant children. The settlor's intentions were also not considered conclusive (indeed, they were overridden).

The courts may go further and approve schemes where there is only a positive disadvantage in material terms. In *Re CL* [1969] 1 Ch 587, the Court of Protection held that there was a benefit to an elderly mental patient in giving up, in return for no consideration, her life interests for the benefit of adopted daughters. The lady's needs were otherwise amply provided for, and the court, in approving the arrangement, was acting as she herself would have done, had she been able to appreciate her family responsibilities.

There are two likely areas upon which examiners might concentrate. One is where no clear financial benefit can be shown, or, if it can, the benefit is postponed into the far future. The second is where, although there might be a clear benefit, there is no certainty of any benefit at all, and indeed a risk of loss.

Non-financial Benefits, and Risks

The following question appeared on a recent examination paper:

The trustees of a testamentary trust, whose investment clause is no wider than the provisions of the Trustee Investment Act 1961, seek a variation under the Variation of Trusts Act 1958. The testator, who died in 1965, was a well-known environmentalist, and the beneficiaries include infants and people who are mentally incapacitated. The variation sought is to allow the trustees to invest a large proportion of the trust capital in Ecological Enterprises Ltd, and Dam for the Future Ltd. Neither investment comes within the terms of the Trustee Investment Act 1961.

In purely financial terms, Ecological Enterprises Ltd do not offer a more attractive rate of return, nor any greater security, than the present investments (authorised by the 1961 Act). The trustees wish to invest in Ecological Enterprises Ltd primarily on ideological (i.e., green) grounds, but would take the view that the investment would make the beneficiaries feel better, and would be in line with the testator's wishes.

Dam for the Future Ltd plan to build a dam across the Bristol Channel to produce wave-powered electricity. They offer an unusually high rate of return, but because of the nature of the project the return is expected only in the very long term (say 30 years). In the short term the investment is expected to perform very badly. While it is likely that most of the infant beneficiaries will survive long enough to see a substantial return, the same cannot be said of those beneficiaries who are mentally incapacitated.

Discuss.

The first point to notice about this question is that the variation sought will extend the trustees' powers of investment beyond those provided by the Trustee Investment Act 1961. Since the 1961 Act was a later provision than the Variation of Trusts Act, it might be thought that its provisions were intended to be conclusive on questions on investment, and that variations would not be permitted under the 1958 Act, to extend the trustees' powers of investment beyond those provided by the 1961 Act.

In *Trustees of the British Museum* v *Attorney-General* [1984] 1 WLR 418, however, Sir Robert Megarry V-C took the view that the powers conferred by the Trustee Investments Act 1961 were becoming outdated, and that the effects of inflation and the character of the trust may amount to special circumstances in which it would be proper to give approval under the 1958 Act. The arguments in that case were all of an economic nature, however, essentially that the trustees could make more money if their investment powers were extended. The decision was based on the changes of investment pattern, including the movement from fixed interest investments to investments in equities and property, that had occurred between 1961 and 1983. In the case, at least, of Ecological Enterprises Ltd, no similar arguments can be advanced here, and it is at least arguable that the principles in *Trustees of the British Museum* do not apply to that type of investment.

So far as Dam for the Future is concerned, arguments of a financial nature could be advanced. Even so, it does not follow that the principles in *Trustees of the British Museum* will necessarily apply, since Sir Robert Megarry V-C's judgment is in quite restricted terms. At the time of the case, investing in equities was relatively risk-free, and there had been a more or less continuous bull market for some eight years. That is not the case today. Sir Robert Megarry V-C also said:

The size of the fund may be very material. A fund that is very large may well justify a latitude of investment that would be denied to a more modest fund; for the spread of investment possible for a larger fund may justify the greater risk that wider powers will permit to be taken.

It is by no means clear, therefore, that a variation beyond the terms of the 1961 Act will necessarily apply here.

This problem also shows the advantage of reading the case fairly closely. Many textbooks do not analyse *Trustees of the British Museum* in much detail, and it would be very easy to fall into the trap of assuming that it covers the present situation, whereas the close reading of the judgment makes the limitations of the case clear.

The other issues in the problem have to some extent already been covered. So far as Ecological Enterprises Ltd is concerned, the variation offers no financial advantage, but may offer moral benefits. Obviously, you are invited to consider *Re Weston's Settlements* [1969] 1 Ch 223, discussed above, which was actually the reverse situation: there was a financial advantage, but a moral disadvantage. You might also mention *Re CL* [1969] 1 Ch 587, above, where in a different context financial benefits were not regarded as conclusive.

So far as Dam for the Future is concerned, there may well be a financial benefit, but it is very risky. Sometimes, a proposed arrangement may involve some element of risk to the beneficiary for whom the court is asked to consent. An element of risk will not prevent the court from approving the arrangement, if the risk is one which an adult beneficiary would be prepared to take. Such a test was applied by Dankwerts J in *Re Cohen's WT* [1959] 1 WLR 865.

In *Re Robinson's ST* [1976] 1 WLR 806, the fund was held on trust for the plaintiff for her life, with remainders over to her children, one of whom was under 21 (the age of majority at the time). The plaintiff was 55 and expected to live for many years. The variation proposed was to divide up the fund, giving the plaintiff an immediate capital share of 52% (the actuarial capitalised value of her share), the children dividing the balance in equal shares. The children who got their share immediately, and those who were over 21 consented to the variation. The court was asked to approve variation on behalf of Nicola (who was 17).

Before the introduction of Capital Transfer Tax in 1975, division of the fund in this way, by giving the children their interests immediately rather than on the death of the life tenant, was almost certain to reduce liability to estate duty, because at that time there was no liability to estate duty on any advance made more than seven years before the death of the life tenant. The same is true today under inheritance tax. However, for a short period following the

Finance Act 1975, which introduced Capital Transfer Tax, all *inter vivos* gifts were also taxable, albeit that liability was lower so long as the transfer was made more than three years before the death of the life tenant.

At the time of *Re Robinson's ST*, therefore, the division would not necessarily have favoured Nicola. The transfer would have been taxed immediately, so that the value of the fund would be reduced. On the other hand, Nicola would get her share immediately, and not have to wait for the death of her mother. Whether this would be to her benefit or not would depend entirely on how long her mother was likely to live. If she died immediately, Nicola's share would be less than she would have received under the unvaried trust, since tax would have been paid on it. It was calculated, however, that, given the mother's life expectancy, the deficiency would be made up in income on her share between the date of the variation and her mother's death.

Templeman J took the view that the court should require evidence that the infant would at least not be materially worse off as a result of the variation. He adopted as the test whether an adult beneficiary would have been prepared to take the risk: a 'broad' view might be taken, but not a 'galloping, gambling view'. The arrangement was approved subject to a policy of insurance to protect the infant's interests.

A different type of case was *Re Holt's Settlement* [1969] 1 Ch 100. The trust provided for a life interest of personal property for Mrs Wilson, and then to her children at 21 in equal shares. The variation proposed was that Mrs Wilson should surrender the income of one-half of her life interest to the fund, but another effect of the proposed variation was to postpone the vesting of the children's interests until 30. The court was asked to approve the variation on behalf of Mrs Wilson's three children who were 10, 7, and 6.

The surrender of the income (the real purpose of which was to reduce Mrs Wilson's liability to surtax) was also clearly to the advantage of the children, since the value of the trust property would be increased. However, the postponement to 30 (on the grounds that it would be undesirable for Mrs Wilson's children to receive a large income from 21) was clearly to their disadvantage. Megarry J nevertheless approved the variation as a whole, on the same test adopted in *Re Robinson*.

Benefit Must Be To Individuals, Not Just Class as a Whole

Another difficulty with the Dam for the Future Ltd investment in the problem question is that some of the beneficiaries who are mentally incapacitated would seem to stand only to lose from the investment, since they would not be expected to live long enough to benefit from the long-term return, and would only suffer from the likely poor short-term performance of the investment.

The 1958 Act requires, in general, that the court must be satisfied that the arrangement will be for the benefit of the persons for whom it is consenting. Stamp J took the view in Re Cohen's ST [1965] 1 WLR 1229 that the benefit must be to those persons considered as individuals, and not merely as members of a class. It follows that if only one member of the class can be envisaged who cannot possibly benefit from the proposed variation, even if the class as a whole will benefit, the court will refuse its consent. This was in fact the outcome in Re Cohen's ST, and would probably be fatal to the second investment in this problem.

Re Cohen's ST is a very interesting case in its own right, and the following recent exam question is based around it:

Under a settlement made in 1940, a large fund was left to Alison for her life, and then to her grandchildren living on her death. Alison was born in 1915, and has a number of grandchildren, some of whom are very young. Consider whether the court will approve the following ALTERNATIVE variations under the Variation of Trusts Act 1958.

ANSWER BOTH PARTS:

(i)   Under the Capital Acceleration Act 1992, a heavy tax is imposed on all capital transfers made after 31 July 2005. A variation is sought substituting for Alison's death 31 July 2005 (or Alison's death, whichever is the earlier), as the date both for ascertaining the grandchildren to take, and for distribution of the fund.

AND

(ii) Under the Capital Stultification Act 1992, a heavy tax is imposed on all capital transfers made before 1 July 2005. A variation is sought postponing distribution of the fund until 1 August 2005 (or Alison's death, whichever is the later), the class being ascertained on Alison's death.

In both parts of the problem the proposed variation appears to offer a clear financial benefit (avoidance of a heavy tax). The problem in part (i) is this, however. Suppose Alison is still alive on 31 July 2005, and a grandchild is born after 31 July 2005, but before Alison's death. The chances of this happening must be fairly low, since by 2005 Alison will be 90 years old, and it may well be thought that the class of unborn grandchildren, as a whole, might be prepared to take the risk of Alison living that long, and having further grandchildren before she dies. Weighed against the substantial tax advantages of the proposed variation should Alison live to be 90, any reasonable unborn grandchild may well be prepared to take the risk.

The problem is that it is not permissible only to consider the position of the class as a whole. If an individual grandchild was born after 31 July 2005, but before Alison's death, then under the proposed variation, he or she would lose his or her entire interest. That individual would clearly not consent, since he or she would have no conceivable benefit, and that will be fatal to the proposed variation: indeed, *Cohen* itself was just such a case as this, and Stamp J refused his consent. It was not enough that the proposed variation would benefit the class as a whole, if it were possible to envisage a single individual who could not possibly benefit.

So far as the infants are concerned, the position is different (as it was in *Cohen* itself). They all stand to gain from the tax advantages of the proposed variation. They can only lose under the variation if grandchildren are born after 31 July 2005, but before Alison's death, since then their share of the fund will be reduced. Even then, a large number of grandchildren would probably have to be born at that time, in order to reduce their interest more than the imposition of the heavy tax on the unvaried trust. The equation is the same for all of them, and each as reasonable individuals would probably consent.

The variation will fail overall, however, because of the possibility, admittedly remote, that there will be persons unborn who would stand only to lose from the variation.

It might be thought that the second part of the question is essentially similar, but it is not. The crucial difference here is that the class is ascertained on Alison's death, even though the date of distribution is postponed should Alison die before 2005. Even if Alison dies in 1993, the class of beneficiaries who will take will be the same, whether the trust is varied or not. It might be thought that a beneficiary who dies in that event, between 1993 and 2005, must lose out, but in fact he or she still keeps the interest, and it will be added to his or her estate. The only evaluation that each beneficiary has to make in such a case is whether the delay outweighs the tax advantages. That is to be decided simply on the principles of *Re Robinson's ST*, above.

It follows that the reasoning in *Cohen* applies only when the date of *vesting in interest* (or in other words the date on closing the class) is altered, and does not apply merely to alterations in *vesting in possession*.

In *Re Holt's Settlement* [1969] 1 Ch 100 (see above), the settlement was in essence that Mrs Wilson gave up part of her income from the fund (so increasing the size of the fund), but vesting of the children's interest in possession would be postponed. If a child was born the year after the variation, and his mother died very soon afterwards, that child could not possibly benefit. The benefit from Mrs Wilson surrendering part of her income under the trust would be minimal if Mrs Wilson died soon after the birth, whereas the postponement would operate entirely to his or her disadvantage. *Cohen* was distinguished, however, because here two chances had to occur: that of the unborn person being born next year, and secondly, that child having been born (and thus become a legal entity), his or her mother dying shortly afterwards. The first chance could be disregarded on *Cohen* principles, but not the second. Both were independently unlikely possibilities, so approval for the scheme was given. Even once the theoretical unborn child had been born, he or she would still have been well advised to agree to the variation, and accept the slight risk of his or her mother dying shortly afterwards.

11 PERSONAL EQUITABLE REMEDIES

The Law Society Foundation definition for equity and trusts places considerable emphasis on remedies. The primary remedy at common law is damages, which are available as of right, whereas equity developed its own range of remedies, which are discretionary. Equitable remedies include account of profits and rescission (e.g., for a misrepresentation inducing entry into a contract). However, the most important equitable remedies are specific performance and injunctions, and the layout of this chapter is to begin by outlining the various types of injunction, and then to consider an essay question on specific performance.

INJUNCTIONS

Prohibitory and Mandatory Injunctions

A *prohibitory* injunction, the most common type, simply orders the defendant to refrain or desist from doing something. A *mandatory* injunction orders the defendant to do some positive act, such as demolishing a building. A mandatory injunction is very like specific performance, but, whereas specific performance usually arises out of contract, a mandatory injunction usually arises out of tort. However, it could be used to force the defendant to undo something which he has done in breach of contract.

Mandatory injunctions are uncommon, and will not be issued when damages would be an adequate remedy, or when the court would be required to exercise constant supervision. Mandatory injunctions will only be issued when it is possible to frame the order very precisely.

Quia Timet *Injunctions*

'*Quia timet*' means 'because he fears', and this type of injunction may be granted if the plaintiff can show that there is a very real danger of substantial damage being done to his interests. The aim is to forestall the defendant from committing a wrong, and since, by definition, the defendant has not yet done anything unlawful, the plaintiff must make out a strong case, described in *A-G v Nottingham Co.* [1904] 1 Ch 673 as 'a strong probability almost amounting to moral certainty' of the threatened or apprehended infringement of the plaintiff's rights.

This type of injunction is rare, and its refusal will not debar the plaintiff from obtaining an injunction if the defendant actually goes ahead and commits the wrong.

Interlocutory Injunctions

High Court cases can take many months to come to court; therefore, courts can, through a swift procedure, grant interlocutory injunctions pending trial. These have the same effect as any other injunction, except that they last only until the full hearing.

If an injunction is not eventually granted at the final trial the defendant may have been restrained from doing something he was perfectly entitled to do. Before 1975 it was thought that an applicant for an interlocutory injunction therefore had to prove not only that there was a serious question to be tried, but also that he had a strong prima facie case and that the balance of convenience was in favour of the grant of the remedy. The last point was likely to be satisfied if, for example, the plaintiff was likely to suffer irreparable damage which could not be adequately compensated by an award of damages were the defendant's actions allowed to continue until the full hearing. For example, any action which seriously affected a plaintiff's ability to trade would qualify on balance of convenience.

In *American Cyanamid Co.* v *Ethicon Ltd* [1975] AC 396, however, the matter was reviewed by the House of Lords and the requirements were relaxed. Lord Diplock noted (at pp. 407–408) that the whole point of the procedure was to allow a remedy to be granted *before* the full trial of the main issues:

> It is no part of the court's function at this stage of the litigation to try to resolve conflicts of evidence on affidavit as to facts on which the claims of either party may ultimately depend, nor to decide difficult questions of law which call for detailed argument and mature considerations. These are matters to be dealt with at the trial. One of the reasons for the introduction of the practice of requiring an undertaking as to damages on the grant of an interlocutory injunction was that 'it aided the court in doing that which

was its great object, *viz* abstaining from expressing any opinion on the merits of the case until the hearing' (*Wakefield* v *Duke of Buccleuch* (1865) 12 LT 628, 629).

Yet the necessity to show a strong prima facie case meant that many of the main issues had to be decided at the interlocutory state. Lord Diplock also noted that if an interlocutory injunction is wrongly granted the defendant may have a remedy at the full trial, because the plaintiff will normally be required to give an undertaking as to damages to cover the eventuality. Except in exceptional circumstances, therefore (which remain undefined), there is no longer any requirement that the plaintiff must show a strong prima facie case. He only has to show that there is a serious question to be tried, although the balance of convenience test remains as before. In general, therefore, the merits of the case are not examined at the interlocutory stage.

Sometimes, however, the interlocutory stage is decisive, because the reality of the situation is that by the time of the full trial there will be nothing left to decide. Thus, for example, where an employer seeks to restrain strike action on the ground that it is tortious, it is unlikely that the industrial dispute will remain live until the full trial, so that success at the interlocutory stage is usually decisive. Yet it became clear as early as the decision of the Court of Appeal in *Hubbard* v *Pitt* [1976] 1 QB 142 that industrial disputes would not be treated as among the exceptional cases envisaged by Lord Diplock in *American Cyanamid*. However, in order to make the trade dispute immunities effective (which were, in practice, more extensive then than they are now), legislation now contained in the Trade Union and Labour Relations (Consolidation) Act 1992, s. 221(2), provided that where a defendant claimed a trade dispute immunity the court was obliged, in deciding whether or not to grant the interlocutory remedy, to consider the likelihood of a defence based upon that immunity succeeding at the full trial.

Since that legislation, which originated in the Employment Protection Act 1975, the House of Lords has held that in cases where the interlocutory stage will, in reality, be decisive, the merits of the case may become a factor to be weighed up in assessing the balance of convenience. In *NWL Ltd* v *Woods* [1979] 1 WLR 1294, an interlocutory injunction was sought restraining industrial action. Lord Diplock noted (at p. 625) that *American Cyanamid*:

... was not dealing with a case in which the grant or refusal of an injunction at that stage would, in effect, dispose of the action finally in favour of whichever party was successful in the application, because there would be nothing left on which it was in the unsuccessful party's interest to proceed to trial.

Cases of this kind are exceptional, but when they do occur they bring into the balance of convenience an important additional element ... the degree of likelihood that the plaintiff would have succeeded in establishing his right to an injunction if the action had gone to a trial is a factor to be brought into the balance [of convenience] by the judge in weighing the risks that injustice may result from his deciding the application one way rather than the other.

The Court of Appeal applied these remarks in *Lansing Linde Ltd* v *Kerr* [1991] 1 WLR 251, upholding a judge's refusal to grant an interlocutory injunction to restrain a former employee from working for a competitor in alleged contravention of a restraint of trade clause in his contract of employment. The trial of the action was unlikely to occur until the period of restraint would have expired or almost expired, and the Court of Appeal held that the judge had been correct, in these circumstances, in assessing the balance of convenience, to take account of the strength of the plaintiff's claim. The case should be contrasted with *Lawrence David Ltd* v *Ashton* [1991] 1 All ER 385, where the action was appropriate for a speedy trial, so that the (two-year) period of restraint would still have a significant time left to run, even after the full trial. In such cases, the Court of Appeal held that it is not open to the judge to consider the merits at the interlocutory stage, but that *American Cyanamid* should be applied directly. However, it should not be assumed that *Lansing Linde Ltd* v *Kerr* is limited to the case where there will be nothing at all left to decide at trial, and a similar approach was adopted by Nolan LJ in *Hanover Insurance Brokers Ltd* v *Schapiro* [1994] IRLR 82, where about one-third of the 12-month period of restraint would have run prior to the trial of the action. Although the earlier case was not explicitly mentioned by Dillon LJ, he was also prepared to consider the merits of the case at the interlocutory stage. Probably little more can be said than that it is a matter of degree, but clearly in restraint clause cases of this type, the length of time prior to trial is relevant to the balance of convenience issue.

Mareva *Injunctions*

The *Mareva* injunction is also a form of interlocutory relief, but its object is to prevent the defendant from removing his assets out of the jurisdiction, or otherwise dealing with them, until the action pending against him has been tried by a court. Although the original basis of the *Mareva* injunction was obscure (like the Anton Piller order considered below), the courts' jurisdiction now has a clear statutory footing, under the Supreme Court Act 1981, s. 37 (powers of High Court with respect to injunctions and receivers), subss. 1 and 2 of which are as follows:

(1)   The High Court may by order (whether interlocutory or final) grant an injunction or appoint a receiver in all cases in which it appears to the court to be just and convenient to do so.

(2) Any such order may be made either unconditionally or on such terms and conditions as the Court thinks just.

The term 'Mareva' comes from the case of Mareva Compania Naviera SA v International Bulk Carriers SA [1975] 2 Lloyd's Rep 509 (although this is not, in fact, the first reported case in which the order appears). In Mareva itself, the plaintiffs were shipowners who time-chartered their ship, The Mareva, to the defendants. The hire was to be paid in instalments, but after the third instalment the defendant defaulted and claimed to repudiate the contract. The plaintiffs were afraid that the defendant would remove his assets from the jurisdiction before the plaintiffs' claim could be heard.

Since the Mareva injunction is a form of interlocutory relief, the courts are reluctant to attempt to make a lengthy and detailed assessment of the strengths and weaknesses of the applicant's case at trial. In Derby & Co. Ltd v Weldon (No. 1) [1990] Ch 48, Parker LJ said (at p. 58):

> It is to be hoped that in future the observations of Lord Diplock and Lord Templeman [in American Cyanamid] will be borne in mind in applications for a Mareva injunction, that they will take hours not days and that appeals will be rare. I do not mean by the foregoing to indicate that argument as to the principles applying to the grant of a Mareva injunction should not be fully argued. With a developing jurisdiction it is inevitable and desirable that they should be. What, however, should not be allowed is (1) any attempt to persuade a court to resolve disputed questions of fact whether relating to the merits of the underlying claim in respect of which a Mareva is sought or relating to the elements of the Mareva jurisdiction such as that of dissipation or (2) detailed arguments on difficult points of law on which the claim of either party may ultimately depend.

Nonetheless, before a Mareva injunction can be granted the plaintiff must satisfy tests which are far more stringent than the American Cyanamid tests considered above, the requirements being summarised by Rattee J (whose views on the grant of the injunction were upheld in the Court of Appeal) in Re BCCI (No. 9) [1994] 3 All ER 764, as follows:

> As has been said again recently by the Court of Appeal, there are three issues on which the court has to be satisfied before granting a Mareva injunction: (i) has the applicant a good arguable case; (ii) has the applicant satisfied the court that there are assets within and, where an extra-territorial order is sought, without the jurisdiction; and (iii) is there a real risk of dissipation or secretion of assets so as to render any judgment which the applicant may obtain nugatory?

Thus, the applicant must show a good arguable case, not merely (as in *American Cyanamid*) that there is a serious issue to be tried. The second requirement, that the applicant must show that there are assets within the jurisdiction, are relaxed where a worldwide injunction is sought: (see further below).

Any kind of property belonging to the defendant may be the subject of a *Mareva* order, and has included cars, jewels, and even aeroplanes. However, the court will not order delivery of the defendant's clothes, bedding, household goods or tools of his trade, livestock, farm implements, or the like. The court should take care not to put the defendant out of business or prevent him earning his living. The remedy is also personal against the defendant, and is not intended to give the plaintiff security so as to place him in a preferential position in the event of the defendant's bankruptcy.

The last decade or so has seen a number of frauds on an international scale, but, until recently, it was thought that *Mareva* injunctions were available only to prevent removal of assets from within the jurisdiction. Since the jurisdiction is personal, however, as we saw in chapter 2, it should not, in principle, matter where the assets are situated, and it is now clear (in particular from *Babanaft International Co. SA* v *Basantine* [1990] Ch 13 and *Derby & Co. Ltd* v *Weldon (Nos. 3 & 4)* [1990] Ch 65) that *Mareva* injunctions can be granted on a worldwide basis. However, since in reality, anybody with notice of the injunction can be affected by it, it is granted only in exceptional circumstances, and the courts are careful to frame the order so as to protect the position of third parties. In *Derby* v *Weldon (No. 1)* [1990] Ch 48, Parker LJ said (at p. 57):

> In [exceptional] cases it appears to me that there is every justification for a worldwide *Mareva*, so long as, by undertaking or *proviso* or a combination of both, (a) oppression of the defendants by way of exposure to a multiplicity of proceedings is avoided, (b) the defendants are protected against the misuse of information gained from the ordinary order for disclosure in aid of the *Mareva*, (c) the position of third parties is protected. Whether, ultimately, the order *in personam* will be converted into an order attaching some or all of the assets disclosed will of course depend on (i) the court here giving the plaintiffs leave to proceed in a jurisdiction in which assets have been found and (ii) the decision of the court in such jurisdiction whether to make an order.

Anton Piller Orders

Anton Piller orders are a type of interlocutory mandatory injunction which (like the *Mareva* injunction) now derives its jurisdiction from the general power of the High Court, cotained in the Supreme Court Act 1981, s. 37, to grant an injunction when it appears 'just and convenient' to do so. The order is named after the case of *Anton Piller KG* v *Manufacturing Processes Ltd* [1976] 2 WLR 162, which was the first case where the Court of Appeal approved the use of this kind of order. *Anton Piller* received House of Lords approval in *Rank Film Distributors Ltd* v *Video Information Centre* [1982] AC 380.

An Anton Piller order is obtained *ex parte* (i.e., in the defendant's absence), so as to catch him off his guard, and is used in cases where the court believes that there is a danger that he will remove or destroy evidence in the form of documents or moveable property, such as money, papers or illegal copies of films. The evidence need not be the actual subject-matter of the dispute. In addition to ordering the defendant not to move or destroy the evidence, the court may require him to allow the plaintiff to inspect the relevant evidence or property at the defendant's premises. It is not, however, a search warrant, and the defendant is required merely to allow the plaintiff to carry out an inspection of the property.

The order is very powerful and the courts are concerned to protect the interests of the defendant. As Lord Wilberforce observed in the *Rank Film* case:

> Because they operate drastically and because they are made, necessarily, *ex parte* — i.e., before the persons affected have been heard, they are closely controlled by the court: see the judgment of Lord Denning MR in *Anton Piller* [1976] Ch 55, 61. They are only granted upon clear and compelling evidence, and a number of safeguards in the interest of preserving essential rights are introduced. They are an illustration of the adaptability of equitable remedies to new situations.

Among the safeguards are that the applicant shows a strong prima facie case, that the damage, potential or actual, must be very serious for the applicant, that there is a real possibility that the evidence will be destroyed, and that the injunction would do no real harm to the defendant or his case.

SPECIFIC PERFORMANCE

For breaches of most contracts the only available remedies are at common law, but sometimes (and subject to the discretionary nature of the remedy) injunctions can be granted to restrain breaches of contract, and some contracts are enforceable by decree of specific performance.

Where the remedy of specific performance is granted, the court orders the party in breach to carry out his obligations under the contract. If he fails to do so, he will be guilty of contempt of court. Traditionally, the remedy has been granted only very sparingly in breach of contract cases, but that seems to be changing. Hence, we will consider the following essay question:

ESSAY QUESTION

The current view is that specific performance can be ordered whenever it is the most appropriate remedy.
Discuss.

This quotation is based, admittedly rather loosely, on a passage in G. H. Treitel, *The Law of Contract*, 9th ed. (Sweet & Maxwell, 1995), at p. 924. The implication is that whatever view may have obtained in the past, today the rigid requirements for specific performance have been abandoned in favour of the simpler requirement that specific performance be the most appropriate remedy. It seems sensible, then, to approach the question by considering some of the more rigid requirements, and seeing whether they have indeed been relaxed.

Damages not Adequate Remedy

The traditional position is that if damages are an adequate remedy then an equitable remedy will not be available. Damages will generally be adequate in sale of goods contracts, because the buyer ought to be able to buy equivalent goods elsewhere, and, indeed, should do so in order to mitigate his loss (if specific performance were generally available then that would significantly weaken the contractual mitigation doctrine). However, it has long been recognised that contracts for estates and in land are enforceable in equity (e.g., *Walsh v Lonsdale* (1882) 20 ChD 9). Even contractual licences are specifically enforceable, as in *Verrall v Great Yarmouth Borough Council* [1981] QB 202. The Great Yarmouth council had agreed to hire out the Wellington Pier pavillion to the National Front, but there were elections before the date agreed for the hire. The Labour Party took control from the Conservatives, and purported to repudiate the contract. The Court of Appeal held this contract to be specifically enforceable, and, although it came as no surprise that contractual licences were specifically enforceable, this was the first case where that was actually part of the *ratio* of the decision.

Although specific performance is not usually available to enforce contracts for the sale of goods, it may be if the goods are unique, for example a Van Gogh painting, or in other cases where the plaintiff could not reasonably be expected to find a substitute. Indeed, the courts are expressly empowered by the Sale of Goods Act 1979, s. 52 (re-enacting a similar provision in the Sale of Goods Act 1893), to grant specific performance of certain contracts for the sale of goods. The courts have been, in general, reluctant to conclude that the goods in question are sufficiently unique. Thus, in *Cohen v Roche* [1927] 1 KB 169, McCardie J refused to decree specific performance of a contract for the sale of a set of eight Hepplewhite chairs, on the ground that such chairs were merely ordinary items of commerce. Ordinary damages for breach of contract were awarded instead.

Arguably, there have been relaxations in recent years, where uniqueness of the goods has been held not to be the only criterion in establishing whether the plaintiff could reasonably be expected to find a substitute. In *Sky Petroleum Ltd* v *VIP Petroleum Ltd* [1974] 1 WLR 576, Goulding J granted an injunction restraining the defendant from withholding supplies of petrol, in breach of his contract with the plaintiff. Although the actual remedy was an injunction, it was accepted that it amounted to a decree of specific performance. Although petrol is hardly unique, the case arose during a worldwide petrol shortage, when the plaintiff could not easily obtain supplies elsewhere. Were the remedy not granted, the plaintiff might have been forced out of business, so that it could not be said that damages were an adequate remedy. Goulding J observed:

> Now I come to the most serious hurdle in the way of the plaintiff company which is the well-known doctrine that the court refuses specific performance of the contract to sell and purchase chattels not specific or ascertained. That is a well-established and salutary rule and I am entirely unconvinced by counsel for the plaintiff company when he tells me that an injunction in the form sought by him would not be specific enforcement at all. The matter is one of substance and not of form and it is, in my judgment, quite plain that I am for the time being specifically enforcing the contract if I grant an injunction. However, the *ratio* behind the rule is, as I believe, that under the ordinary contract for the sale of non-specific goods, damages are a sufficient remedy. That, to my mind, is lacking in the circumstances of the present case. The evidence suggests, and indeed it is common knowledge, that the petroleum market is in an unusual state in which a would-be buyer cannot go out into the market and contract with another seller, possibly at some sacrifice as to price. Here, the defendant company appears for practical purposes to be the plaintiff company's sole means of keeping its business going, and I am prepared so far to depart from the general rule as to try to preserve the position under the contract until a later date. I therefore propose to grant an injunction.

Beswick v *Beswick* [1968] AC 58 is another case where damages were considered inadequate, and specific performance granted to the estate, even though the obligation was only to pay money (an annuity). The problem was that the annuity was to be paid to a third party, and damages to the contracting party would therefore have been nominal only (because he personally had suffered no loss). There are, however, other justifications for the remedy in *Beswick* v *Beswick*. Lord Pearce thought that damages would not have been an adequate remedy even had it been an ordinary two-party contract, because a single award of lump sum damages is not appropriate where the contractual obligation had been to provide a continuing annuity. Further, the contract satisfied the mutuality requirement, since the obligation of the innocent party (whose personal representative was suing) was to transfer the goodwill of a business, and if he had failed to do so specific performance could have been awarded against him.

If, however, the courts regard the fact that a contract is intended to benefit a third party *per se* as a strong ground for the grant of the equitable remedy, then that provides support for the view that the requirements for specific performance have been relaxed.

Remedy Discretionary

It may be relevant to observe that specific performance will not be awarded where it is not the most appropriate remedy, and this may follow from the discretionary nature of the remedy. The remedy of specific performance is, in principle, available to enforce contracts for the sale of land, but it will not be granted, for example, where, due to some special circumstance, to grant specific performance would be grossly unfair to the defendant. *Wroth v Tyler* [1974] Ch 30 concerned a contract to sell a bungalow, for which specific performance would normally be available. As far as both parties to the contract knew, the only encumbrance on the title was the vendor's mortgage, which would ordinarily not matter, as the vendor would use the purchase price to pay it off. Unfortunately, the vendor's wife objected to moving, and subsequently tried to stop the sale by entering a notice of her right of occupation under the Matrimonial Homes Act 1967. This put the vendor into an impossible position, since in order to fulfil his contract, he would have had to sue his own wife in order to get the notice removed, and he withdrew from the sale. Megarry J refused to grant specific performance, and awarded the purchaser damages instead, which were based on the difference between the market value of the bungalow at the date of the contract, and its value at the date of the judgment (since house prices had risen considerably in the meantime, the award was substantial).

Specific Performance of Employment Contracts

One area where there has been a noticeable relaxation in the requirements in recent years is in specific performance of employment contracts, and injunctions which have the same effect. Until recently, it was generally thought that this remedy was not available in this situation. It is worth beginning by considering the justifications for this.

As is discussed further below, employment contracts cannot be specifically enforced against employees, partly because this would be tantamount to legalising slavery. The usual rule is that equitable remedies are not available to employees either. Clearly, the same reasoning does not apply where an employee is suing, and the justification for the rule appears to be that employment contracts are contracts for personal service, and that (since employers cannot obtain specific performance) the mutuality requirement is not satisfied. One reason for not enforcing contracts for personal service is that constant supervision is required. We should start, then, by considering the general position, that specific performance is not granted where constant supervision is required, and that the mutuality requirement needs to be satisfied.

Not Granted where Constant Supervision Required

A one-off sale is one thing, but an order requiring the defendant to perform a series of acts over a period of time is quite another. The courts have no machinery for exercising continuous supervision to make sure that the defendant carries out an order, and rather than risk the law being flouted, they will refuse to grant an order in such circumstances.

In *Ryan* v *Mutual Tontine Westminster Chambers Association* [1893] 1 Ch 116, the lessor of a flat agreed in the lease that he would appoint a porter who would be constantly in attendance to clean the passages, deliver mail, etc. In fact, the lessor appointed a porter who also worked as a chef in a nearby club, and who was consistently absent. The plaintiff sought specific performance, but the Court of Appeal held that his only remedy was damages for breach of contract: the court would not attempt to supervise the daily goings-on in a block of flats.

Contracts to build or repair will not normally be specifically enforced. This is partly because the courts will not supervise, but also because the wronged party can normally find another builder to do the work (in other words, damages are an adequate remedy, on the principles discussed in the previous section). Nevertheless, there are exceptional cases where specific performance has been awarded. One such case was the Court of Appeal decision in *Wolverhampton Corporation* v *Emmons* [1901] 1 KB 515, where the plaintiff corporation had actually sold the land to the defendant, who had contracted to erect a number of buildings on the land, in pursuance of a scheme of street improvement. The defendant had defaulted on his obligations regarding the buildings, but, as purchaser, had gone into possession of the land, so that the corporation could not have sent in a different firm of builders without committing a trespass. In this case, the court held that the corporation could not adequately be compensated by damages, and ordered the defendant actually to carry out the work. Another material factor was that the building obligations had been defined in detail in the contract, so that the court could see what was the exact nature of the work required.

There are also a number of old cases involving railway companies. If a railway company built a railway through a farmer's land, having undertaken to build a bridge to allow the farmer to go from one part of his farm to another, the courts regarded damages as an inadequate remedy, and decreed specific performance. The most important single factor in these cases was that the defendant was in possession of the land, so that it was impossible for the injured party to provide for the work to be carried out by other means.

Mutuality Requirement

In any case involving land the contract is specifically enforceable by *both* parties (vendor as well as purchaser), and, generally speaking, any contract which is specifically enforceable by one party is also specifically enforceable by the other. This is termed the mutuality requirement, and, although there are exceptions, a common ground for specific performance of a contract being refused is that the contract could not be similarly enforced by the other party.

In *Flight* v *Bolland* (1828) 4 Russ 298, for example, a minor failed to obtain a decree of specific performance, since specific performance will not normally be ordered *against* a minor. A contract is specifically enforceable, however, as long as there is mutuality at the date of trial — it does not matter if mutuality did not exist at the time the contract was made. In *Price* v *Strange* [1978] Ch 337, the defendant had agreed to grant to the plaintiff a lease, which contained a provision that the plaintiff should carry out internal and external repairs. The courts will not normally enforce a contract to repair, so there was no mutuality at the time the contract was made. However, by the time of the trial, the plaintiff had carried out the internal repairs and although the external repairs had been carried out by the defendant, the plaintiff had expressed willingness to pay for them. By the time of the trial, therefore, repairs were no longer an issue and the only question was whether the agreement to grant the lease should be enforced. The Court of Appeal held that mutuality was now satisfied, and that specific performance could be granted.

An exception to the mutuality requirement is that a victim of misrepresentation may enforce a contract, even though the contract could not be enforced against him because the misrepresentation would entitle him to avoid the contract.

Specific Performance against Employers

It is clear from the preceding paragraphs that the principle that specific performance will not be granted where constant supervision is required implies that employment contracts will not be enforced against employees, and that a rigid application of the mutuality requirement implies that the equitable remedy is not available against employers either, and indeed this is generally the case. The general rule was stated by Lord Reid in *Ridge* v *Baldwin* [1964] AC 40 (at p. 65): '... there cannot be specific performance of a contract of service, and the master can terminate the contract with his servant at any time and for any reason or for none'.

This was described as 'a statement of general principle to which there are exceptions', implying that in exceptional circumstances, specific performance *can* be granted in favour of an employee. The leading case is *Hill* v *CA Parsons Ltd* [1972] Ch 305, the facts of which were highly usual, however. The employer was pressured, against his will, to dismiss the employee, by a union (DATA) attempting to impose a closed shop, and purported to dismiss the employee on one month's notice (whereas he was entitled to six months' under his contract of employment). The employee obtained an interim injunction (the effect of which was identical to a decree of specific performance), restraining the employer from dismissing him without the proper notice. The main effect of the remedy was simply to continue the employment relationship until the Industrial Relations Act 1971 came into force a few weeks later (s. 5 protected employees by providing that a dismissal for non-membership of a trade union would be an unfair dismissal). The Court of Appeal held (Stamp LJ dissenting) that there was no rule of law against enforcing employment contracts using the remedy of specific performance (or injunction). It is a question of practice, and there are a number of exceptions to the general rule. Lord Denning MR noted that damages were not an adequate remedy in the case.

Hill v *Parsons* appeared to create only the narrowest of exceptions, however, Lord Denning MR commenting (at p. 316):

> If ever there was a case where an injunction should be granted against the employers, this is the case. It is quite plain that the employers have done wrong. I know that the employers have been under pressure from a powerful trade union. That may explain their conduct, but it does not excuse it. They have purported to terminate Mr Hill's employment by notice which is too short by far. They seek to take advantage of their own wrong by asserting that his services were terminated by their own 'say-so' at the date selected by them — to the grave prejudice of Mr Hill. They cannot be allowed to break the law in this way. It is, to my mind, a clear case for an injunction.

Three factors that were considered relevant by the majority in *Hill* v *Parsons* were that the employer retained confidence in the employee, his dismissal being brought about by third-party pressure, that the employee was not seeking actually to return to work, and that the only effect of the remedy was to give the employee protection (here a statutory provision which was about to come into force) to which he might reasonably have felt entitled.

Stamp LJ, dissenting in *Hill* v *Parsons*, was not prepared to create an exception to the general principle (that equitable remedies are not available to enforce employment contracts), even on these unusual facts. The case was treated as exceptional, and virtually limited to its own facts in later decisions; Megarry J commenting, for example, in *Chappell* v *Times Newspapers Ltd* [1975] ICR 145 (at p. 159):

> There were three main grounds for [the decision in *Hill* v *Parsons*]. First, there was still complete confidence between employer and employee; the defendant did not want to terminate the plaintiff's employment but had been coerced by the union. Second, the Industrial Relations Act 1971 was expected to come into force shortly: it had been passed but the relevant parts had not been brought into operation. As soon as the Act was in force, one probable result would be that the closed shop would no longer be enforceable and the plaintiff would be free to remain a member of the union of his choice. He would also obtain the rights conferred by the Act to compensation for unfair dismissal if he was then dismissed. Third, in the circumstances of the case damages would not be an adequate remedy.

By the middle of the 1970s, therefore, it was beginning to look as though *Hill* v *Parsons* would never be followed, but to the surprise of a number of commentators, Warner J applied it in *Irani* v *Southampton and South West Hampshire Health Authority* [1985] IRLR 203. *Irani* did not, of itself, however, extend the principle of the earlier case by much.

The employee was a part-time opthalmologist, and a dispute arose between him and the consultant in charge. The defendant authority set up an *ad hoc* panel of enquiry, the results of which the plaintiff was not allowed to see, and, on the basis of the panel's report, the authority wrote to the plaintiff purporting to terminate his contract of employment. The effect of the purported termination would also have been to take away the plaintiff's right to use the procedures for resolving disputes contained in the Whitley Councils for Health Services Great Britain, Conditions of Service ('the Blue Book'), the terms of which were incorporated into the plaintiff's employment contract. The plaintiff would have been unemployable in the health service if his dismissal had stood.

There was no complaint as to the conduct or professional competence of the plaintiff, and the pressure for his dismissal came from the consultant. The plaintiff sought, and was successful in obtaining, an interim injunction restraining the defendant authority from terminating his contract without first exhausting the procedure set out in the Whitley Councils Conditions of Service. The interim injunction, whose effect was similar to that of a decree of specific performance, was granted subject to him not presenting himself for work at any of his employer's establishments.

As in *Hill* v *Parsons*, the employer had no complaint against the employee, but was under pressure to dismiss him from a third party, and the effect of the remedy being granted was not to force the employee upon an unwilling employer, but to ensure that proper disciplinary procedures were applied, in accordance with the contract. The point of remedy was to force the employer to comply with the statutory provisions derived from Whitley Councils Conditions, incorporated into the contract of employment as part of the dispute procedure. The employer should not be able to 'snap his fingers' at statutory appeal rights. In addition, as in *Hill* v *Parsons*, there was no evidence that mutual trust and confidence between employer and employee was destroyed.

In *Powell* v *London Borough of Brent* [1987] IRLR 165, Ralph Gibson LJ regarded the continuing existence of trust and confidence between the parties as the decisive factor, and followed *Hill* v *Parsons* even where the pressure for dismissal did not come entirely from a third party, and where the effect of the remedy was actually to allow the employee to continue at work. It should be noted, however, that this was an interlocutory appeal, and that if Powell had later won her claim at trial, she would have been needlessly disadvantaged by being forced to give up her new post in the meantime.

Mrs Powell had been employed by the council for a number of years, and applied for a post which was a promotion. She was interviewed and told that she had been appointed. Subsequently, another candidate complained about the procedure, and the council took the view that its selection procedure might have been in breach of its equal opportunity code of practice. Mrs Powell was accordingly told that it was not possible to appoint her, that she had not been properly appointed, and that she should resume her previous duties. Meanwhile, the council proposed to readvertise the post. She claimed that the council was acting in breach of her employment contract, and sought an interlocutory injunction preventing it from readvertising, and to treat Mrs Powell as employed by it in the post. The council claimed that she had never been properly appointed.

On receiving the original writ the council undertook that it would treat Mrs Powell as employed in the new post for a month. During this period there were no complaints as to her competence or her working relationships.

The Court of Appeal held that there was a good arguable case that Mrs Powell had been properly appointed to the new post, and granted an interlocutory injunction (the effect of which was identical to a decree of specific performance), on the principles of *American Cyanamid* v *Ethicon* [1975] AC 396.

In holding that this was an appropriate case for enforcing an employment contract by injunction, Ralph Gibson LJ noted that damages would not be an adequate remedy for Mrs Powell, and continued:

I must state the principle which must, I think, guide our decision. It is clear to me that part of the basis for the general rule against specific performance of contracts of service is that mutual confidence is normally a necessary condition for the satisfactory working of a contract of service. If one party refuses to allow the relationship to continue the mutual confidence is almost certainly missing ...

For my part I am not able to derive much assistance from the words 'complete confidence' for the purposes of this case. I prefer to state what I think the applicable principle to be in this way. Having regard to the decision in *Hill* v *Parsons* and to the long-standing general rule of practice to which *Hill* v *Parsons* was an exception, the court will not by injunction require an employer to let a servant continue in his employment, when the employer has sought to terminate the employment and to prevent the servant carrying out his work under the contract, unless it is clear on the evidence not only that it is otherwise just to make such a requirement but also that there exists sufficient confidence on the part of the employer in the servant's ability and other necessary attributes for it to be reasonable to make the order. Sufficiency of confidence must be judged by reference to the circumstances of the case, including the nature of the work, the people with whom the work must be done and the likely effect upon the employer and the employer's operations if the employer is required by injunction to suffer the plaintiff to continue in the work.

The only requirement, therefore, was that the employer had sufficient confidence in the employee, and this was treated as a question of fact.

Powell was followed by Taylor J in *Hughes* v *London Borough of Southwark* [1988] IRLR 55, where the employer wished to redeploy the plaintiff employees (social workers) in breach of contract, because of a shortage of funds. As in the earlier cases there was no question of the employers doubting the competence of the employees, and their decision was influenced solely by financial considerations. Taylor J was prepared to grant an interlocutory injunction although there was a dispute between employer and employees:

There are *dicta* to the effect that specific performance of a contract of service will not normally be ordered. On the other hand, my attention has been drawn to *Powell* v *London Borough of Brent* [1987] IRLR 466. It is accepted by counsel on both sides that it is the latest authority on the subject and it is clear from the case that there are circumstances in which an injunction can be granted in relation to a contract of service. The important criterion is as to whether there is mutual confidence, the point being that it would be inappropriate to grant an injunction against an employer requiring him to keep on in service on certain terms a servant who has lost the confidence of the employer. There is no question of that here. It is quite clear that the defendants have great confidence in these social workers ... So I accept here that the court has power, if it is thought appropriate, to grant an injunction and indeed to grant an interlocutory injunction of the kind sought.

In all the cases considered so far, the mutual confidence between the parties remained intact. *Powell* was distiguished in *Wishart* v *National Association of Citizens Advice Bureaux Ltd* [1990] ICR 794 where there was no mutual confidence between the parties. An appointment which had been made subject to references was cancelled when the employee's absenteeism at her previous job became apparent. The Court of Appeal held that even if there had been a breach of contract by the employer, damages were an adequate remedy, and the contract would not be specifically enforced.

Nor was an interlocutory award made in *McPherson* v *London Borough of Lambeth* [1988] IRLR 470, where the plaintiffs, who were backed by NALGO, claimed that their contracts did not require them to operate the new computerised technology which had been introduced by the employers. Vinelott J refused to grant an injunction, in spite of the fact that the employers had not lost confidence in the plaintiffs. The plaintiffs could not, however, continue to discharge their contractual obligations without using the new computer, and Vinelott J did not think that the employers should be forced to reorganise their administration so as to enable the plaintiffs to carry out their duties without using the new computer.

The requirement for mutual confidence has itself been relaxed recently, however, and *Powell* was again followed by Mervyn Davies J in *Wadcock* v *Brent London BC* [1990] IRLR 223, where the employee no longer enjoyed the confidence of his employer. The council had allegedly wrongfully reallocated the plaintiff social worker's work from both child care and special needs to special needs alone. The plaintiff was not prepared to accept the reallocation and was dismissed. On an unreserved undertaking from him that he would, in fact, obey orders and work in special needs, he would be granted an interlocutory injunction restraining the council from acting on the purported dismissal pending trial. The test was whether a 'workable situation' could be achieved. Any other result would have deprived the plaintiff of the protection of the disciplinary procedure.

The 'workable situation' test was also adopted by Morland J in *Robb* v *London Borough of Hammersmith and Fulham* [1991] ICR 514, where, however, the sole point of the injunction was to force the employer to pursue disciplinary proceedings. Trust and confidence had been lost, and this was not a case where any pressure to dismiss had come from outside. The test was whether the injunction was workable. Trust and confidence would have been relevant if the employee had wanted actually to go back to work, but was not necessary in this particular case.

In spite of the weakening of the general rule in recent years, however, all the cases where an equitable remedy has been awarded are exceptional, to a greater or lesser extent, and the general rule is still that equitable remedies are not available to enforce employment contracts. It remains necessary to show that damages are not an adequate remedy, and either that mutual confidence between the parties remains, or that the employee is not intending actually to remain at work, but is using the remedy, for example, to ensure that the employer complies with contractual disciplinary procedures.

Equitable Remedies against Employees

An area where there appears to have been no relaxation in the rigid requirements is in respect of equitable remedies against employees. Indeed, employment contracts cannot be specifically enforced against employees at all. This is expressly provided by the Trade Union and Labour Relations (Consolidation) Act 1992, s. 236, re-enacting the Trade Union and Labour Relations Act 1974, s. 16, but the 1974 Act merely puts into statutory form an old principle of equity: to grant specific performance against employees would be tantamount to legalising slavery. As Fry LJ observed in *De Francesco* v *Barnum* (1890) 45 ChD 430, 'The courts are bound to be jealous, lest they should turn contracts of service into contracts of slavery'. In any case, an aggrieved employer can almost always find someone else to do the work, even where the employee in breach has rare qualifications or skills. Usually, therefore, damages are an adequate remedy.

However, although specific performance may not be awarded against an employee, injunctions may be granted to stop an employee working for anyone else, if to do so would involve a breach of employment contract. This line of authority begins with *Lumley* v *Wagner* (1852) 1 De GM & G 604. The plaintiff theatre had engaged the defendant, an opera singer, to appear at his theatre for three months, and the defendant had agreed not to use her talents at any other theatre during that time. The defendant broke her contract by accepting engagements elsewhere, for a higher remuneration. Although the court would not have compelled her to continue to sing for the plaintiff, it was prepared to grant an injunction forbidding her to sing for any other theatre during the three-month period of the contract.

The courts have shown a considerable reluctance to extend *Lumley* v *Wagner*, and, indeed, in recent years, they have tended to tighten up the requirements before granting the equitable remedy against the employee. The main concern is to avoid forcing the employee to work for the plaintiff employer and, therefore, the courts are not prepared to grant an injunction for a long period, or one whose terms are too wide. In *Lumley* v *Wagner* itself, the defendant was restrained only from performing at another theatre during the remaining two-month period of the contract, and her contract left her free to take other kinds of employment, apart from singing. In *Whitwood Chemical Co. v Hardman* [1891] 2 Ch 416, however, the Court of Appeal refused to enforce by injunction a contract whose effect was to prohibit the employee from working for anyone else in *any* capacity (the contract required a manager to give the whole of his time to the plaintiff's business for the contract period of 10 years, approximately four of which remained to run).

Lindley LJ commented (at p. 427) that the court would not put a man into the position where he would have either to be idle or perform the agreement with the plaintiffs. *Lumley v Wagner* was regarded by Kay LJ (at p. 431) as defining the extreme limit of equitable intervention. In principle, a promise not to work for anyone else in any capacity ought not be enforced by injunction, since that would be tantamount to specific performance (because unemployment would then be the only alternative).

The issue is what is meant by being compelled to continue working for the plaintiff? In many cases it may be possible to get alternative work, but only at a significant cost to the employee. However, in *Warner Bros Inc v Nelson* [1937] 1 KB 209, Branson J, following *Lumley v Wagner* was unimpressed by the argument that this meant, in reality, being forced to continue working for the plaintiff. In that case, a film actress (Bette Davis) was restrained from making films for anybody apart from the plaintiffs, with whom she had an exclusive contract. Warner Bros regarded her as a difficult star to work with, and for a long time they failed to offer her parts which were suited to her ability. When she attempted to obtain work with another studio, Warner sought and obtained an injunction, whose maximum duration could have been as long as three years. Branson J commented that the defendant was a person of intelligence, capacity and means, and that even if restrained from making films for anybody apart from the plaintiffs, she would be able to employ herself both usefully and remuneratively in other spheres of activity. This decision has not gone uncriticised, since a film actress's earning capacity depends heavily on how far she can remain within the public eye, and employment elsewhere would have involved a significant financial loss, so that the practical effect of the injunction may well have been to force her to continue working for the plaintiffs. Bette Davis chose not to give evidence, however, which may go part of the way towards explaining the decision.

Generally speaking, *Warner Bros v Nelson* has been distinguished, or even referred to with disapproval, in subsequent cases, the principle in *Whitwood Chemical Co. v Hardman* being extended to cases where, *in practice*, the effect would be to force the defendant to work for the other party. The courts also seem to be reluctant to force gifted professionals to choose between performing the agreement, and earning a living in unsuitable employment.

Similar principles apply to management and agency agreements. In *Page One Records Ltd v Britton* [1968] 1 WLR 157, equitable relief was refused where the effect, *in practice*, of an injunction would have been to force Britton, who was trading as 'The Troggs' pop group, to continue to engage the plaintiffs as their sole and exclusive managers, agents and personal representatives for five years, or go out of business, since it was recognised that pop groups cannot operate without an agent. The contract in question was for five years, and another reason for distinguishing *Lumley* v *Wagner* was that in the earlier case the plaintiffs had been obliged only to provide money, whereas here, of course, the plaintiffs' obligation was much wider, and the relationship could work only if trust and confidence remained between the parties. It is now clear, however, that this is unlikely to be a ground for distinguishing *Page One Records Ltd* v *Britton* in a future case.

Another similar case is *Nichols Advanced Vehicle Systems Inc.* v *De Angelis* (unreported, 21 December 1979). The Italian racing driver Elio De Angelis, then 21 years old, was under contract to drive in Grand Prix events exclusively for the plaintiffs' Shadows team for the 1980 season. Upon receiving a better offer from Team Lotus, he entered into a contract to drive for them instead (a practice that appears from the motoring press to be common in Formula One motor racing circles), and Shadows sued for an injunction, the duration of which would have been a little over one year. Oliver J refused to grant the injunction, confessed to finding difficulty in reconciling *Warner Bros* with *Page One Records* v *Britton*, and preferred the approach taken by Stamp J in the later case, except perhaps where, as in *Lumley* v *Wagner*, the period of the injunction was short (in *Lumley* v *Wagner*, less than two months remained of a three-month engagement). It seemed to have been accepted by all parties that the effect, *in practice*, of granting the injunction would have been to force De Angelis either to drive for Shadows or to give up his career for the period of the injunction.

Another factor weighing with Oliver J, as it had with Stamp J in the earlier case, was that even if the injunction were granted, the employee's trust and confidence in his original employer might no longer exist. Oliver J also placed reliance on the fact that the contract involved a very high risk to life and limb on De Angelis's part (who was, in fact, killed some years later in a motor racing accident).

Similar principles appear to apply where the wronged employer sues not the employee himself for breach of contract, but the rival employer for the tort of inducing breach of (or interference with) contract, since otherwise it would be possible for the wronged party to obtain relief by the back door which would have been unobtainable through the front. In *Lotus Cars* v *Jaguar Cars* (unreported, 1 July 1982), Mr Putnam, who was a sales director of Lotus, intended to break his contract with them by moving to Jaguar, with 18 months of his contract left to run. An injunction, in very wide terms, was sought not against Mr Putnam, but against Jaguar, for inducing breach of contract, but the same principles were applied by Nourse J as in the ordinary contract cases. The evidence suggested that for someone with Mr Putnam's skills, the only possible employers were Lotus and Jaguar (a rather surprising conclusion, one might think). To grant the injunction against Jaguar would therefore have effectively tied Mr Putnam to Lotus, or forced him to remain idle. The injunction was therefore refused on the principles established in *Whitwood Chemical Co.* v *Hardman.*

Lotus Cars v *Jaguar Cars* was followed by the Court of Appeal in *Warren* v *Mendy* [1989] 3 All ER 103. The boxer Nigel Benn was under contract to Warren, a licensed manager and promoter of boxing matches, and had undertaken not to fight for any other promoter for a period of three years. Disagreements arose, and Benn expressed his intention of acting as his own manager in future, assisted by Mendy, a financial consultant. Warren sought an injunction (the duration of which would have been approximately two years) not against Benn, but against Mendy, to prevent him from acting in a managerial capacity on Benn's behalf. There was, in fact, considerable doubt as to whether Benn's reliance on Mendy's financial advice could have amounted to a breach of his contract with Warren, but, in any case, the Court of Appeal upheld Pill J's refusal to grant the injunction sought. The principles applied were the same as if Benn had been sued directly (i.e., it was assumed that the principles applicable were the same whether the action was for an inducement to break a contract or for breach of contract itself).

The importance of the case lies in the court's extensive review of previous authority, and the view taken of *Warner Bros* v *Nelson*, which was regarded as wholly out of line. Nourse LJ noted that *Warner Bros* v *Nelson* was the only case where an injunction of more than a few months' duration had been granted, and shared Oliver J's doubts in *Lotus Cars* about Branson J's approach in the earlier case. He restated the general principle that equity will not normally grant an injunction the effect of which is to debar a person from selling his services to anyone other than the plaintiff, and described the view taken by Branson J in *Warner Bros*, that Bette Davis could employ herself usefully elsewhere for three years, as 'extraordinarily unrealistic'. He did observe, however, that Miss Davis did not give evidence, and inferred that in the absence of evidence the court might have been reluctant to assume that she was not otherwise employable elsewhere. Whatever is the true explanation, it is clear that little reliance can now be placed in *Warner Bros* v *Nelson*.

Nevertheless, *Warner Bros* v *Nelson* was applied and followed recently in *Evening Standard Co.* v *Henderson* [1987] IRLR 64, a Court of Appeal decision not cited in *Warren* v *Mendy*. Henderson was employed in the production room of the *Evening Standard* on one year's notice. He was approached by a rival newspaper which was being started by Robert Maxwell, and wrote to his employers purporting to terminate his contract on two months' notice. The employers successfully obtained an interlocutory injunction to prevent Henderson from working for Maxwell during the period of his notice.

The case is not directly comparable to those previously discussed, however, since an important factor was the plaintiffs' willingness to pay Henderson his full salary during the notice period, regardless of whether he did any actual work for them. The case was therefore not one in which Henderson was faced with a stark choice between working for the plaintiffs or being reduced to a condition of starvation or idleness. Otherwise the case would have been difficult to distinguish from *Page One Records* v *Britton*. Lawton LJ also emphasised that this was only a interlocutory appeal, and that it was unnecessary to reach any final view of the law, since the plaintiffs could succeed on *American Cyanamid* principles (see above).

Evening Standard Co. v *Henderson* is probably reconcilable, therefore, with the views set out above.

Quite apart from the above discussion, a further limitation on the use of injunctions in this context is that the promise not to work for anyone else must be *express*, whereas in the case of some other types of contract such negative obligations can be implied and enforced by injunction (e.g., a shipowner can be restrained by injunction from using a ship inconsistently with an implied term in a charterparty). The requirement for the express term derives from *Whitwood Chemical Co.* v *Hardman*, where it would have been necessary to imply the term from the requirement that the employee must 'give the whole of his time to the company's business'. The lack of an express term was another ground for distinguishing *Lumley* v *Wagner*.

Injunctions may also be obtained to prevent breach of particular *terms* of employment contracts, for example to prevent confidential information from being disclosed to a rival (see, for example, *Lansing Linde Ltd* v *Kerr* [1991] 1 All ER 418, and *Lawrence David Ltd* v *Ashton* [1991] 1 All ER 385, above).

Conclusion

It seems, therefore, that whereas there may have been some relaxation in the traditional rigid requirements, the quote upon which the exam question is based is certainly too sweeping a statement as it stands.

DAMAGES IN LIEU OF INJUNCTIONS AND SPECIFIC PERFORMANCE

We finish the chapter with a short discussion of damages in lieu of injunctions and specific performance.

Damages in Lieu of Specific Performance

Before the Chancery Amendment Act 1858, the Court of Chancery had no power to grant damages in lieu of specific performance, and a disappointed plaintiff was obliged to start his action all over again in the common law courts to recover damages. The 1858 Act gave the Chancery courts power to award damages in lieu, or even in addition to, specific performance. Additional damages are awarded only if there has been some special damage to the plaintiff.

The 1858 Act was repealed in 1883, but the power to award damages was preserved through a series of later enactments, and is now to be found in the Supreme Court Act 1981, s. 50.

Like specific performance itself, damages granted in lieu of specific performance are discretionary, and the plaintiff will be able to obtain equitable damages only where the court could have granted him specific performance at the date when the action was begun.

Damages in Lieu of Injunction

As with specific performance, a court can award equitable damages in lieu of an injunction, by virtue of s. 50 of the Supreme Court Act 1981. Since, in this event, the defendant is able to carry on as before, subject only to a payment of damages to the plaintiff, the court must take pains to ensure that the defendant cannot use damages in lieu simply as a licence to continue committing a wrong.

In *Shelfer* v *City of London Lighting Co.* [1895] 1 Ch 287, A. L. Smith LJ took the view that damages should be awarded in lieu only where the injury to the plaintiff is small, is capable of being estimated in money terms, and would be adequately compensated by a small payment, and where it would be oppressive to grant an injunction. The Court of Appeal there granted an injunction restraining excessive vibration despite the fact that this might interfere with electricity supplies.

The *Shelfer* principles are open to interpretation (for example, what is meant by small?), but the courts are generally very reluctant to grant damages in lieu, especially where a continuing trespass, or a continuing nuisance is complained of. For example, in *Kennaway* v *Thompson* [1980] 3 WLR 361, the Court of Appeal set aside the trial judge's refusal to grant an injunction against power-boat racing, where damages of £16,000 were awarded in lieu, and substituted an order restricting the racing to certain times and limited noise-levels.

SUGGESTED ADDITIONAL READING

Pearce and Stevens, *The Law of Trusts and Equitable Obligations* (Butterworths, 1995), especially chapter 2.

On *Mareva* injunctions and Anton Pillar orders, see also Goode, *Commercial Law* (1995), pp. 1164–1170.

On specific performance, see G. H. Treitel, *The Law of Contract*, 9th ed. (Sweet & Maxwell, 1995), pp. 918 *ff*.

BIBLIOGRAPHY

H. G. Hanbury and R. H. Maudsley, *Modern Equity*, 14th ed. by Jill E. Martin (London: Sweet & Maxwell, 1993).

B. W. Harvey, *Settlements of Land* (London: Sweet & Maxwell, 1973).

D. J. Hayton and O. R. Marshall, *Cases and Commentary on the Law of Trusts*, 9th ed. by D. J. Hayton (London: Sweet & Maxwell, 1991).

R. H. Maudsley, *The Modern Law of Perpetuities* (London: Butterworths, 1979).

R. H. Maudsley and E. H. Burn, *Maudsley and Burn's Trusts and Trustees: Cases and Materials*, 4th ed. by E. H. Burn (London: Butterworths, 1990).

A. J. Oakley, *Constructive Trusts*, 2nd ed. (London: Sweet & Maxwell, 1987).

P. H. Pettit, *Equity and the Law of Trusts*, 7th ed. (London: Butterworths, 1993).

P. Todd, *Textbook on Trusts*, 2nd ed. (London: Blackstone Press, 1993).

INDEX

TITLES IN THE SERIES

SWOT Constitutional and Administrative Law
SWOT Law of Evidence
SWOT Company Law
SWOT Law of Contract
SWOT Family Law
SWOT Land Law
SWOT Criminal Law
SWOT Equity and Trusts
SWOT Commercial and Consumer Law
SWOT A Level Law
SWOT Law of Torts
SWOT Jurisprudence
SWOT Employment Law
SWOT English Legal System
SWOT EC Law
SWOT Conveyancing
SWOT Law of Succession
SWOT Intellectual Property Law
SWOT International Law